Christian Consolations.

SERMONS

DESIGNED TO

FURNISH COMFORT AND STRENGTH

TO

THE AFFLICTED

BY

A. P. PEABODY,
PASTOR OF THE SOUTH CHURCH, PORTSMOUTH, N. H.

Sixth Edition.

BOSTON:
WALKER, WISE, AND COMPANY,
245 WASHINGTON STREET.
1864.

University Press, Cambridge:
Welch, Bigelow, & Co., Electrotypers and Printers.

PREFACE.

The following volume is a selection from the author's common parish sermons, written with no view to future publication, at wide intervals of time, and many of them with reference to individual cases of affliction. They are given to the public, not because they are deemed of peculiar value as discussions or as rhetorical compositions, but solely in the hope that they may indicate the true sources of consolation and strength to the afflicted. The range of subjects may seem wider than the title would authorize; but it has been thought that an additional interest might on that account attach itself to the work for readers in general, while the afflicted themselves may often derive more benefit from the adaptation of some one of the great doctrines of the Gospel to their peculiar condition and wants, than from discourses which treat directly of suffering, sorrow, and death. With this view, the sermons on the Life of the

Affections, the Kingdom of God, and the Lord's Supper, have been deemed no less conducive to the general aim and purpose of the work, than those which relate solely to the discipline of an afflictive Providence. The volume is submitted to the Christian public, with the earnest prayer that it may be made the means of conveying to a few at least of the sorrow-stricken elsewhere the consolations which it is the author's duty and privilege to dispense among the people of his charge.

PORTSMOUTH, N. H., December 5, 1846.

[Sermons XXI. to XXV. inclusive were added in the second edition. Sermons XXVIII. to XXXIII. inclusive appear for the first time in the present edition.]

CONTENTS.

SERMON I.

SERMON II.

SERMON III.

SERMON IV.

SERMON V.

SERMON VI.

SERMON VII.

SERMON VIII.

SERMON IX.

SERMON X.

SERMON XI.

SERMON XII.

SERMON XIII.

SERMON XIV.

SERMON XV.

SERMON XVI.

SERMON XVII.

SERMON XVIII.

SERMON XIX.

SERMON XX.

SERMON XXI.

SERMON XXII.

SERMON XXIII.

SERMON XXIV.

SERMON XXV.

SERMON XXVI.

SERMON XXVII.

SERMON XXVIII.

SERMON XXIX.

SERMON XXX.

SERMON XXXI.

SERMON XXXII.

SERMON XXXIII.

SERMONS.

SERMON I.

OUR NEED OF THE FATHER.

I WILL ARISE AND GO TO MY FATHER. — Luke xv. 18.

We need a full perception and deep sense of God's fatherly presence and love, more than all things else, to keep us safe from the snares of life, and to make us happy under its trials; and, had I only a range of illustration and a power of impression corresponding to the glimpses of this great truth which flit before my mind, I would seek no other theme, but should deem my ministry best accomplished by pointing you continually to your Father above, and reiterating the exhortation, — "Beloved, now are ye the children of God; — see that ye bear the hearts, and lead the lives, of children." This exhortation we all need. The parable of the Prodigal Son not only depicts the condition of the profligate and the irreligious, but represents too faithfully the state of many Christians. For how few of us dwell constantly with Jesus "in the bosom of the Father"! To how few of us, as regards the flow of our daily thoughts, could God say,— "Son, thou art ever with me"! Though we have knelt before him in penitence, and daily draw nigh to him in praise and prayer, do we not at times forget the joy of his presence and the bread of his house, and let our hearts wander off into the far country, and hanker for its husks? Still I believe that an infinite Father is a want of our nature,—a want felt by all, alike by the saint and the sinner, the glad and the wretched. Our souls are so made that they cannot lead fatherless lives without a sense of destitution and loneliness. The language of every heart that will interrogate itself is,—"Show me the Father." It is to this conscious need of a Father above that I would now direct your attention; and I may be able to interpret feelings to which you have given but little heed, or which you have experienced without understanding them.

1. I would first recall your attention to seasons which must have marked more or less frequently the lives of all who hear me,—seasons of inward uneasiness without any outward cause. They come sometimes in the dim solitude of evening

or the quiet night-watches, sometimes in the yet deeper solitude of a heartless human throng. Though only voices of joy may be around us, an unbidden and irresistible melancholy steals over us. The dark side of life shows itself, however hard we strive to keep it out of sight. The outward objects which we are pursuing come up before us, stripped of their gay coloring, and in their utter flimsiness and frailty. We see what mere bubbles we are chasing; — they burst and vanish from our sight; and when we look again, it is upon a future void and blank. We can promise ourselves nothing. Weariness and doubt creep over our spirits; courage to run the race of life fails us; giant difficulties and perils rise before us; and we cannot help saying to ourselves, — "How happy would it be, could we turn our faces to the sunny past, and lie down to our last sleep before the clouds now gathering meet, and the thunders break over our heads!" At such times we hear from every connection and pursuit and trust upon earth the admonishing voice, — "This is not thy rest." We feel that our desire and toil have been for that which satisfied not; and all seems "vanity and vexation of spirit." You have, I doubt not, my friends, passed through such seasons; and, unless you have come to God in them, you have found no relief but in forcibly diverting the current of your thoughts by the bustle of business or of mirth, to have them flow in upon your next lonely hour with added bitterness and gloom.

But these seasons have a most important religious significance. They are times when the soul asserts her right to higher goods and joys than earth can give, — when "the heart and the flesh cry out for God," — times, too, when the Father comes forth to meet us, and bids our weary and laden spirits repose on him. And at such seasons, when everything seems frail and fluctuating, and there is nothing earthly on which we can rely or calculate, we do need an unchangeable point of support, — something on which we may fix our swimming and bewildered eyes, till they recover their steadiness of vision. We need the unslumbering eye, the undying love, of the Almighty. We need to have the voice sent home to our spirits, — "Fear not thou, though the earth be removed, though the heavens be no more; for He who laid the foundations of the earth and meted out the heavens is thy Father and thy Friend. This, thy God, shall be thine for ever. The Most High is thy refuge, and underneath are the everlasting arms." Nothing but this assurance can light up the hours when we muse and are sad, and change the spirit of dark reverie into that of praise and gladness. But there are no seasons when the Christian more heartily enjoys the luxury of communion with God, than during these hours which begin with melancholy. They are indeed the soul's night-seasons; but they are like those glorious nights in our northern sky, when the bright bow of God spans the firmament and floats among the stars, and the lambent fires from the horizon shoot up to meet it, and the whole heavens are telling of the glory of the Most High.

Jesus constantly made little children examples for his disciples; and in our hours of weariness and sadness, we may well take pattern from them. The infant has his seasons of weariness, when the day has been long, his sports have all been tried in their turn, and his slender resources are exhausted. He grows vacant, restless, and unhappy. But to what does he have recourse? He buries himself in his mother's arms; and then his tears are dried, his smiles return, and the fountain of gladness wells up anew from his heart. Thus the true child of God, when dazzled and wearied by the glare of day and the phantoms of life, casts himself on the bosom of his Father in the prayer of faith, and receives from the spirit never sought in vain such peace as the world cannot give.

2. We feel, it seems to me, peculiar need of a Father in heaven, in our communion with the fair and glorious scenes of nature. Did you ever see a little child taken by his father to see some glittering pageant, which seemed to the child immensely vast and grand? And have you not

marked how the child will at short intervals look away from the gay show to his father's face, as if to fortify himself by a glance of love? And, in these glances, does he not tacitly confess himself dazzled and bewildered by the sight, and able to look upon it only as supported by his father's eye? Not unlike emotions many of you must have felt, when you have stood by the ocean or on the mountain-top, or when you have considered the heavens, and beheld the stars, as "at the commandment of the Holy One they stand in their order, and never faint in their watches." You have felt bewildered and lost, lonely and desolate; you have been overwhelmed by a sense of vastness and immensity; and a silent, shuddering awe has come over you. These emotions are the child's yearning for the father's eye. You feel thus because you cannot support the consciousness of solitude and desertion in the boundless universe. You cannot bear to find yourself mere atoms in the outward creation, filling a smaller place in the great sum of being than a single leaf in the forest or a drop in the ocean, unless there be revealed to your distinct consciousness One who numbers the hairs of your heads and the sands of your lives. Were I an atheist, I would cut myself off from every grand view of nature, would shun the mountain and the ocean, and shut my eyes against the crimson sunset and the gemmed vault of night;

for all these things would tell me what a solitary being I was, and how unsheltered, — they would speak to me of a stupendous machinery beyond my control, of gigantic powers which I could not calculate, of material forces which my boasted intellect could neither comprehend nor modify.

This sinking of heart, which I see not how an atheist could ever subdue, we all feel, when we look at the works of God for the mere gratification of curiosity or taste. There is always a straining of the eye and thought beyond what we can see, — a yearning for a spiritual presence in the heights and depths of nature. When we contemplate the heavens, when we mark the paths of the deep, when we ascend to the birthplace of the rivers and the fountains, we are not satisfied, unless we meet some intelligent response to our earnest, searching glances; — it wearies and repels us to think of these things as mere lifeless forms. The inquiry almost mounts to our lips, —

"Live not the stars and mountains? Are the waves
Without a spirit? Are the dropping caves
Without a feeling in their silent tears?"

But how does it fill and warm the heart to see a fatherly presence in the glow of night, in the mist upon the mountain-top, in the waterfall and the ocean, — to look upon all these forms as but the varied God!

3. In our domestic relations, we also deeply

feel the need of a Father in heaven. How short-lived the family on earth! How frail the tie that here makes us one! In the most painful emergencies, how little can we do for each other to heal disease, to avert sorrow, to roll back the shadow of death! One after another of the circle is called away; but our hearts only cleave the more closely to those that remain. We draw out our whole power of love; yet the objects of our love seem the mere sport of fickle elements, and may be taken from us at a moment's warning. How deep, then, our need of one to whom we can look as the Father of us all, — to whom, together or apart, we can commend each other with unfaltering faith, — and in whose house, though the departed and ourselves may for a while tenant different mansions, we cannot feel divided!

To a parent, above all, is this faith in the Supreme Father of unspeakable value. To have a helpless being intrusted to one's care, with hosts of diseases and accidents thronging around the very gates of life, to know that a rude breath may quench the flickering vital spark, to be so often baffled in one's own plans and measures, and then to look around upon the multitude of early graves, — who could, in view of all these things, find courage to go forward in the discharge of a parent's duties, without the assurance that the little flock have a Heavenly Shepherd, whose breath will feed their life, whose staff will guide their steps, and who, both on earth and in heaven, bears the lambs in his arms and carries them in his bosom? Then, too, when we think of their moral exposures, of the snares that are laid for them, of the evil that they must encounter, of the many whose first steps are in the ways of death, whence should we derive confidence to place them on the theatre of moral action and discipline without trust in the Father, who loves them better than we can, who will make us sufficient for our work if we lean upon his counsel, who will not suffer the prayer of faith to return to us void, and in whom we can look forward to a distant harvest season, if the seeds of Christian instruction do not spring up and bear fruit at once? O yes! we need the protecting providence and the regenerating spirit of our Father for the ground of immovable trust, at every stage of our domestic experience, — else we might well resign our charge and remit our efforts, exclaiming in despair, "Who is sufficient for these things?"

4. Finally, as sinners, we need a Father in heaven. There is one class of inward experiences in which every Christian feels this need. It is the class to which St. Paul refers, when he says, — "The good that I would, I do not; but the evil which I would not, that I do. I delight in the law of God, after the inward man; but I

see another law in my members warring against the law of my mind." How often, my Christian friends, do our attainments fall short of our aims! How often are we betrayed into sudden sins of thought or speech! How frequently will the very frame of temper which we have the most earnestly striven to subdue rise, on some unforeseen occasion, and surprise us into some form of speech or conduct to be looked back upon with unfeigned sorrow! And at such times, it seems as if all our toil had been in vain; and we are ready to cry out in bitterness,—"O wretched man that I am! who will deliver me from this body of death?" Often, when we look back upon a day, we see that through its hours the spirit has been willing, but the flesh weak,—the law of love and fidelity for the most part present to the mind, and yet little unkindnesses and negligences strewn here and there, testifying to momentary victories of impulse over principle. With our holiest efforts and desires, with our best services, there are blended so many imperfections, as to leave no room for a self-complacent thought, and to fill our hours of self-recollection with the consciousness of infirmity and short-coming. We find, also, that our besetting frailties and sins often place us on a false footing with our fellow-men. Under transient impulse, we often manifest traits that form no part of our established characters. We may have hearts full of love; and yet some constitutional infelicity may often check or pervert the utterance of our kind affections. We may have glowing religious zeal, and an earnest longing to render active and effectual service to the cause of piety; and yet diffidence or unreadiness may tie our hands and palsy our tongues, and we, with full hearts, may seem cold and dead, while others, with even less inward fervor, can tell their joy, and bear about the message of their God.

Under such experiences, we need to turn from our own frailty to our heart-seeing Father, with whom our witness is in heaven, our record on high. We need to appeal from the malign judgment of the world, nay, from the self-reproach of our own baffled and discouraged hearts, to Him who "knoweth what is the mind of the spirit." To him we may say,—"Thou, O God, hast searched me, and known me. Thou hast seen my aims; thou hast beheld my failures and my transgressions. Judge thou me, O my Father, not according to my sins, which are ever before me, but according to my desire for thy service and my delight in thy law." How quietly does the little child rest in the spirit of filial confidence, implicitly trusting his father's readiness to forgive! He may often have failed and fallen. Yet did he have all the while a filial spirit? did he desire to do right? was it his prevalent wish and aim to obey? In all his self-reproach for his transgressions, however frequent, he still, with the rectitude of a filial heart, reposes on his Father's love, and knows that he is forgiven and accepted. Thus may we, children of God's great family, though we proffer no claim of merit, and bow under a deep sense of unworthiness, cherish an undoubting confidence in the Father, whose forgiving mercy breathed in the words, and flowed in the reconciling blood, of the Lord Jesus.

I have thus, inadequately I fear, but in the language of deep conviction, set before you our need of a Father in heaven. Could we but lead a strictly filial life, could we walk, as Jesus did, ever in the felt presence of our Father, how would the spirit thus given us satisfy our worthy desires and repress our aimless strivings, sustain us in trial and comfort us in sorrow, quench the terror of the grave and make death an angel of light! In God's fatherly care and love, there ever comes to us the voice,—"Be thou careful for nothing, but in everything give thanks. Cast thy burden upon the Lord. Move on in the path of duty; and calmly wait, till the Father calls thee from thy service on the dusty pavement of earth to minister before him in the starry courts of heaven."

Brethren, are we partakers of this spirit of adoption? Have we felt its blessedness in our homes, on the bed of languishing, at the grave-side? How, then, can we be indifferent to the desolation and misery of those who live in spiritual orphanhood? For them let us pray, let us labor; and thus fulfil the law of Christ, and manifest ourselves the true children of Him who lights his sun and sends his rain upon the unthankful and the evil.

SERMON II.

PATIENCE.

LET PATIENCE HAVE HER PERFECT WORK, THAT YE MAY BE PERFECT AND ENTIRE, WANTING NOTHING. — James i. 4.

I NEVER feel more strongly the divinity and perfectness of the Christian system, than in reading the works of those classic authors whose morality makes the nearest approach to the Christian standard. There is always some rough point which juts out to mar what might otherwise seem faultless, — always some essential virtue lacking in the catalogue, or some vice, like Satan clothed in robes of light, placed in strange companionship among the virtues. I have of late read much, and with both pleasure and profit, in the moral treatises of Seneca, who has been often and justly styled the *almost* Christian moralist. But in morals, that one word *almost* is a fatal word. The omission of one cardinal virtue, or the glorification of a single vice, is enough to give sin free entrance and an established foothold. The chief fault that I find with Seneca is his omission of patience from his list of virtues; and from this omission, unessential as some might deem it, there flow the most revolting and fatal consequences. He gives many admirable precepts, worthy the heed of the Christian warrior, for contending with the evils of life, and destroying their power by exterminating them. But, if they exceed mortal strength, and cannot be overcome, he represents it as beneath a wise or a brave man to bear them, when it is so easy to leap out of existence. The duty of suicide in preference to unavoidable and incurable outward evil is one of his favorite topics, and frequently forms the nauseating close of a paragraph, on which, up to that point, you are ready to exclaim, "How truly Christian!" He is perpetually citing as the paragon of virtue Cato, whose principal achievement was his deliberate self-murder.

The very field of discipline, which the heathen moralist thus precluded for his disciple, is that on which the precepts and example of Jesus are the most full and clear. The necessary evils of life are the pavement of precious stones on the highway to heaven. Patience occupies a place second to no other grace of the Christian character. It clothed our Master like a robe on his weary sojourn, and sat on his brow like a jewelled diadem in the hall of Pilate and on the mount of crucifixion. The Gospel, indeed, excludes not courage; but prefers in honor its gentler sister virtue. Courage is an occasional act or effort of the soul; patience, a continuous habit. Courage is the mission of some; patience, the duty of all. Courage courts observation, and sustains itself by every possible outward prop and stimulus; patience is lonely and quiet, — its warfare is within, — its victory, without sound of trumpet, for the eye of God and the award of heaven. Courage may give its strength to evil, and may nerve the arm of the thief or the manslayer; patience dwells only in the bosom of piety, and always beholds the face of her Father in heaven.

I now ask your attention to a few remarks designed to illustrate the necessity and the means of cultivating the virtue of patience, and the mode in which it so reacts upon the whole character as to make the patient disciple "perfect and entire, lacking nothing."

The necessity of this virtue can hardly be overrated. Our Saviour said, with literal truth, — "In the world ye shall have tribulation." Who escapes it? No one can feel more fully than I do, that God has placed us in a good world, and has put within the reach of us all a large preponderance of happiness over misery. With most of us, life rolls on calmly through childhood and early youth, and for long portions of our later years. But few approach middle life without some experience of sorrow, — seasons of sickness and infirmity, heavy disappointments, weary vigils with suffering parents, children, and kindred, — times when the floods lift their angry voice and the billows break over us, — times when nothing seems stable but the throne of God and the hope of heaven. And these visitations of Providence are not momentary, so that they can be met by a sudden and defiant effort; but they are prolonged, continuous, spreading out into the future, and the end is not yet, but is beyond our foresight and calculation. For some, also, the sun is darkened long before midday; and they, though not without kind reliefs and rich blessings, must move on beneath clouds which only the resurrection morning will scatter. Poverty, desolation, or chronic infirmity is their appointed sphere of duty, their only portion, till they exchange it for Abraham's bosom and the inheritance of the righteous. And these darker scenes and portions must be met either in ceaseless discontent, murmuring, and distrust, or in that spirit of quiet, trustful patience, which says, — "Father, not my will, but thine, be done!" But for those that murmur, blessings left and comforts sent are wasted, and there hangs over their dwellings and about their spirits an impenetrable gloom; while to the patient and confiding soul light arises in darkness, — the cloud cannot hang so thick and heavy, but that rays of divine love struggle through its fissures and fringe its edges,

— it is spanned by the bow of promise, with the inscription, — "I will never leave nor forsake thee."

Among the means of cherishing patience, I would first name a deep and enduring sense of the love of God, and of the merciful purpose of all his dispensations This we all confess in words; but we must feel it. Our theoretical faith is right and sound; the great object is to bring our feelings up to the standard of our avowed belief. This faith must work itself into the whole texture of our souls, pervade and fill our hearts, and be as the life-blood of our inward being. "God is love," — "God is our Father," — these divine words must enter into our consciousness, be inwardly digested and assimilated. And this can best be done in those early, happy days which are bathed in the Creator's smile, on all whose moments hang the dew-drops of his blessing. This needed faith in a fatherly Providence parents should teach their children, when they are full of joy; and the young, prosperous, and always happy should grow into it more and more in daily adoration and thanksgiving. We should look back upon the way in which our Father has led us, and mark its special deliverances and favors. We should look around us, and trace back through their earthly sources to their eternal fountain the streams of mercy flowing hourly upon our homes and our daily walks. There has been, there is, enough in the life of each of us, if we would only ponder upon it, to draw forth the confession, with gratitude too full for utterance, — "God has nourished me as a child, — in ways and times without number he has revealed himself as my Father and my friend, — I individually am the distinct object of his care and love, — how precious are thy thoughts of mercy towards me! how great is the sum of them! — should I count them, they are more in number than the sands of the sea."

This spirit will give us patience, when the evil days come. We shall know that disease and affliction are but altered forms of mercy, ordained with kind purpose and for a blessed ministry, — that outward trial is sent to heal inward disease, to establish the soul in firmer health and fuller strength, to shed into it the peace of God and the spirit of heaven. We shall lean in faith upon a Father, whose ways seem dark to us only because we are children and fall short of our Father's wisdom. We shall calmly yield ourselves to the guidance of Him whose appointed way must needs be the surest, safest path to heaven. Our trust will be confirmed by exercise and deepened by experience, so that every new period of trial will give to patience its more and more perfect work. Our early trials, if submissively borne, will leave in our hearts a work of grace, which we can mark and recognize. We shall see and know that they made us better,— that they made our prayers more fervent and more constant, our love to man more tender and enduring, our sympathies quicker and stronger, our tempers more meek and gentle, our tastes more pure and spiritual. We shall bear so consciously these blessed fruits of an afflictive Providence, as to leave no room for doubt and misgiving, and to fortify our faith in the word of God by a voice within, which we can neither suppress nor gainsay.

Again, patience derives nourishment from the hope of heaven,—not from the mere belief in immortality, but from the personal appropriation and consciousness of it. What makes courage a much easier virtue than patience is, that it is called into exercise for a crisis which will soon be passed, and beyond which hope easily extends; while patience belongs to those protracted trials which offer no immediate or definite hope of their termination. We think little of a rough road or a bad inn, if the end of our journey is near and attractive. We cheerfully encounter temporary inconveniences and troubles, if fully assured that they are to be followed by long and unbroken quietness and prosperity. Did we let our contemplations rest habitually on eternity, all our earthly trials would in like manner seem light and short, and not worthy to be compared with the joy set before us. This consideration enters largely into all patient and submissive suffering. Many there are, indeed, who well know that their first bed of rest will be the grave, but who are made cheerful and happy by a near and constant view of the home where sickness, pain, and sorrow can find no entrance.

Patience receives, also, ample support from the life and example of Jesus. In him the disciple learns that whom the Lord loves he chastens. He sees that trials cannot be sent in anger, when the best beloved Son had their full weight laid upon him. He feels strengthened to tread the path and to bear the lot which Jesus has made illustrious by his own victory and triumph. Poverty, desolation, acute bodily suffering, have all been consecrated by his homeless wanderings, his rejection, agony, and cross.

None find themselves so severely afflicted, but that in the outward circumstances of his toilsome and painful pilgrimage they can see traces of yet severer suffering and agony. Yet we behold him calm, patient, submissive, trustful. Not a murmur escapes him, not an unconditional prayer for relief. His patience is tried at every point, both by the mysterious hand of an afflictive Providence, and by the malice and scorn of the wicked. He encounters ingratitude in its most revolting forms, persecution from those whom he had striven to bless, insult and ignominy alike from the supercilious great and the sycophantic mob. The Jew gives him over to the Gentile; the Gentile hands him back, scourged and buffeted, to the Jew; and the Jew again transfers him, lacerated and mangled, to the foreign executioner. But, beneath their jeers and taunts, tossed from one coarse hand to another in the crowd, grasping the mimic sceptre, with his temples torn by the thorns, he wears in his unmoved serenity a kingly aspect, which strikes admiration and awe into many rude hearts, and constrains the man of blood, who watches by the cross, to exclaim, — "Surely this was the Son of God." This beautiful example of patience the Christian contemplates, till it transfuses itself into his own soul, till the cross gives him strength, till he can enter into the secret of the Saviour's submission, peace, and joy, and can say with him, — "Not as I will, but as thou wilt!"

But this life is a school for heaven, and we are accustomed to believe that we learn lessons here to practise there, — that the virtues which we are here to acquire most sedulously are those of which we shall have the greatest need in the life to come. Is not patience an exception? We can have no occasion for its exercise in heaven; — why, then, assign it so prominent a place in the Christian character? This question will be best answered by considering the uses of patience.

Under this head I first remark, that there is one work which we must all accomplish, would we enter heaven,—namely, the formation of spiritual characters, the establishment of the supremacy of the inward over the outward, of the soul over sense, of things unseen and eternal over things seen and temporal. The world, in one way or another, must be overcome,—the preference for external and perishing goods subdued,—the overmastering love of what is inward and spiritual planted firmly in the soul. It is to accomplish this warfare that we are placed here, that by means of it the soul may grow and get strength, and all its higher powers be drawn out in hardy and self-sustaining vigor. This, however performed, is an arduous process; but perhaps not more so for those whose discipline is that of frequent or protracted suffering, than for the prosperous and happy. Nay, I doubt not that in the sight of Heaven seemingly opposite lots may occupy the same level as to actual enjoyment, if connected with similar moral developments; and, for one who would win heaven, it may be that the trials of health, prosperity, or riches are no less severe than those of sickness, adversity, or penury. They are, indeed, of a different class; and because they are not so frequently regarded as occasions of moral discipline, they appear less. But for those who are rich, and full, and strong, if they would reach favored places in the heavenly kingdom, there must be a course of self-restraint, self-denial, and self-renunciation, — there are numberless allurements to be resisted, innocent desires to be kept innocent by their moderate indulgence, an engrossing world, with its countless attractions, to be pushed back, by constant effort, from the inmost citadel of the affections to that second place which it rightfully occupies. Most of this work Providence performs for the suffering disciple, — appointing him, indeed, a discipline of a different kind, no less arduous, but I believe not more so, than those of us who are prosperous and happy would no doubt feel, if we did our work as faithfully as we love to see the afflicted do theirs. And herein lies one essential office of patience, in the spiritualizing of the character; and how beautifully and effectually it does this many of us can testify, from our having felt nearer heaven in the abode of penury, or by the bed of chronic illness, than in the gayest and brightest scenes that have fallen within our experience.

Then, again, in no form does a Christian example seem more attractive, and win more honor to the Christian name and character, than in patience under severe trial and suffering. Piety, indeed, is in the sight of God the same, under whatever form; but by man it cannot be equally appreciated in all conditions of life. In prosperity and joy, there will always be the sneering and sceptical, who will repeat Satan's question, — "Doth Job serve God for naught?" But touch the disciple in his dearest earthly interests, bow him down under severe affliction, and if he then holds fast his faith and trust, if he is serene and happy, if he talks of the goodness of God, and manifestly dwells in inward peace and quietness, there is no room left for cavilling. We can see and calculate the burden under which the spirit rests, and the obstacles against which it struggles; and we may estimate the strength of its faith and principle by the weight which it can lift and bear with ease and joy. No examples are so powerful as these in commending the religion of the cross. Multitudes have been reclaimed by them from indifference and scepticism. Multitudes have been led by them to meditate, as they never had before, on the sufficiency of the Gospel, and to believe and confess it the power and wisdom of God unto salvation.

God means that we should all be examples to one another; that, while we save our own souls, we should shine for the salvation of others; and that thus the world should from generation to generation become more and more filled with lights on the heavenward path. We read in the Bible of the integrity of Joseph, the patience of Job, the early piety of Samuel, the firmness of Daniel, the zeal of Peter, and the love of John. God means that the life of each one of us should be, for those around us, and for those to come after us, such a scripture as is the life of each of these holy men. In Jesus his whole will and law were written out in living characters. What he was, God means that each disciple should be in his own sphere and measure, — each the special embodiment of some part of his communicable attributes, mingled, as they must appear, in different proportions, and with different degrees of lustre, according to the theatre on which they are to be displayed. Each living gospel, by its own peculiar blending of divine traits and manifestations, may have a peculiar charm and power for some soul, which others will not reach, and may thus do its part towards leading fellow-men to righteousness and heaven. This office, as I have said, seems to be performed with superior felicity and power by those whose mission it is to suffer rather than to do. In their humility and self-distrust, their only regret often is, that they can do nothing for the glory of God and the honor of their religion; while, from the retired scene of their calm and trustful endurance, as from a tribunal of world-resounding eloquence, there may be constantly going forth the most deep-reaching and effectual lessons of truth, duty, and piety.

I remark, in closing, that patience is not a virtue to which even death sets limits. It belongs to heaven and to eternity. What! you ask, — patience in heaven? Will there be suffering there? By no means. But what is patience?

It is implicit faith and trust, exercised in the darker scenes and vicissitudes of life. These scenes will brighten into the perfect day, — these vicissitudes will be merged in the great change, when the corruptible puts on incorruption; but the faith and trust of which they were the theatre will live for ever, and be for ever needed. There will be mysteries in heaven as well as here, things to be taken on faith before they can be fully known, portions of the vast administration of God, in which, in our ignorance, we must cast ourselves in humble reliance on his wisdom and goodness. Our faith, our trust, must go before us on our career of growing knowledge, power, and holiness, always hovering on the limit of what we already see and know, and harmonizing and equalizing to our apprehensions what we cannot fathom or understand.

I have thus spoken of the necessity, the aids, and the uses of patience. It makes life beautiful. It sheds a calm and heavenly glory upon the bed of death. As we watch the passage hence of one who has been baptized into the likeness of our Saviour's sufferings, in the hushed stillness of entire submission, in the peace of God and the atmosphere of prayer and praise, we seem in a heavenly presence, and almost listen for the angel wings that bear a kindred spirit to the throne of God and the communion of the unsuffering and the ransomed, while every regretful thought is checked by the voice that bade the seer of Patmos write, — "Blessed are the dead that die in the Lord; for they rest from their labors, and their works do follow them."

SERMON III.

OLD AGE.

THE RIGHTEOUS SHALL FLOURISH LIKE THE PALM-TREE: HE SHALL GROW LIKE A CEDAR IN LEBANON. THOSE THAT BE PLANTED IN THE HOUSE OF THE LORD SHALL FLOURISH IN THE COURTS OF OUR GOD. THEY SHALL STILL BRING FORTH FRUIT IN OLD AGE. — Psalm xcii. 12–14.

AMONG my hearers are many who have passed or are passing the meridian of life, and of those still young almost all look forward to length of days upon earth. I would now address those who feel that they are growing old, or who hope to become old, and would offer them such counsels as may save them from the misery of a barren and hopeless age, and make them like those cedars of Lebanon, around which generations, states, empires, have been born and have passed away, and which still clothe themselves with the verdure and the fruit of their youth.

We are accustomed to think of the prospect of death as full of the most solemn and sad interest.

It seems to me that the prospect of a lengthened life upon earth may well awaken even a deeper seriousness and pensiveness of spirit. And in saying this, I cast no reproach on the Creator or his world. I regard both the old age and the death which God means for us, and for which his spirit ripens us, as blessed and desirable. But old age, where the youth and prime have been passed in frivolity or worldliness, and death, where God has not been owned in the life, cannot be regarded with excessive dread, or warded off with a diligence too early or too constant. Let us now look at some of these inevitable experiences of advancing years, which evince the need of some principle of greenness and vitality beyond the power of time or of earthly change.

In the first place, if we live long, we must outlive the keen enjoyment of mere pleasure, — of the lighter and gayer portions of life. While the elasticity of youth lasts, before the freshness is worn off from scenes and objects that early grow familiar, before care presses heavily, or sorrow teaches its first hard lessons, one derives conscious gladness from the round of amusement, from whatever wears a festive aspect, from song, laughter, and merriment. But before the noon of life, most persons find these things becoming burdensome. They cannot raise their spirits to so high a level. Growing responsibilities have subdued their former buoyancy of soul. Affliction, while, so far from deadening, it has only rendered the more intense the capacity for calm and sober enjoyment, has infused a lasting pensiveness, with which loud and gay music makes a repulsive discord. The feeling rapidly grows upon one, that the game of life is too doubtful, and its stakes too desperate, for trifling; and many of the voices, much of the laughter, which used to make him glad, and on which in early life his free soul could float forth in entire sympathy, have become as vapid as the crackling of thorns. Those who still retain the livery of youth for the most part find it irksome, and deem it a galling necessity, an incessant burden and weariness, to continue in the routine in which they once found their chief pleasure.

With regard to the more serious pursuits of life, a man very early ascertains and exhausts the capacities of his condition, knows all that he is likely to be and do, and sees but little unattained for which he can reasonably hope. Before middle life, most persons have found their own level and their own measure. They have exhausted the charm of novelty in their profession or avocation, and yet feel that any essential change in their mode of life is growing more and more improbable. They have already abandoned many of the aims and hopes with which they started on their career, — expect only a competence instead of wealth, or mere mediocrity instead of eminence. Golden visions have grown dim, wide and far-reaching prospects have been narrowed, and the horizon is fast shutting in on every side. Then, too, whatever rewards of enterprise or effort have been won appear, when attained, but slight and small, compared with what they were in expectation. What would once have been deemed an ample estate, when possessed, seems paltry. The station which was once a goal almost too distant to be striven for, when reached, dissatisfies; for some envied Mordecai holds a higher seat. Even in the generous and ennobling walks of mental culture, a conviction of our own ignorance grows upon us with our growth in wisdom, and the proportions and dimensions of truth enlarge to our view faster than its details reveal themselves to us. In point of mental acumen and vigor, too, there must come a period of decline and stagnation; at least, there have been no exempts from this law, except where a devout and loving heart has embalmed the intellect in its freshness, and kept the old man young. Then how eagerly do younger men remind their seniors that they are growing old! Crowding close upon one another's heels, the generations rush on, and each thrusts itself, with irreverent haste, into the place of that which preceded it, saying, — "Stand aside, and give us room; for we were born under better stars, and are more abundantly the children of light and wisdom than ye." The foremost places in society, the commanding posts in public life, are constantly usurped by younger and still younger claimants, so that instead of the fathers are the children and the children's children.

Then, again, though the domestic life of the aged is often serene and happy, it is made so only by the hallowing power of a higher world; for, in an earthly point of view, it is but little that we can promise ourselves in declining years as to our social and domestic relations. If we live long, there will drop away from our circle one after another of those who seemed essential to our very being; and we must be left as solitary barren trunks, or with here and there a decaying branch, in place of the green and verdant boughs that now seem so full of promise. If we live long, it will be to survive a thousand deaths, — to see those that started with us gradually wasting away; nay, more, to have those that still remain, and are inexpressibly dear, far or often divided from us, — to be oppressed with numberless anxieties on their account, to have their burdens and sorrows added to our own, and perhaps to incur the keenest disappointment in the moral delinquency, the blighting and spiritual death, of the once innocent and lovely.

In fine, waning life must continually part with outward advantages which early years had given. Decrease as to all things earthly is the inevitable law of man's latter days. We must have less and less in prospect, must have our strongest holds upon life one by one broken off, and, beyond a certain point, can hope only for days whose strength is labor and sorrow. And now take the only view which can present itself to the old man who has no interest in things above, no hope beyond the grave, and who already feels in his own frame that the evil days are drawing nigh and the pleasureless years are at hand. What lies before him? A prospect, every feature of which is worn and faded, and beyond which rises a black, impenetrable wall, — a heritage almost squandered, and with no reversion for his benefit, — a future, an eternity blank and void. And are you willing to see life thus slipping away from you, and to know that what is gone is irretrievably gone, and yet to have no hold on a higher and better life? But there is only one Master who remains faithful to the hoary head, and "forsakes not his servant when his strength faileth him." Let us look, then, at some of those things which we shall need for our happiness, under the full consciousness of declining years.

In the first place, we must feel that we have lived for some worthy purpose, accomplished some satisfying and permanent results, laid up some treasure that cannot be taken from us. The work of life must have been such, that we can regard it with pleasure in our lonely and our solemn hours. It must be such as will abide, and go with us from the busy scene, and go with us, too, from the life that now is. We must see the work within in chastened affections, pure tastes, a heavenly temper, a heart familiar in its converse with God and at peace with man. Our choicest possessions must be those which retreating health and strength cannot bear with them, or the failure of our active intellectual powers destroy, or treacherous memory hide from us. And here we may trace a beautiful arrangement of divine mercy, and a pledge, too, that the moral nature shall survive the grave, in the fact, that, when the sight grows dim through age, and energy is palsied, and recollection fails, the moral traits generally remain unobscured, nay, grow in mellowness and beauty even to the confines of eternity. A friend once gave me an account of his father, since deceased, who had then added seven to a full century of years. His communion with the outward world had at that time entirely ceased, except when objects were for a moment, and with the utmost effort, forced upon his attention. But having been from his youth up gentle, contented, happy, and devout, he still manifested the utmost cheerfulness, patience, and gratitude; his lips were moving, the greater part of his waking hours, in the language of half-uttered prayer; and the only form of conversation that he had retained was that of a fervent benediction, whenever the voices of his children or friends could pierce the thick walls of sense that shut in the soul of the blind and deaf old man. Who can doubt that such a soul has that within it which keeps it in perfect peace and gladness, — that it is cheered in its solitude by celestial visitors, by the communings of God, and Jesus, and justified spirits, even as the lone mountain, inaccessible to the steps of mortals, has the nearest view of heaven? Let us walk with God now, — and then, should the days come when we can no longer walk with men, we shall still retain our hidden life with him; and in hoary winter, when the harvest of our earthly life has passed, and its sheaves are all gathered in, the fruits of piety shall still be ripening for a better harvest in heaven.

Again, would we enjoy a happy old age, let us make kindness and love the law of our lips and our lives. Let us bind ourselves by ties of mutual benefit with as many of our fellow-beings as we may. Let us not have lived in vain for those among whom we dwell; but let us so order our lives, that the eye that sees us shall bless us, and the ear that hears us shall bear witness for us. Selfishness withers the heart prematurely, and makes a young man old, while a kind and beneficent life keeps the heart young, and makes old age flourish like a palm-tree. Generous age is deserted neither by God nor by man. Its own kindred and coevals may grow few; but strangers perform the part of kindred, and youth delights to blend its morning beams with the rich sunset of a benevolent life. Gratitude and affection smooth the tottering steps, and lighten the infirmities, of the merciful man. God and all good angels are with him. The fruits of his charity in part remain to refresh and nourish him till his change comes, while those not to be found on earth are garnered for him in heaven.

Again, would we pass a happy old age, let us not forsake the communion of our departed friends. If we live on, their number must soon equal, and then exceed, that of the surviving. However assiduous and tender may be the ministry of newer and younger friends, there will still be vacant places near and about us, which they can never fill. The nearest places may be made void, and others can then move around us only in an outer circle. Let us learn, therefore, of the spirit of Jesus to regard those who have gone as still near and with us, as separated from us but by a thin veil, which faith may make transparent, and as forming a goodly company to welcome us to our final rest, and to shed over the majestic courts of heaven a familiar, homelike aspect.

Let us, my friends, by these Christian means of preparation, fortify ourselves against the years of decline and infirmity. Let us not hope for length of days, without making the gift worth praying for and worth having.

Let me, in conclusion, commend the train of thought in the preceding discourse to the diligent heed of the young who may have listened to me. You will all think early of some provision for the comfort and happiness of old age. The best provision for your latter days, — that without which hoarded wealth will be a weary burden, — that with which poverty will be no curse, — is the provision which memory may furnish, — the retrospect of a life of piety, integrity, and kindness. You see those whose early lives were given to worldliness or profligacy; and there surely is not in their ranks an advanced post which you could think of occupying without a shudder. But how beautiful, how reverend, the hoary head which crowns a pure and virtuous youth and prime! This world presents no sight so heavenly as the serene sunset of a well-spent life, when the testimony of a good conscience is loud and clear, — when the eye can glance back on duties faithfully performed and conflicts well sustained, — when the veteran soldier of the cross can say, in godly sincerity, — "I have fought a good fight, I have finished my course, I have kept the faith." He may have borne severe trial and desolating sorrow. He may be left alone by those once his best beloved. He may seem to have been a mark for the keenest shafts of adversity. But he is still calm and happy. His repose is on the bosom of eternal Love. His peace is that which Jesus gives, and which the world cannot take away. How gently blend for him the visions of memory and hope! How tranquil and kind is nature's decay! For him the evening shadows fall gently, and they all "point to the dawn." For him the silver cord is softly loosed, not cut; the golden bowl crumbled, not rudely broken at the fountain; and death at length is greeted with a solemn welcome, as bearing the faithful servant to that better home, where, in the beautiful language of the prophet, "they that wait upon the Lord shall renew their strength; they shall mount up on wings as eagles; they shall run and not be weary, they shall walk and not faint."

SERMON IV.

A PROTECTING PROVIDENCE.

(Preached on the day of Public Thanksgiving, 1843.)

THOU SHALT REMEMBER ALL THE WAY WHICH THE LORD THY GOD LED THEE. — Deut. viii. 2.

THIS is emphatically a day of remembrance. Parted families meet, and recount the course of Providence since they were last together. The long absent return, each to bear testimony to heavenly guidance and protection. Griefs, too, come up with vividness, and wounds are reopened. Vacant places at the festival dim the eye of the bereaved, and thoughts of those no longer with us mingle deep hues of pensiveness with the gayety and gladness of the season. What can be more appropriate, at once to hallow the joy and to soothe the sad remembrances of our festival, than for us to do together what will be done separately in every house, (Heaven grant that it be religiously done!) — namely, to look back upon the way in which the Lord our God has led us, and to recall some of the grateful views of a kind Providence which are or ought to be common to us all?

The monuments of divine love are crowded so closely together, that we are prone to pass them by unnoticed. The experience of all of us is so much alike, that we cease to marvel at it. The Lord our God leads us all in a way so wonderful and so merciful, that it seems a worn and common path, with nothing upon it to excite our special interest. Were any one of us the sole recipient of favors of which we all partake, that individual would stand forth as a miracle of mercy to himself and to every one else, and would be regarded, day by day, with the same amazement with which the sisters of Bethany saw Lazarus stepping forth from the tomb. But because the Father of all leaves none unblessed, we often neglect the religious review of his Providence, so that this duty, than which there is none more imperative or more sanctifying, is, perhaps, one of the rarest to be faithfully discharged.

In helping you in the performance of this duty, I would first ask you to reflect on the amount of happiness which you as an assembly represent. You have come hither from more than a hundred different dwellings; and in those dwellings a very few are left at home on account of the chronic infirmities and gentle decline of age, and one or two laboring under more acute disease, but not one so ill as to be incapable of enjoying many of the common bounties of Providence, — not one to whom this day will not have given a very considerable preponderance of enjoyment over suffering. Of those here, how few have come with anxious or grief-worn countenances, or with sad hearts! The hue of health, the glow of cheerfulness, is on almost every face. True, there are many of you who have chronic troubles, — disappointments and sorrows, which you do not regard, and probably never will regard, as healed. But these take much less than at first thought might seem from the enjoyment of life. Probably those who feel the poorest are those of you who are only less rich than you once were, who have met with great losses, yet have never lacked fitting food, raiment, and shelter, or even the comforts and luxuries which you enjoyed when you called yourselves richer. Your consciousness of poverty, therefore, is by no means constant, but comes to you only at moments when you are forced to compare yourselves with others, and casts no cloud over the better portion of your lives. Those of you who have been bereaved of kindred nearest to your hearts are, indeed, mourners every day. But still there are so many of the beloved left, and so many sources of joy still open, that your moments of poignant grief bear a small proportion to the gladness which a kind Providence forces upon you in spite of the sorrow that you so carefully nourish. It is not that your hearts are ever unfaithful to the memory of those that are gone; but your joy-giving Father will not leave his children a prey to enduring grief. There is probably not one of you to whom, in the sight of God, this is not a happy day; not one, whose glad do not outnumber his regretful thoughts; whose mercies spared do not exceed those withdrawn, by a proportion beyond our power to calculate;—for our sorrows we can count, and tell our wounds, but thy thoughts of love, O God, how great is the sum of them!—should we count them, they are more in number than the sands of the sea.

How many sources of happiness flow for us this morning! While we slept, the stars faded from their night-watches, and the misty dawn prepared a softened, mellow light for our waking eyes. The sun rose in beauty on our day of glad festivity. The autumn air has breathed health and vigor into our frames. The rich, yet chastened, hues of the autumn sky have sent their spirit of repose into our hearts. The notes of the dying year reach us, not as those of a dirge, but as an anthem of praise and hope. When the night-curtain was uplifted, we came forth from our rest to the tables which our Father had spread for us; and the table of the poorest of us bore testimony to his blessing on commerce and on harvest toil, on skill and handicraft. We met in our respective families. No watch had we kept by night, but we feared no evil; we abandoned ourselves and one another to the unslumbering Shepherd of Israel. Yet danger may have been near. The shadow of death may have passed over our dwellings; but God averted it before we waked to fear it. There were in our houses numerous frail infant lives, which might be crushed before the moth, and the sparing of which through so many gates of death seems an unceasing miracle; yet they slept unharmed, and awoke full of health and gladness, for they rested under the good Shepherd's eye, and beneath his arm.

Home, — how many springs of joy does that one word comprise! It is created by the very events which we most dread within its enclosure. It is the offspring of sickness, suffering, and death. It is our exposure to these (so called) calamities, which makes it necessary for each to have that retreat, that ark of protection, where others shall help him ward off the evil day, or bear and survive it when it comes. It is death that calls for successive generations of men, and creates families for the nourishment and defence of each new race. Take suffering and death away, and mankind would be at once resolved into isolated units, and the shrine of the purest joy would be laid waste and desolate for ever. Yet how kindly are these essential portions of the beneficent system arranged, so that they often darken not for years the home that they make glad, and, when they come, come almost always with gentle preparation, and with unexpected sources of relief and comfort! How much is implied in the tranquil and healthful condition in which most of our families have found themselves to-day! So many living lyres in time and tune, so many marvellous tides of life kept flowing, — and yet these lyres strung as with threads of gossamer, these tides flowing in the frailest vessels, and liable to be shed by the slightest accident. In a thousand forms and ways must an incessant Providence watch, guard, and guide, avert peril and bestow aid, in each of our households, with every new day, to make health the rule, disease and death the rare exception, — joy the current, grief the transient ripple on its surface.

I have spoken of common blessings. Have we not each special mercies which we would own with devout gratitude, — mercies adapted to our peculiar wants, stamped and sealed as for us individually, as distinctly marked, so to speak, with our names, as keepsakes from a friend might be? How often have we received the very favors which we most needed, yet foresaw not, and dared not anticipate, sent at the only moment and in the only mode in which they could have been availing! How many way-marks have we had reason to set up all along the path of life for peculiar interpositions and deliverances, for the hand of love outstretched at our seasons of greatest need, for those blessings so exactly timed, that, sent sooner, they would have been useless, or, given later, they would have come too late! Often, too, have slight events become the parents of great; and conjunctures of trivial circumstances have seemed to sway the whole course of our destinies. Often has our entire future appeared to hang as on a single thread, and to be modified as by the turning of a straw. Thus has God, by the feebleness of second causes, laid bare his own guiding arm, and shown himself the gracious arbiter of our fortunes. At times, too, the path has seemed shut up against us, mountains of difficulty have obstructed our way, or we have been, as were the Israelites of old, with foes behind and the deep sea before them. But just as we have halted in despair, not knowing where to plant our next footstep, God has cleft the mountain, or made the sea to stand in heaps on either hand, thus opening a straight path before us, and giving us the garment of praise for the spirit of heaviness.

In the way in which the Lord our God has led us, we may also cherish our gratitude by marking the footsteps of things that have almost happened. How close have we all often come to trial, suffering, or death, which Providence has averted when just hanging over our heads! The shadow darkens on our path; but the hand of love rolls it back before we feel its gloom. The safe way, by which we have been led, is a narrow road, often on the brink of fearful precipices, and crossing chasms and abysses as by a single plank. The slightest misstep to the right hand or to the left, and we are lost. Yet, amid hidden pitfalls and lurking graves, God has kept our feet from falling, and our souls from death.

In this connection, it is well for us to consider how little we can do for ourselves. We are too prone to feel as if our own industry, energy, and forethought could accomplish much. We are apt to take credit to ourselves for the security in which we dwell, and for the comforts which we multiply around us. But think how many sources of joy must all flow together, how many departments of nature and of being must all be brought into harmony, in order for us to pass a single hour in comfort. Is this, my hearer, an hour of peace and happiness? Are you sound in body, free from pain and infirmity, without any heavy burden on your mind, any outward source of grief, or any secret sorrow preying on your heart? If so, you may count the stars in the sky more easily than you can number the blessings of this moment. Your complex frame, consisting of myriads of parts, demands nutriment from every element, levies contributions on all surrounding nature, and pines and suffers the instant its claims are denied. Your mind takes simultaneous cognizance of a vast variety of objects and topics, and is thus constantly open at all points to anxiety and corroding care. Your heart interweaves its fibres, not only with a cherished few, but, more or less closely, with a great number of relatives, intimates, or dependents, whose lives are bound up in the same bundle with your own, whose griefs you bear, whose sorrows you carry, who can none of them be in immediate and deep distress, and leave you at your ease. But though you depend on all these things, you can yourself do but one thing at a time; and, while seeking your own good in one direction, you are obliged to leave all your other interests uncared for, all the other avenues to your peace unguarded. Your own counsel and might cannot be instrumental in doing for you a millionth part of what is every moment done for you. How deep, then, should be the gratitude with which you now set up a new pillar of thanksgiving, with the inscription, — "Hitherto hath the Lord helped me!"

We have thus taken, under a few obvious, yet too much forgotten heads, a cursory view of the way in which the Lord our God has led us. What are the duties to which this review calls us?

Does it not make the gratitude of the most thankful seem cold? What but unceasing praise can worthily respond to this incessant flow of mercy? And yet, my friends, do not some of us live without thanksgiving, — receiving unnumbered benefits, and yet never rendering the sacrifice of praise, — with mercies ever new compassing their path and their lying down, and yet their way unblessed, their rest unsanctified, by the incense of a grateful heart? O that every soul might feel the love in which it is embosomed, and might send heavenward the blended anthem of all its powers and affections, — "Bless the Lord, and forget not all his benefits!" May the smile of our Father rest upon us, and sink deep into our hearts, as we enjoy the festivities of this day. With those that we love best at our sides, in homes made happy, at tables spread by our Father's bounty, may the rich gifts lead us to the Giver, and may every fireside and every heart be an altar of praise.

In these mercies, hear we not also the voice of religious exhortation, — "My son, give me thy heart"? Why is it that our outward life is thus passed as in the bosom of the Infinite Father, if it be not that our souls may also live in him? From our happy homes and our bountiful boards, from the children, like olive-plants, around our tables, from the uncounted blessings that encompass our daily path, from the watchful love that guards our nightly rest, come there not invitations, loud and many-voiced, to consecrate our lives to Him who loves us all, and whose tender mercies are over all his works? And shall not these voices of Providence blend in beautiful harmony with that of Him who bore upon earth, and displayed among the dwellings of men, the image of the Father's love?

God's providence in all the past invites and exhorts us to implicit trust in him for all time to come. In our littleness and lowliness, we may feel that we are individually the objects of the Divine interest, care, and love; that "he knoweth our path and our lying down, and is acquainted with all our ways." We may dismiss care; for he careth for us. We may repose even on the mountain billows; for "the Lord on high is mightier than the noise of many waters, yea, than the mighty waves of the sea." We need never apprehend for the morrow, or cast looks of doubt or fear along the path of life; for we are assured that the pillar of cloud will shield us by day, and the fire-signal guide us by night.

SERMON V.

DESPONDENCY.

WHY ART THOU CAST DOWN, O MY SOUL? AND WHY ART THOU DISQUIETED IN ME? HOPE THOU IN GOD. — Psalm xlii. 5.

THE lesson of implicit trust in Providence is, even to many who call themselves Christians, hard to learn, and easy to forget. Some of us habitually, and most of us at times, cherish a foreboding spirit with reference to the future, and afflict ourselves with the evils and calamities that may come. In our text the Psalmist rebukes himself for this anxious, distrustful spirit, and, in a season of doubt and disquietude, urges upon his own soul the exhortation, — "Hope thou in God." The text will suggest the division of my sermon. I would first illustrate the unreasonableness and virtual impiety of the over-anxious, foreboding spirit manifested by so many, and would then inculcate the lesson of implicit trust in a wise and paternal Providence.

Do I address any of the foreboding and distrustful? I would first remind you that this spirit is rebuked by your whole experience. The vast preponderance with you has always been on the side of happiness. You have probably never passed an utterly wretched day,—a day which did not give you more enjoyment than suffering. If you have been long of this foreboding habit, not one in a hundred of the sorrows that you have apprehended has reached you. Those, also, that have overtaken you have been lighter than you would have feared. The stone may have been great, and as you drew near, you said,—"Who will roll it away?" But an angel's hand has helped you lift it. Why should you look for darker days than you have passed through? Why should you expect a more afflictive experience than you have had? Why do you fear that the goodness and mercy which have followed you all your days will forsake you now? Do troubles seem close at hand and inevitable? So have they seemed before, and yet a way of escape has been opened. We have all of us been as was Isaac on Mount Moriah. The sacrifice has been ready, the knife lifted, and ourselves the victims; but, as the stroke descended, an unseen hand turned it from us. "The thing that hath been shall be." The Divine presence, which in cloud and fire has guided your path thus far, shall be your guide even unto death.

Again, what can your anxiety do for you?

Can it avert what you dread? No. But it may hasten it. Under Providence, there are many evils which it is within our own power to ward off. In many respects, our health, our outward well-being, and that of our households, are committed to our own keeping, and can be safely kept only by a self-collected mind and a quiet heart. But the foreboding, desponding spirit is apt to be thrown off its guard; it loses the just balance and healthy tone of its mental powers; it becomes incapable of forethought, and rushes headlong into the evil which it fears, or remains in the track of calamities which, if in a more tranquil state, it would foresee and escape. Then, too, your solicitude, even where it cannot hasten, cannot prevent trial; and if the dreaded evil comes, your previous anxiety will have weakened the fortitude with which you might otherwise have borne it and triumphed over it, and will give it the victory over you in a conflict, in which it is your Father's will that you should come off more than conqueror.

I would also remind you that sorrow in prospect is much more bitter and grievous than it is in actual experience. When it comes to us as the cup which our Father gives us, it comes ready mingled, and mingled with elements of relief and comfort. God sends no unmitigated sorrow; but always enables us to sing of mercy in the midst of judgment, — never suffers us in the spirit of heaviness utterly to cast off the garment of praise. He smooths for us the descent into the vale of tribulation; and we go down into it laden with covenant mercies, and with the assurance, — "I will never leave nor forsake thee." Every trial comes with its alleviating circumstances, its mild preparatives, and abounding consolations. Sickness summons sympathy and patience for its ministers. Unmerited disesteem fortifies itself by the testimony of a good conscience. Poverty moves on under the guidance of health and hope. Bereaved affection meets the risen Saviour at the grave-side. In every form of sorrow, God draws near to the stricken spirit, and offers his own joy-giving presence in the place of the blessings taken; and many of the afflicted have had in their severest trials far deeper, more heart-swelling views of the Divine love than they ever had in their seasons of gayety and gladness. But if we borrow trouble, we seize the cup in its untempered bitterness, before the time has come for the infusion of what may sweeten, bless, and sanctify it.

But there are some who are perpetually dreading for themselves calamities, which they say they would not fear so much for others; but such is their lot, — they are the doomed ones, — they are marks for the shafts of adversity, — the cup may pass from others, but not from them. Have I a hearer who cherishes such feelings? If so, I would ask him, Do you deem God partial, as man is partial? Do you believe that he will send you one trial more than you need? And if you really have more trials than others, may they not be sent in part to break up your habit of complaining and foreboding, to lead you to a calm and quiet self-commitment to the Divine protection, and to fix in your heart the spirit of cheerful confidence?

Let me again ask those who permit themselves to cast fearful and gloomy looks into the future, Why do you dread aught that can befall you, when none of these things can take place without your Father? You must feel assured that under him all things will work together for your good. You are as little children under his guidance; and to your short sight there may be deep mysteries in many of his dispensations, as there always are to a child in the course of discipline chosen by a judicious earthly parent. Lean, then, as children upon his arm, and commit yourselves as children to his keeping. Let him lead you in a way which you know not. Say with the Psalmist,—"I will fear no evil, for thou art with me." Make yourselves, so far as may be, independent of outward calamity. Seek those treasures of the inner man, that property of the mind and the affections, which can be neither frittered away by change nor destroyed by death. Let your true life be that hidden life of the heart, which is "most vigorous when the body dies." Let your souls be renewed by the transforming power of your Saviour's spirit, and then shall no outward trouble have power to harm you.

> "The man resolved and steady to his trust,
> Inflexible to ill and firmly just,
> Should the whole frame of nature round him break,
> In ruin dire and wild confusion hurled,
> He unconcerned would meet the mighty wreck,
> And stand secure amidst a falling world."

I have thus spoken of the folly and the remedy of a disquieted and foreboding spirit. Let me now urge upon you, and upon my own soul, the Psalmist's self-exhortation, — "Hope thou in God." An unexplored future is before us. There hangs over it a veil, which no hand can lift, and behind which no eye can look. But, as Christians, we have every possible ground for trust and hope; for that unexplored future is in the hands of our Father. And in saying this, consider how much we imply, — a providence minute, perfect, constant, — a care for us individually, extending itself to our least interests and wants, — an unslumbering watchfulness for our good, — a particular adaptation of whatever befalls us to our true and highest welfare. This doctrine of a minute paternal Providence is often on our lips, and were we assured that it is false, I doubt whether one of us would be willing to incur the risks and responsibilities even of a prosperous life for a moment longer. But who among us gathers from this thought the support and consolation which it might and should afford? Who feels the slightest insecurity, so far as he can have his interests cared for by an earthly parent? Who distrusts the future as to any point in which human love can make it blessed and happy? Yet is there not, in many hearts, a vague, undefined, latent feeling of insecurity under the Divine government? Let us cast out this feeling, as at war both with our intellectual belief and with the teachings and spirit of Jesus. God is our Father. On this one blessed truth let us repose. Here let us cast down our cares and drop our burdens. There is a burden-bearer with us, who fainteth not, neither is weary. Let us suppress the thought of murmuring and repining, and say of every appointment of Heaven,—"It is the Lord; let him do what seemeth to him good." True, like Jacob when he left his father's house, we may often have to lie down in desolateness and sorrow. Our pillow, like his, may often be a hard and a lonely one. But near us, as near him, will the mystic ladder be reared, and the angels of God descend with blessings for us; faith will set up the bleak and barren rock on which we rested for a pillar of thanksgiving; and when from the heights of heaven we mark the spot, we shall call "the name of the place Bethel."

Again, we have under God one object of hope

continually in view, namely, the growth of our characters; and this is the great end for which, were we wise, we should desire to live. It is not merely in the sanctuary that we find testimony borne to the truth, that the outward condition of itself presents no adequate object of hope. We see those who bear the heaviest burdens perfectly happy, — those whose burdens are few or none, often wretched. And as to ourselves, we cannot but be conscious that our chief need is of that inward principle of holiness, that reign of God in the heart, which is complete in itself without any outward addition. This, we believe, is the ultimate purpose of all our Father's dispensations. Does he send outward favors and mercies? It is that gratitude may engrave his image on our hearts, and write his law on our lives. Does he remove from us cherished blessings? "Every branch that beareth fruit he pruneth, that it may bring forth more fruit." He takes from us what is not ourselves, that the hidden man of the heart may have a more free and rapid growth. He takes gifts which we were in danger of loving more than the Giver. He takes wealth that bound our souls to the sordid pathway which he bids us leave. He takes friends, whose unquenched love and undiminished loveliness may unite our spirits by new and more intimate bonds with the unseen and eternal world. He guides us where we dread to go; but we find, as we move on, new energies of character, new strength to do, to bear, and overcome, called forth. He leads us through deep waters; but their baptism is that of the Holy Spirit. His waves and billows go over us; but they bear our souls nearer to their true rest. The outward he makes subservient to the inward, the body to the soul, time to eternity. This, then, let us hope without the shadow of a doubt, — that, if we are only faithful, every change, and trial, and cross will make us better, will increase that treasure which is within and indestructible, will render us more and more what in our best moments we wish and pray that we may become.

Finally, heaven and eternity, brought to light by Jesus, re-echo the exhortation, — "Hope thou in God." Have we the testimony of his love within? Are we living by the law and in the spirit of Christ? Have we the consciousness of pardoned sin and of souls at peace with God? If so, however heavy our outward burdens or sorrows, we may well ask, in self-rebuke, — "Why art thou cast down, O my soul? and why art thou disquieted within me?" How brief the longest space which earthly trials can cover! How short the period during which changes can come! How, in comparison with eternity and with ever-growing joy, does all that flesh and heart can bear, on this side of the grave, shrink into utter nothingness! But this inheritance above is revealed, that faith may use it here,—that hope may bridge over the few doubtful years that remain with an arch, that shall repose at once on a past full of mercy, and a heaven where all is sure, cloudless, and eternal. The time is indeed short, to some very short. Duty, love, faithfulness, these endure for ever, while the world passes away, with its desire and its fashion. Let us seek those things that are unseen, that live through death, that are born, and grow, and ripen for eternity.

SERMON VI.

THE DEATH OF THE RIGHTEOUS.

LET ME DIE THE DEATH OF THE RIGHTEOUS, AND LET MY LAST END BE LIKE HIS. — Numbers xxiii. 10.

THESE words were wrung from a heart in rebellion against God, and at enmity with his people. Balaam had been sent for to curse Israel, and went into the neighborhood where the covenant people had encamped on their way to the promised land, full of malignant passions, and prepared to utter railing and imprecation. But as he cast his eyes over the nation that God had blessed, and saw their tents "spread forth as gardens by the rivers, and as cedar-trees beside the waters," — as he beheld the marks of their undecaying vigor and prosperity, notwithstanding their lengthened wanderings in the desert, — and then, as he looked across the Dead Sea to the distant hills of the fair land that God had given them, the curse died upon his lips in an earnest longing for the inheritance upon which they were going to enter. "O that I could yet cast in my lot among them! Let me not remain for ever an alien from their God, an outcast from their ranks. O that my name were written among their tribes, that I might die the death of those whom God loves, and that my last days might be like theirs!" The feeling that thus burst forth from the seer of Moab cannot but enter every mind, however thoughtless, in witnessing the calm and hopeful departure from life of those to whom it was Christ to live, and we know that it must be gain to die. As we behold them resigned, cheerful, and happy, while the death-shadow steals over them, and see God's own peace reflected from their countenances as they draw near the land of promise, whatever our lives may have been, we for the moment breathe the prayer,—"Let me die the death of the righteous, and let my last end be like his."

Why is it that the event of death occupies so small a space in most men's thoughts and calculations, surrounded as they are by its memorials, its knell ringing in their ears every week, its signal and impressive voices, in the removal of conspicuous and active members of society, succeeding each other at very brief intervals? I apprehend that much of the prevalent thoughtlessness with reference to death results from the absurd, unchristian idea, that preparation for death is something entirely distinct from the work of life.

There are in every Christian community scores of people who have no doubt, that, when they are about to die, they shall have ample warning, and can then, amid the last scenes, hasten through certain stereotyped forms of death-bed penitence and devotion, which will insure them a passport to heaven. And if they know when death is near, they will be hurried through these forms, they will have everything that Christian assiduity can proffer to awaken religious faith and trust, they will lay hold with trembling eagerness on the merciful words of the Saviour, and will pass away with expressions of feeling, to which fond and partial friends cannot help giving a hopeful interpretation, but on which the observing and experienced Christian is constrained to look with full as much doubt as hope, apprehending that they flow from the diseased action of a feverish brain.

The thought which I wish to inculcate in the present discourse is, that a Christian life is the only sure ground of hope in death. I would represent the work of life and the preparation for death as one and the same thing; and would attach to every portion of healthful, active, busy life the associations of deep solemnity, which are commonly grouped around the closing moments of one's earthly pilgrimage. Nay, I believe, that, could we look at things in the light of eternity, the shop, the counting-room, the fireside, the social party, the scenes of temptation that are scattered up and down the wayside of life, would seem more solemn than the death-chamber; for it is in those that the soul wrestles with death, and often falls and dies, while through what we call the mortal agony the soul passes unscathed.

In pursuing my present design, let me first ask your attention to an invariable law of our being, of which we are too prone to lose sight, namely, that our success and happiness in every new condition of life depend upon our preparation for that condition. We continually reap as we sow, and are both sowing and reaping every day. Our earthly life is made up of a series of states and relations, each of which derives its character from the next preceding. Thus, "the child 's the father of the man." The faults, follies, omissions, and sins, or the attainments and virtues, of youth determine our condition, seal our misery or happiness, as men and women. Were our early steps in the way of transgressors, "the iniquities of our heels compass us about" through life, and we cannot escape them. Were we consecrated from childhood to God and duty, we still walk in our uprightness, and God's peace and blessing rest upon our homes and our daily ways. Multitudes there are who can bear sad and joyful testimony to the working of this law, — those whom sincere repentance has not saved from keen suffering, mortification, and besetting sin, on the score of early delinquencies, — those who bless God to the day of their death for the virtuous auspices which attended their opening youth. And old age, which lives upon the past, which cannot but feed on its remembrances, whether they yield the bread of heaven or apples of Sodom, — old age is altogether what youth and manhood have made it. Where can you point to a happy old age, where the prime of life was not marked by purity, honesty, diligence, and usefulness? Where can you find the hoary head bereft of peace and hope, where earlier days were passed in the fear of God and on the post of duty?

The case is similar with the various relations of business, and of domestic and social life. A man's success and happiness in his worldly avocation depend, as you all know, not on his advantages, but on his preparation to use them aright. Splendid advantages only lead to a splendid failure, where they are not connected with previous training and self-discipline. It is not his capital that makes the merchant, or his tools the mechanic, or his acres the farmer; but it is the mind, that patiently yields itself to the culture and the preliminary trials which create experience and skill.

The same law holds good in domestic life. The families in which we are born are our nurseries for the families of which we become the heads. We are, as husbands, wives, and parents, what we were as children, brothers, and sisters. The most felicitous connection cannot make the undutiful son a good and happy husband, or the frivolous daughter and selfish sister an honored wife, or a mother worthy of the name. In society, too, in extended trusts and large responsibilities, how often are we reminded of the early traits of those who have grown up at our side! The little republic of the school or the playground trains the neighbor, the citizen, the public functionary. Those whom their young companions trusted and loved, who were the peacemakers in the petty quarrels of children, the friends of truth and right on the humble, yet spiritually momentous occasions of our early days, are now, for the most part, the true, peaceful, upright, and trustworthy men and women, whose virtues adorn and bless the smaller or larger circles in which they move. On the other hand, the petulant, quarrelsome, untruthful, ill-nurtured children, whose influence and example were to be deprecated among their schoolmates and playmates, are now the talebearers, mischief-makers, brawlers, double-dealers, unloving and unloved, distrustful and distrusted, in every social and public office and relation.

Now, how is it that men will not apply this same law to that future state of being on which they hope to enter? How fail they to perceive and understand that the heavenly society, like every other state of being, needs and demands preparation, and that preparation for it cannot be a mere formula of holy words mumbled by dying lips, but must run through the habits, the feelings, the affections, the entire character? Think not, my friend, that a mere name above reproach among men, mere honesty and kindness, and a reputable walk in your outward relations and duties, will suffice for the dying hour. The great question is, Where is your heart? What are your prevalent tastes and habits of thought? Whence flows your enjoyment? Where rest your hopes? Is your whole soul fixed on things outward and earthly? Is your whole life bound up in the world that you must leave? Are you, in the spiritual world, living as an orphan and a stranger,—with God, as though he were not, without prayer, without the consciousness of his venerable presence? Are your desires and plans all earth-bounded, as earth-born? If so, you must acknowledge that you have not within you the possible elements of happiness in the life to come. With such a character as this, did no change take place in you, but only around you, were the outward scenes which engross your thoughts and affections swept away, every pleasure of sense cut off, every form of outward activity suspended, and then were the spiritual world made clearly manifest, new means of moral growth afforded, new avenues of communion with God opened, the serene heights of virtue and of piety made to rise in divine beauty before your sight, all this could only render you wretched; for you would lack the preparation of spirit, without which these high privileges must remain unenjoyed, these lofty attainments unattempted. You must have entered here upon the duties and the joys of the spiritual life, in order to make them even tolerable to you hereafter. And spirituality of thought, temper, and feeling must, in some measure, have detached you from earthly objects, and made them seem inferior and unessential goods, in order for you to resign them without intense suffering. If you have not learned to live above them, if you have not elements of character which make you independent of them, it will be utter misery for you to be parted from them.

This view demands, as a preparation for death, not only a decent formalism, but a strictly spiritual religion, — a religion which has its seat in the affections, its throne in the heart of hearts. Now, why are we not all diligently fitting ourselves for the home where we hope to go? Were it some distant city or foreign country upon our own planet, where we expected to fix our residence, how earnestly should we seek an interest in its scenes, its resources, and its life! How eagerly should we avail ourselves of every opportunity of exercise and training in whatever might be peculiar in its condition and modes of living! How fast, in the interval before embarking, should we become, in desire and feeling, citizens of our future home! And shall the city of God form the only exception to this rule? Shall we turn our backs upon it till driven to the shore where we must embark, and then go we know not whither? Shall not prayer, and faith, and hope lay up treasures against our arrival thither? Shall we not take in our hands and to our hearts the map of the inheritance which God has given us, survey its fair proportions, range in thought among its many mansions, so that, when we must go, it shall be to familiar scenes, to joys already begun, to accustomed duties and a long cherished life?

Such, surely, is the dictate of right reason. And does the word of God leave us the choice of any other ground? Our relation to the New Testament is one of the most solemn import. It is in this record that we think we have eternal life. This is the charter of our immortality and our heavenly citizenship. Take this away, and what, where, is our assurance of a life to come, — what, where, our hope for ourselves or our departed friends? We are all willing, glad, to go to it for the words of immortal life. When the beloved die, we delight to think of the grave-side of Lazarus, and to listen to the voice which the realms of silence heard and gave up their dead. But if we thus gladly receive, and would not for worlds abandon, the hope of heaven, — if we would shrink with horror from the atheist's icy creed, and would rather never have seen the light than to have it quenched in utter annihilation, — are we not sacredly bound to embrace our Saviour's doctrine of immortality as a whole, its conditions no less than its promises? But the same voice that proclaimed that the dead live for ever has also taught, that, "except a man be born again, he cannot see the kingdom of God." The same hand that led Lazarus from the land of shadows back to the home of the living points to heaven as destined for those alone who cheerfully bear the cross, who lay up treasures above, who do the will of the Father, and love one another as he has loved us all. On no other condition has the New Testament a word of hope or promise for us; nor has Jesus given the slightest ground for confidence or peace as to the future to those who now are willing aliens from the life of heaven. If, then, you believe that Jesus spake with authority from God, let his words as to judgment and eternity rouse you from your supineness to do the work of life, and enlist all your powers and efforts in the only path which can lead you to fulness of joy.

Thus do the law of human life and the word of God, while they make us solicitous to die the death of the righteous, unitedly urge upon us the essential importance of living his life. The same lesson must have impressed itself upon all who have been in any degree familiar with the closing scenes of life. It is not the opportunity of a death-scene, not the hurried and unnatural utterances of a last hour, but the whole previous character, the direction which the face and steps had borne before death seemed near, that cherishes or crushes our hope for the departed. Of those not personally religious, many die and leave no sign; sometimes they are cut down in unwarned dissolution; and when the approaching footsteps of death are perceived, it often creeps over the soul before it chills the limbs, and the patient sinks into a lethargic ease and self-complacency, from which no appeal can rouse him. Others are awakened, alarmed, agitated, pass through a paroxysm of fearful agony, emerge from it with words of exultation and triumph, and then die fearless and happy, with a louder and more elastic confidence than often falls to the lot of the mature and experienced Christian. When this unwonted manifestation of feeling comes at the close of an innocent, serious, dutiful life, though there may have been no previous religious profession, it is no doubt frequently to be regarded as the rush for utterance, at the last moment, of thoughts and emotions which diffidence had previously suppressed. But when a careless, worldly, sinful life closes with this spasmodic semblance of piety, there is reason to apprehend that the utterances of the last hour are unmeaning words, caught up in a state of mental imbecility from surrounding friends, or copied from the remembrance or record of similar scenes, or the result of a nervous excitement too strong for the shattered body and enfeebled mind to restrain. They do, indeed, suggest hope; for we remember the malefactor upon the cross, we think of the overflowing mercy of our Father, and may thus be led to cherish and offer more encouragement than calm reflection would warrant. But why, by such a death-bed, do we listen so anxiously for the last words, and catch so eagerly at whatever stimulates the expression of calm and rational faith or of filial trust? Why do friends question each other so earnestly as to every word, and look, and gesture of the dying? It is because we feel so sensibly the discrepancy between the life that is closing and the life of heaven, — because the two have nothing in common, but a broad and deep gulf lies between them; and we long for something, shadowy though it be, to fill up the chasm, — we would bridge the gulf with a rainbow, rather than not see it spanned, — we will accept almost anything, however vague and unsatisfactory in itself, which may go towards softening the discrepancy and establishing some faint show of connection between the life which the dying one has led and that which we hope for him. This hanging upon last words indicates a latent consciousness that we need and crave some better evidence, — that the testimony of the life alone can satisfy us as regards those that die.

But there is a life which terminates naturally and necessarily in heaven. There sometimes pass away from us those whose death-chamber seems an ascension-mount, and we can almost see them go, so sure we are that they go home to God. From them we need no parting words, — nay, we sometimes feel glad that no strongly marked closing scene intervenes to rival the beautiful testimony of a holy life, and to distract our thoughts from their free range over the successive stages of a heavenward pilgrimage. We ask not added proof that they are happy. We desire not that the closing days should wear a different complexion from that of their days of active duty. We prefer witnessing till the last moment the same blending of social and religious traits and affections, which we have seen in them for months and years. Our best prayer for them is, that they may die as they have lived. Should the call come suddenly or unperceived by them, there is nothing wanting, nothing left to be wrought in a hurry and agitation of impending death, no expiring torch to be trimmed, no wedding garment to be sought, and fitted, and hastily thrown on, when the king comes in to see the guests. They waited not to trim their lamps, till the cry arose, — "Behold, he cometh!" Their robes were long since washed white, and made ready for their

Lord's appearing. Our assurance that they have found it gain to die dates back even to early years. It flows from a youth redeemed from vanity and consecrated to the Most High,—from virtues that grew with the growth and strengthened with the strength,—from successive occasions and posts of duty met and filled with unshrinking fidelity,—from years of hallowed effort, example, and sacrifice in every relation of domestic life,—from kindness, sympathy, and love extended throughout the larger circle, from the homes of the poor and the hearts of the fatherless,—from a walk with God in a manifestly prayerful and devout spirit,—from a walk with man, to which religion always gave its unction and its glow. Where but in heaven can such a path have ended? Where else can such features of spiritual life have gone? What possible doubt, what short of a certainty not to be made surer, can rest upon their present condition? Their characters were of heaven; their virtues were such as have honor in the presence of God; and "the Father seeketh such to worship him."

Nor can our friends have lost in heaven aught of those traits of character which endeared them to us here, and which all find room for exercise, and for still fuller, loftier development, in that better home. Were they true and faithful? On God's holy mount they still "walk uprightly and work righteousness." Were they the friends of

Jesus? They now "follow the Lamb, whithersoever he goeth." Were they lovely and happy in every home relation and duty? They have kindred there, whom they have rejoined, — those of their earthly home, who have gladly welcomed them to the heavenly household. Were they known in the dwellings of the poor, and did prayers go up for their longer life from stricken hearts that had been blessed through their ministry? There are works of love to be wrought by the redeemed, — divine offices of mercy, for which the walks of earthly charity are ordained to train and perfect the Christian soul. Did they love and keep the commandments of the Most High? Now "he that sitteth upon the throne shall dwell among them," and they go no more out from his felt presence for ever.

SERMON VII.

MEMORY.

A BOOK OF REMEMBRANCE WAS WRITTEN. — Malachi iii. 16.

I HAVE taken these words as an appropriate motto for a sermon on memory, considered in its moral and religious bearings, in its connection with critical seasons and emergencies of life, and in its relation to God's retributive justice in the future world.

I would first remark, that there is abundant reason to believe that memory never loses anything, but that it retains, and may reproduce, when the right string is touched, every thought, impression, and event of our whole past lives. The well-ascertained phenomena of delirium, insanity, and other unusual forms of consciousness, furnish ample demonstration of this statement. In these conditions of mind, it has been found that the most minute and remote circumstances, complex trains of thought, series of words or musical notes, words even in an unknown tongue, have been recalled after an interval of years, and flooded the soul with its rememberings. In our usual state of mind, things do not indeed return to us uncalled, nor yet do they come at once when sought, but obey certain laws of suggestion or association, which retard the action of the memory, as the balance-wheel does the movements of a watch. But in the modes of consciousness now referred to, the balance-wheel is taken off, the usual laws of suggestion are suspended, the full flow of memory takes the place of the scanty jet of recollection, and the whole past rushes spontaneously upon the mind, foreshadowing the day when death will snap asunder the earth-spun threads of association, and pour the accumulated treasures of the past into the lap of the boundless future.

But we need not go beyond our own familiar experience to verify this view. Revisit some scenes of early life, from which you have been absent twenty, thirty, or forty years, and what intensely vivid remembrances take shape, hue, and voice! The faces and tones of the long forgotten, the very trees and stones now dislodged, the prattle and the day-dreams of infancy, every evanescent frame of thought and feeling, will be recalled, and you find yourself again a child. There is not a reverie that ever flitted across our minds, not a dream that ever haunted our pillows, which has gone beyond return. Nor is there a single day, when strange and isolated facts, fragments of conversations, vague, floating images of ancient and forgotten things, do not thus rise before us, like ghosts of the unburied.

Thus the past never dies, though, in the common routine of life, we have to a degree the keys of memory in our own hands, and may admit or exclude recollections at pleasure. But there are seasons, and those not rare, when the keys are taken from us, and, without the power of choice, we are liable to inundations from the good or evil, the sweet or bitter, of the past, promiscuously. Indeed, these seasons are so frequent with us all, that a large part of our happiness is placed irrevocably out of our own keeping,—transferred from our present to our past selves. Our unoccupied time, our vacant hours by day, our sleepless night-watches, are thus given over to the genius of memory; and whatever there may be worthy of regret in the past is then unfailingly brought up to arm the passing moments with daggers' points, or to plant thorns in our pillows. The more harassing the remembrance, the more closely it besets us. The visitings of any one such phantom may indeed cease, or at least its sting may become mollified, after a long lapse of time, but not till we have exorcised it, not only by reiterated repentance, but by entire conversion, by the thorough alienation of the temper and the character from what thus gave us trouble. And even then, like an old wound long healed, which an east wind will fill with neuralgic pain, may not this unwelcome remembrance be revived with afflictive power, at intervals we know not how remote?

In seasons of sorrow, the past always utters its voices. At such times God brings every work into remembrance, and enters into judgment with our spirits. When the hand of Providence is heavy upon us, if the past has been stained with guilt, we need no inscription upon the wall to make our knees smite together and our souls tremble. The handwriting is upon the fleshly tablets of the heart,—"Thou art weighed in the balance and found wanting." There is nothing more true to universal experience than the self-reproaching communings of Joseph's brethren when they felt themselves surrounded by imminent perils in a strange land. Their memory glided over the long period for which they had led self-complacent and generally dutiful lives, and rested on the one damning sin of former years; "and they said one to another, We are verily guilty concerning our brother, in that we saw the anguish of his soul when he besought us, and we would not hear; therefore is this distress come upon us." A vast amount of remorse mingles with human grief, and drugs to the utmost with gall and wormwood the cup of sorrow. When ill-gotton and ill-used wealth departs, the remembrance of numberless breaches of good faith and charity arms penury with a scourge of scorpions, which she never wields when she enters the dwellings of God's chosen ones. When the unfaithful and unloving are separated by death, with the sorrows of bereavement there blend the embittering recollections of violated duty, variance, and discord.

But compare with the sad retrospect which Providence forces upon the guilty the rich reminiscences which crowded Job's mind, when health, riches, and children were at once taken from him. "When the ear heard me, then it blessed me; and when the eye saw me, it gave witness to me; because I delivered the poor that cried, the fatherless, and him that had none to help him. The blessing of him that was ready to perish came upon me, and I caused the widow's heart to sing for joy. I was eyes to the blind, and feet was I to the lame. I was a father to the poor." And with a past so full of consolation in the review, no wonder that he could break forth in those noble words of undoubting faith and hope, —"I know that my Redeemer liveth, and will stand up at length on the earth; and though with my skin this body be wasted away, yet in my flesh shall I see God."

Most of all, death, as it is passing the book of memory over to the register of eternity, rehearses its records in the ear fast closing to the outward world. I have often been startled by the keen recollection of the fatally sick, the declining, and the dying. The mind, as death draws nigh, cannot be diverted from the past; but will scan it with the most wakeful, earnest scrutiny, will wait for it to utter all its voices, whether of approval or of condemnation, and will not resign itself in perfect peace, unless the past wear a smiling aspect, and be contemplated with a conscience that approves much more than it condemns. True, we are saved by hope. Heaven is ours, "not for works of righteousness that we have done"; yet such works are the only seal of God's pardon and acceptance that will satisfy us in the dying hour. Under the gnawings of fatal disease, new work is seldom done, new ideas are seldom acquired, new resources seldom opened. The mind is thus thrown back upon its remembered experience, and acts upon it with unabated keenness and strength. Then, too, in all its consolations and hopes it seeks to be supported and confirmed by memory. With those who cherish religious sentiments and affections at the close of life, and who desire to fall asleep in Jesus, there is frequently witnessed an anxious and painful self-questioning to which memory alone can respond. The inquiry is,— "Is there nothing unusual, unnatural, in my present feelings? Are they the fruit of true piety towards God; or are they the mere wanderings of a sickly, dreaming imagination?" This is a question which none can happily answer, except those who can look back upon days of active and healthful piety, and make these their term of comparison; — who can say, — "This is indeed no new glow, no strange fire, but the same that warmed me for duty and for conflict while my health was firm, — the same that gave fervor to my daily prayers, burned in my soul at the public altar, and inspired me for the words of Christian counsel and sympathy, and the labors of a willing charity. My joy in God, my trust in Jesus, my hope of heaven, which now sustain my sinking spirit, have been the staff of my life, — I have tested their genuineness, I have made full trial of their power, I know that they are from the Father, and cannot fail me." This, my friends, is no fancy sketch. Such questionings I have often heard from the perilously sick and the dying. They themselves are prone to distrust new-born faith and piety. They need memory for a witness in their behalf. This testimony a deathbed repentance lacks; and therefore it finds no medium between vehement, self-forgetting excitement and utter despondency.

But it is asked, Is it within our own power to lay up remembrances that will give peace and pleasure? Are not many of the events of life (and some of them such as we can never forget) entirely beyond our own agency? May not an always frowning Providence, without our fault, fill the book of memory with dismal and mournful entries? I answer, No; for it is not events, but our own traits of character and conduct alone, that are capable of giving us anguish in the remote retrospect. It is astonishing how smooth the roughest ways of Providence look at a little distance. Sickness, bereavement, disappointment, though agonizing in their immediate pressure, are remembered without torment, — nay, if they were submissively borne, their place, in the way that we have been led, is marked by a pillar of gratitude, with the inscription, BETHEL. If shadows gather about our dying bed, they will be the shadows of our negligences, follies, and sins. But if our lives have been faithful, devout, and loving, then will the remembrance of what we were through the grace of God, and the testimony of a good conscience glancing to and fro through the years that are gone, give peace and triumph to our departing spirits, and enable us to feel that God is taking us to a rest for which he had first fitted us.

These thoughts evince the necessity of laying up remembrances for the hour of death. Most emphatic are the lessons to this effect which have gone forth from the death-beds of those that have passed away from our own circle. I have heard the pure and devout regret even having read what was unedifying and frivolous; for, said they, "there is hardly an evil or foolish thing that has ever met our eyes, however little hold we meant to give it upon our minds, that does not come back to us now." Nor is it barely enough to have an empty conscience, and to look back upon a life free from reproach, yet void of spiritual good. A merely worldly life cannot present a satisfying retrospect from the bed of death. We shall then need remembrances of duty, virtue, love, and piety. Life must have had its work, and must in some good degree have fulfilled its mission. There must be a past filled with those things by which character grows, man is served, and God glorified. A recent German writer, in a fictitious sketch, introduces a worthy youth as compiling a book of pleasant experiences to be read for his comfort at the hour of death. Such a book it concerns us all to write, not on paper, but on the surer and more lasting tablet of a memory that cannot die. When we lie down to our last sleep, let our thoughts, as they must needs run back, rest upon a life of fidelity and devotion, upon frequent visitings of angels and the felt smile of Heaven, upon a growing and deep experience of that love of God through Christ Jesus from which neither life nor death can divide or alienate us.

I wish now to present the bearing which this view of memory has on the doctrine of a future righteous retribution. "I saw the dead," says St. John, — "I saw the dead, both small and great, stand before God. And the books were opened, and the dead were judged out of those things which were written in the books, according to their works." And out of what books can they be thus judged, except those of memory, — books written by themselves, but preserved by God, and opened at the solemn hour of death for their acquittal or condemnation? If the past is thus to be brought to light, may not memory be the prime-minister of God's retributive justice, — the worm that never dies, the fire that is never quenched, in the sinner's soul, — the peace of God, that passeth all understanding, to the pure and faithful spirit? Of the power of memory for good or evil we have in this life ample experience from the torn and scattered leaves of its book, with which recollection furnishes us. What anguish can be compared with the remorse that gnaws the breast of the betrayer of innocence, — of him whose profligacy has brought the gray hairs of parents with sorrow to the grave, — of him whose every retrospect is rayless and guilt-stained? What more apt type does earth afford of heaven, than in the calm and honored decline of a faithful and devout life, which consecrated to God the dew of its youth and the fulness of its strength, which grew in virtue as in years, which ripened steadily for heaven as its summer leaf grew sear? How deep, then, must be the despair, or how full the joy, of those before whom the veil is all rolled away, and every secret or forgotten thing, be it good or evil, brought to light!

Imagine the abandoned sinner full in the presence of his God, no sentence passed upon him but that which he is constrained to pass upon himself, no fire let loose upon him but that which memory can kindle. What is the view upon which he cannot close his reluctant sight? The God, whom he now sees to be merciful as well as holy, whose very judgment-seat is a throne of love, who hides not even from the reprobate and hell-doomed the paternal aspects of his character, — that God, that Father, he has set at naught, neglected, scorned, perhaps blasphemed. Showers of blessing fell thick on every portion of his earthly pilgrimage, unacknowledged, unheeded. Voices of love were daily, hourly, wooing him heavenward; but he has turned a deaf ear to all of them. His ingratitude, seen in memory's clear light, seems black as midnight. He turns from an insulted God to the company of his fellow-spirits. And here memory again torments him. It brings up numerous violations of the law of justice and of kindness, neglected opportunities of mercy, successful conflicts of selfishness with brotherly love. He is in the midst of the injured and the outraged, and knows not where to look for sympathy and love. Memory thus isolates him, makes him both afraid and ashamed to trust either God or man, bids him dread the frown of the Almighty and shrink from the scorn of his brethren. Apply to this quiet outline the several degrees of coloring which belong to the different shades of human guilt, and though I say not that this is all, have you not even here a hell, in which the workers of iniquity cannot fail to receive according to their works?

Pass now to the right hand of the Judge. Contemplate a truly humble, devout, exemplary Christian, with the holy thoughts and good deeds of a long life of piety spread out before him, not veiled, as they were on earth, by the self-abasement of a lowly spirit, but sparkling in heaven's pure sunlight, seen of angels, owned by the benignant Redeemer, approved by God, the Judge of all. Moreover, as his earthly life is thus reviewed in heaven, he sees not only each act itself, but its happy, glorious, perhaps still widening and brightening results. Did he sow a seed of humble charity? He sees not the seed, but the tree which has sprung from it. Did he cast his bread upon the waters? He sees not the bread, but the hungering souls whom it has nourished. Did he labor, and pray, and live, for the salvation of souls? He sees not his efforts, but their fruits, going forth, it may be, even for the healing of the nations. For these fruits are a part of his prayer of faith and labor of love. They were so in the determined counsel and foreknowledge of God. They are so in the undecaying memory which dwells with him in the home of the blessed. I say not, indeed, that these remembrances constitute the sole or the chief happiness of heaven. They are but the beginnings of celestial joy,— the starting-point on the career of eternal glory; and thence there is a constant pressing onward and upward on the path which waxes brighter and brighter to the perfect day.

There is one question which, I doubt not, has suggested itself to some of you. The best of men have been, to a greater or less degree, sinners; and, if memory be perfect and entire, while the pious look back with pleasure upon their good deeds, must not the remembrance of their follies and sins cloud their joy, and mingle strains of sadness with their songs of rapture? For those who deem piety the work of a moment, and who rely strongly on death-bed penitence, I care not to answer this question. I am entirely willing to leave their difficulties unsolved; for the more numerous the doubts that hang over the fate of him whose first sighs of contrition are the last of life, the better is it for the living, while, with all our doubts, we can commit such a one, when dying, to the overflowing mercy of God, and hope for the best. But for those who understand by piety the frame of the life, not the hasty utterances of the death-agony, who mean by it faith and love made manifest in a sober, righteous, and godly conversation, I have a ready answer. To the awakened memory of the consistently virtuous, in the world to come, worthy and holy thoughts and deeds must so occupy the foreground as to throw follies and sins completely into the shade. Then, too, against every disobedient purpose and act there will be written in the book of memory the cancelling vows of contrition that succeeded it, and the holy resolutions that forbade its repetition. The sins of the exemplary and devout will be to them in heaven as the sins of our infancy are to us now. We recollect our childish follies, and the chiding and the pain which attended them; but if they were outgrown, forsaken, and forgiven, and if, while they lie back in the dim distance of many years, we have built fair and pleasing structures in the foreground, these so occupy the view as to prevent the eye from resting painfully on earlier guilt. But experience shows that in no other way can early sins be kept out of distinct and appalling view; nor can we conceive of any other way in which even repented sin can fail to disturb our peace in the world to come. The grovelling edifices of iniquity cannot conceal each other. Nor can virtue cover sin; but, at best, can only eclipse it and cast it into the shade.

If the views which I have now presented be just, they are of vast practical importance. They expound, and at the same time invest with a momentous interest, such declarations of Scripture as these:—"God will bring every work into judgment, with every secret thing, whether it be good or whether it be evil." "For every idle word which men shall speak they must give account at the day of judgment." If a book of remembrance is kept, and if every entry on its pages is to be brought to light, how vigilant should this prospect make us in the least things as well as in the greatest, in the government of our hearts as well as in the conduct of our lives,—how prayerful against secret faults,—how watchful against besetting sins! For the young, our doctrine has encouragement and promise, offering them, if they will keep their youth undefiled, a stainless and beatific retrospect as the rich first-fruits of heavenly joy. For those who have wandered from the path of rectitude, it utters a voice of warning, bidding them trust not to a late repentance, which will still leave the book of remembrance stained and blackened, and may not suffice to save them from a communion with the past, which will fill their disembodied spirits with horror and despair.

God also has a book of remembrance, composed of the fair and unspotted leaves from men's books; and it is written "for them that fear the Lord, and think upon his name." May our books of remembrance be so pure and stainless that their record shall be transferred to his, that thus we may be among those of whom it is written,—"And they shall be mine, saith the Lord of hosts, in that day when I make up my jewels; and I will spare them, as a man spareth his own son that serveth him."

SERMON VIII.

SUDDEN DEATH.

YE KNOW NEITHER THE DAY NOR THE HOUR WHEREIN THE SON OF MAN COMETH. — Matthew xxv. 13.

NATURE has her times and seasons. Throughout her inanimate and irrational kingdoms, bloom and decay, youth and age, life and death, succeed each other at periods that can be foreseen and calculated. The flowers discharge their bright ministry of love, elaborate their seeds, and die not till their work is done. The hoary oak retains its vigor for ages, is ages more in dying, and falls at last amid a giant progeny that has grown up to fill its place. The insect race fade with the leaf and die with the dying year. Their span is brief; but they have grown old in it, have finished their work, and drop into timely dissolution. Thus is it with all the tribes of animated nature. No infantile diseases prey upon them; no fever throbs in their young veins; no palsy blights their active powers; death, except by violence, comes not at cock-crowing or in the morning, but only at eventide. But for man death chooses all seasons. The cradle is his; and the first ecstasy of maternal joy is subdued into bitter wailing. Childhood and youth are his; the laughing eye is quenched, the gleeful shout hushed. The prime of manhood and womanhood is his; he blights the freshness of hope and promise, and clothes in the garments of the grave those bound the most closely by the ties of life. He often sends no summons before him; but floats unseen on the breeze, and has aimed his shaft before his approach is perceived. The morning is full of happy plans and bright visions; at nightfall the cry goes forth, — "Make ready the shroud, prepare the pall." In the midst of life we are in death. Like the demoniac of old, we have our dwelling among the tombs. Hardly is there a spot or an object which the shadow of the grave has not hallowed to the memory of the deeply loved and early lost. Premature and sudden dissolution has its voices for the living. To some of them let us now give heed.

Such instances of death are a proof and a pledge of man's immortality, and are adapted to make us feel this truth, as well as believe it. Here is a child, budding with golden promise, the mind just awakened to self-consciousness, the heart twining its young affections around all that is fair and good, native innocence just ripening into a virtue of choice and effort. Suddenly the decree goes forth, — "Cut it down." A wind passes over it, and it is gone. But why? It cumbered not the ground. It blessed the soil where it grew, and has left a balmy fragrance where it fell. Can it have become extinct, while so many clodlike existences, inane as the earth they tread, are suffered to live on? O, no! Its root cannot have withered, though its stem is crushed. It has only been transplanted, where softer zephyrs, warmer suns, richer dews, shall make its bloom perennial.

Here, again, is a man of ripe mind and noble heart. He fills a large and honored place in the public eye. Science, humanity, and piety all rejoice in his light. Weighty interests are confided to him, and momentous cares rolled upon him. It is high noon with him in his path of progress and of usefulness. But his sun is darkened at noonday, and he "goes to the grave in all his glorious prime," while charity weeps and the ways of Zion mourn. Yet, is he dead? Can the caprice of powers above have extinguished such a burning and shining light, while the smoking flax still glimmers, and the feeble lamp of age still trims its flickering blaze? We cannot thus believe. A new star in the firmament above was needed, and that which glowed with the purest lustre here was transferred to the galaxy around the throne of the Eternal.

Once more, here is a woman of pure mind and chastened affections, rich in good works, the ornament of her household, the staff and stay of her parents, the tenderly loved of many hearts, with new scenes of happiness and spheres of duty just opening before her, and the fondest hopes just glimmering and dawning. At the very moment when life offers the most for her to do and to enjoy, the arrow is sped, and she lies silent in unwarned dissolution. But can so much loveliness have died? Can God have suffered a spirit so full of blessed influences, so radiant with intelligence and kindness, to drop out of being, while he burdens the earth with so many of the selfish and depraved, who have lived unhonored, and might have died unwept? This cannot be. There was a vacant mission of love in heaven, waiting her acceptance. She was found faithful in a lower sphere, and her Master has said to her, "Friend, go up higher."

Thus only can we interpret these sudden and premature removals of the pure and good. Without a higher life, man is the greatest anomaly in existence, — the only broken column in creation. Everything else lives its span, and does its work. But man "cometh forth as a flower and is cut down; he fleeth as a shadow, and continueth not." With him everything is incomplete and unfinished. A human life that seems entire in itself, reaches a natural period, and comes to the grave in full age, like a shock of corn in its season, is the rare exception, not the rule. And as God, having endowed man more highly than the rest of his creatures, cannot love him less, the mere light of nature might prompt the belief in a higher state of being, where this seeming incompleteness will be filled up, where defeated aims, broken plans, and unfinished works may all be consummated. Everything else we can comprehend in the cycle bounded by earth and time. If man comes not within that cycle, it must be because his interests and fortunes belong to the larger cycle of eternity. It is this only that brings man into harmony with the rest of the creation, and makes his being anything else than an insolvable enigma.

I next remark, that sudden and premature deaths among the innocent and holy are precious, as giving us a nearer view of heaven than we can otherwise gain. When the chariot and horses of fire bore Elijah to paradise, think you not that it brought the home of the blessed very close to the mental vision of those who saw him go? One who had just walked with them in the beauty of holiness, and spoken to them in the name of the Lord, whose wise and pious counsels were yet recent in their ears, the impress of whose energy and love was still fresh upon their hearts, had passed from them to heaven, and they could follow him thither, behold him the same there as here, and feel that the traits of character which had so closely bound them to him were congenial with the world which he had entered. Similar is our feeling, when our worthy friends are suddenly translated from our homes. The sky remains parted; we trace their passage; we follow them within the veil; and, through the vivid impressions which they have left us of their characters, we seem to see them still, the same in all that was good, entering upon the joys of paradise, sweeping the harps of heaven. It is as if a gem of unearthly radiance, which had shone in our dwellings, which we had handled and sported in the sunlight, and gazed at in all its rainbow tints, had been snatched from our grasp, planted in the sky, and made a star. Impressions of this kind cannot be so strong, where long decay or infirmity has preceded death, so as to suspend the active energies of the soul, and to give scope only for the passive virtues. In such cases, our last converse has been with but a part of what our friend was, with an intensely interesting part indeed, with faith, patience, and submission; but still there has been a change, — the remembrances of health have become clouded, — sad associations of groans, weakness, and ghastly disease have clustered around the loved form, so that we are but dimly conscious that it is the bright, energetic, happy being of former days, that has entered into rest. Even our contemplations of heaven take a sombre hue, when we have been for weeks and months conversant with the gloom and suffering of its antechamber. But when death comes ere the eye is waxed dim or the natural force abated, when our friend is removed in the prime of energy and fervor, our last remembrances of the departed are of all that our friend was, and whatever there was in him of rare, and various, and well-developed moral strength and beauty remains in our minds as an abiding memorial of the spirit and the life of heaven.

Yet once more, the sudden, and what we call the untimely, death of those who are prepared to die, may be regarded as a relief and blessing to them. To survivors it is, indeed, unspeakably appalling. The contrast, the revulsion of feeling, the instantaneous prostration of plans and scattering of hopes, the blight which it seems to cast on every familiar scene and object, all conspire to aggravate the severity of the stroke. But from how many conflicts and sorrows has the departed one been saved! He has not seen earthly objects fade one by one from his sickening gaze. His heart has not bled anew each day in the sundering of cherished ties. He has not known the bitterness of death. He has been spared the last adieus, the parting throes, the sight of agonized friends about his bedside, the anxieties for those to be left, which intrude themselves on the soul the best prepared to die. Perhaps, too, though he dreaded not the world to come, he shrank from the passage to it, feared the moment of dissolution, and felt, that, with all the joys of heaven in full prospect, the pains of death would still fill him with terror. But from this trial of his faith he has been exempted. The battle was fought, and the victory won, without his consciousness. He knew not that he was dying, till he found himself alive from the dead. His Master came at an hour when he thought not; but found him watching, his lamp trimmed, his "feet shod with the preparation of the gospel of peace." And happy was that servant to have been borne, as on angels' wings, across those turbid waves which so many of the righteous must ford with fear and trembling.

I cannot sympathize with the dread of sudden death, as such, which many feel. Only give me the full assurance that I am prepared to meet my God, that I am leading a Christian life, that my prevalent frame of mind is spiritual and heavenly, and I would even pray to be spared the slow decay of nature or disease, the sad farewell, the parting conflict,—I would beg of my Master to let me work in his vineyard till the very last moment, and close my life with my labors. But such wishes, so far as we cherish them, let us breathe with submission, and with the willingness, if such be Heaven's decree, to glorify God in the pains of a last illness and a lingering death; for the cause of piety needs such suffering witnesses, and for the service which some must render all should hold themselves in readiness. If the chariot of fire comes for us, we will deem it a blessed privilege thus to go; but if it be our lot to tread the dark valley with slow and painful steps, "even so, Father, for so it seems good in thy sight." And when,

"Cast as a broken vessel by,
Thy will we can no longer do,
Yet, while a daily death we die,
Thy power we will in weakness show,
Our sufferings shall thy glory raise,
Our speechless woe proclaim thy praise."

But, my friends, what means this almost universal shrinking from sudden death, as if the very words were a fearful talisman, synonymous with all that is terrific and nothing that is bright and happy in the world to come? It is because we are so ill prepared for death. When the thought of removal without warning presents itself, our sins stare us in the face, and we cannot read our title to heaven clear. When some such visitation of Providence takes place among our kindred or neighbors, the warning is most thrillingly sent home to our hearts, — "Be ye also ready." We then feel our liability to depart at any moment. The ground seems to quake beneath us. We own that we have here no continuing city, and resolve to seek that city which hath foundations. But with the terror, the resolution fades away, and very soon we are again living on as if the voice of Providence had not arrested us,—just as the frightened bird returns, the moment after, to the covert from which the fowler's step had startled her. But we are always in peril, and the most so when we are farthest from the thought of danger; for the longer it is since the last event of the kind, the nearer at hand must the next be. Our daily path is by hidden pitfalls and lurking deaths. The puncture of a pin, the sting of an insect, a slight misstep, a flash from a storm-cloud, may send us at once from our bloom and prime to the judgment-seat of Christ. A sudden hemorrhage, from the very excess of health, or from some wanton feat of strength, may shed life's current from its broken bowl, when our mountain stands the firmest. Or soon insidious disease may prey secretly upon the seat of life, and we suspect it not till our hearts have throbbed their last pulse. There is not one of you who could pronounce himself less likely to die before nightfall, than could thousands whom the morning has beheld full of vigor, and the evening in their shrouds. And are we ready? The decree may have gone forth concerning some one of us. Who knows but that preacher or hearer may make his next appeal in the silent eloquence of death? I say these things not by way of rhetorical exaggeration, but because I feel them. When I reflect on the many causes of death latent within me and around me, on the many avenues by which the breath of life may at any moment be expelled, on the frailty of every part of this complex frame, on its thousand strings, not one of which can be broken without the harp's becoming a tuneless ruin, on the numberless conditions which must all be fulfilled in order to keep the springs of being in motion for a single moment, I seem a wonder to myself, life becomes the mystery of mysteries, and God's guardian care an incessant miracle. When I think of these things, so far from being surprised at an occasional instance of sudden dissolution, I marvel that it should occur so seldom. But I would not hold forth this event as the object of blind terror. I would rather urge you to that constant preparation of spirit, without which the slowest dissolution will seem too soon, with which death cannot come too soon or too suddenly.

Let me, then, urge you to live prepared for the sudden sundering of domestic and social ties. Unreconciled enmities, open wounds, unquenched anger, arm death with a sting of tenfold sharpness. They have often cost bitter weeping for years over the graves of the injured. Is one who was the subject of other than kind sentiments called away from our circle? However ready we were in his lifetime to cast all the blame upon him, death will soften his faults and heighten his virtues to our view, so that we shall feel ourselves alone guilty; and love, reviving over the lifeless dust, will vent itself in vain longings to grasp the shadowy spirit in our reconciling embrace, to ask forgiveness of the ear for ever sealed, to call forth the once wonted glow of affection on the cheek for ever pale. And if we ourselves go hence with such wounds unhealed, must they not rankle in our disembodied spirits, cloud the light of eternity as it dawns upon us, embitter the streams of paradise as they roll by us? But "we know neither the day nor the hour when the Son of Man cometh." Our earthly household may be dissolved at any moment; and when we think the least of it, the parting hour may be near. With what a solemn emphasis, then, should the counsel be sent home to our souls, — "Let not the sun go down upon your wrath"! How careful should we be to keep the unity of the spirit inviolate, the bond of peace unbroken, lest the gall of bitterness be instilled into some early cup of sorrow! Let us so walk together, in our smaller and larger circles of kindred and intimacy, that no remembrances of broken faith or wounded love may haunt us at some future grave-side, or in the spiritual home to which we may soon be called. Let us go to our rest each night in peace with all men; for we never know, when we lie down, but that it is on our death-bed, or, when we rise up, but that it may be to the scene or tidings of another's unwarned doom.

Above all, let us keep our hearts at peace with that God in whose unveiled presence we may at any moment find ourselves, — with that Redeemer at whose judgment-bar the great account of life may be so speedily demanded. We are too prone to think of sudden death as if it were dropping into a frightful abyss. To the reconciled and prepared spirit, to the experienced and mature Christian, it is falling from the cradle of its infant being into everlasting arms of love beneath. But are we ready? We know not the day or the hour; but, come when it may, will it find us waiting? Is there one of us who could receive, without a shudder, a final summons so sudden as has often been sent to those around us? I trust that there may be some of us over whom surviving friends would feel no fear, and whom God and Jesus would own and welcome. But is our every day spent as we could wish, were it to be our last? This ought to be our standard, this our rule of life. Not that we should be of a sad countenance, or wear a funereal aspect; for to live thus takes from death all its sadness and its bitterness. But every day should be marked by as earnest diligence in duty, as fervent a spirit of devotion, as careful a heed to the dictates of conscience, as faithful a walk in the Redeemer's footsteps, as if on that one day were suspended all our interests for eternity. Happy is that servant whom his Lord, when he cometh, shall find thus living.

But am I wrong in saying that some of you live with no more reference to death and eternity than if you had a lease of life at pleasure? Every other contingent event you foresee and provide for. Disasters in business, fire, fraud, and shipwreck, are the subjects of your most diligent precaution. You ground plans, hopes, and fears on the death of others. All but yourselves seem mortal to you. But you are strong and well. You are not constitutionally liable to acute disorders. Sudden death, while it has laid low your neighbors, has not actually entered your own doors. You are exempts. The destroyer may rage around you, but you feel that he cannot cross your threshold. O, let multiplied warnings arouse you from your fatal security, your apathy at death's door, your slumber among the tombs! The sands are fast running. The days of privilege are drawing to a close. With some of you, this may be the last; would to God that it might be an effectual appeal, bidding you, in the words of holy writ, — "Turn ye, turn ye; for why will ye die?"

Let us not dismiss these contemplations without lifting our hearts in gratitude for that hope of immortality which gilds the shadow of death and the caverns of the grave. Do we mourn over virtuous friends, suddenly snatched from the large and cherished place which they filled in our affections? Glory be to Jesus, that we mourn not without hope! Our homes are made desolate; but the grave is desolate also. It imprisons not the beloved who have parted from us. We go thither to weep, and the angel of the resurrection meets us; the voice steals over us, — "They are not here, they are risen." Death is swallowed up in victory. They die no more, but are as the angels of God. The Lamb, who is in the midst of the throne, shall feed them, and shall lead them unto living fountains of waters, and God shall wipe away all tears from their eyes. A veil, indeed, must hang for a while between them and us. They and we must, for a season, pursue separate paths of duty, in separate mansions of our Father's house, — yet not divided. It is still one house and one family. Yet our faith is weak. We think too much of the dark coffin and the lonely grave, with which the departed have far less connection than ourselves. But could we lift our thoughts to the abode of their glory, could we catch the hymn-note of their joy, could we get a momentary glimpse of their blissful state, it would arm us with fortitude to bear our loss, fill us with thankfulness for their unspeakable gain, and urge us ever onward and upward with unfaltering steps in the path which they trod before us. God grant to the deeply afflicted among us, that faith and patience may have their perfect work, that they may come forth as fine gold from the furnace, and may be found among those who through much tribulation have entered into the kingdom of God!

SERMON IX.

THE TRANSFIGURATION.

WE HAVE NOT FOLLOWED CUNNINGLY DEVISED FABLES, WHEN WE MADE KNOWN UNTO YOU THE POWER AND COMING OF OUR LORD JESUS CHRIST, BUT WERE EYEWITNESSES OF HIS MAJESTY. FOR HE RECEIVED FROM GOD THE FATHER HONOR AND GLORY, WHEN THERE CAME SUCH A VOICE TO HIM FROM THE EXCELLENT GLORY, THIS IS MY BELOVED SON, IN WHOM I AM WELL PLEASED. AND THIS VOICE WHICH CAME FROM HEAVEN WE HEARD, WHEN WE WERE WITH HIM IN THE HOLY MOUNT. — 2 Peter i. 16 - 18.

MY subject is our Lord's transfiguration. We know not the scene of this miracle. Monkish tradition has assigned it to Mount Tabor, but without any good ground. It probably occurred on one of the mountains north of the Sea of Galilee, in the region of Cæsarea Philippi. It was on the Sabbath, less than two weeks before our Saviour's death. It was his uniform custom, when he passed the Sabbath in any city or village, to attend the service of the synagogue; but now, in the wilderness, he leads his three most intimate companions up into a secluded place of worship, probably in the evening, when, by Jewish reckoning, the day of rest began. He spends the hours in prayer. Meanwhile the weary disciples fall asleep. And while they sleep, a glorious change passes over the form and features of their Master. A supernatural brightness shines from his face. His garments become a robe of light. There appear in familiar converse with him Moses and Elijah, the founder, the restorer, of the Jewish faith, the two great men of the ancient dispensation, — the one august and venerable as a leader and lawgiver, the other the loftiest of those sublime old seers who had thundered the decrees of Heaven into the ears of an apostate and rebellious nation. They talk with Jesus of his approaching sufferings and death. The apostles awake, and listen with amazement and intense interest to their communings. They are reluctant to quit this heavenly society for the dusty world beneath. On this lofty, secluded mountain they would have their Master hold his court. "It is good to be here," cries the ardent, impulsive Peter; — "let us, then, pitch three tents for our Master and his illustrious guests, and let us sit at their feet and hear their words." But while they speak, the heavenly visitors vanish in a luminous cloud, and from the cloud comes the voice of the Eternal, — "This is my beloved Son; hear ye him."

We may trace, I think, with distinctness, two

express purposes which the transfiguration was designed and adapted to serve.

1. It installed our Saviour in his true place and glory in the eyes of these three chief apostles. They had begun to look upon him as the promised Messiah; but their conceptions of the Messiah were as yet low and narrow. They thought of him merely as a powerful Jewish king, who should mount the throne of David, govern by the law of Moses, keep alive the daily sacrifice, restore the decayed majesty of the ritual worship, and bring all the kindreds of the earth to bow with offerings and hosannas at the temple in Jerusalem. Thus was the Messiah in their gross conceptions subordinated to the law and the prophets; and his instructions were not to constitute a new religion, but merely to be engrafted on the old stock of Judaism. With these notions, they were ill prepared to receive from him any teachings which looked far beyond the creed of their fathers, and would have regarded with utter scepticism anything that might come in conflict with the perpetual obligations of the Levitical law. But the scene now before them is adapted to enlarge their views of their Master's mission and office. He is the chief personage; and the great lawgiver, the mighty prophet, appear but as ministering spirits to him, passing over to him their insignia of authority, resigning to him their supremacy over God's people.

They stay not with the awe-stricken disciples; for their commission has expired. They had prepared his way, had heralded his coming; and now they vanish from his glorified presence, as stars fade before the sun. They were the servants, faithful in their day and for their work; but of him comes the voice, — "This is my beloved Son; hear ye him." The apostles thus saw the three in their true places and relations, and were prepared to receive the new religion as an independent revelation, and to regard their Master as a teacher who, so far from borrowing light from those that went before him, reflected back light upon them, making it their highest glory that they foresaw and foretold the day of his appearing.

This lesson of the transfiguration many Christians need. There is, there always has been, in the Church of Christ a great deal of Judaism, — a clinging to what is worn out, outgrown, and done away, — a preference for that which is in part over that which is perfect. Many stop at Moses, instead of going on to Christ. There are prevalent in many parts of the Church unchristian notions of doctrine and duty, derived from the Old Testament, which represent a certain stage of progress from darkness to light, but fall short of the revelation made in the Gospel. Thus there are certain harsh, stern views of the Divine character entertained by many, which have no support in the New Testament, nor yet any in the Old, properly understood, but which mark the point of attainment reached by the covenant people in passing from polytheism and idolatry towards the sublime conception of God as a Father, which first had its full development in the words of Jesus. Thus, also, many Christians deem the retaliation of injury, even to blood for blood, a Christian duty, because it was enjoined by Moses; whereas under him the enactment of literal retaliation, and nothing more, was but a stage in the humanizing process by which men were gradually reclaimed from the practice of reckless and unmeasured vengeance, and prepared for Christ's law of perfect love and prompt forgiveness. Let me not be misunderstood. I cherish a faith which has no room to grow stronger in the divine origin of the Old Testament revelation and religion. But it was not the whole truth, — not absolute truth; else there had been no need of a more perfect law. It was truth with reference to the sins which it rebuked and the errors which it dispelled; but on every point it left undisclosed much that is essential to the perfect culture of the race. On every point Christ reveals more, and goes farther, than Moses. And Christ is our law and our authority. The law and the prophets are but steps to his throne. On his face rests the brightness of heaven; his are the robes of light; and Moses and Elijah shine only in the rays that go forth from his countenance. In our theology let us not, then, build the three tabernacles, but one holy of holies to the great high-priest who has passed into the heavens; for in him all preceding dispensations have their completion and fulfilment.

2. The second great purpose of our Saviour's transfiguration had reference to himself. It was one of the agencies employed by God for the development of his moral perfection, of his power of effort and endurance. That Jesus, though he knew no sin, was yet gradually fitted and perfected for his arduous and world-embracing mission, for the agony of his cross and the triumph of his death, the testimony of Scripture leaves us no room to doubt. St. Luke speaks of his growing in wisdom, and in favor with God and man. The writer to the Hebrews says, — "It became him, for whom are all things, and by whom are all things, in bringing many sons into glory, to make the Captain of their salvation perfect through sufferings." And again, — "Though he were a Son, yet learned he obedience by the things which he suffered, and, being made perfect, he became the author of eternal salvation unto all them that obey him." That he felt the need and experienced the power of aid from heaven would appear from the frequency of his seasons of prolonged supplication to God, and from the

instances in which, at striking emergencies of his life, there were special interpositions for his support and relief.

Our Saviour was now going to die. His warfare was well-nigh accomplished. There was everything before him to fill the prospect with anguish and dread. Physical torture and suffering were to form but a small part of the bitterness of his cup. His bosom friends were to be left as sheep without a shepherd in the season of their greatest helplessness and need. Those whom he had invited, warned, and cherished, those whose sick he had healed, whose dead he had raised, whose maniacs he had restored, were to be his accusers and his murderers. He was to pass from among the living under circumstances the most revolting to that deep moral sensibility, to those sentiments of piety and love, which his exalted character and mission can have rendered only the more intense and delicate. By every vile form of impiety and blasphemy was his pure spirit to be kept in protracted torture.

The scene now under consideration was one of the instrumentalities ordained to strengthen our Saviour for conflict and for agony. Those who had overcome were sent to minister to him who was to suffer. They spake of his approaching death. They, too, had been sufferers; and their deepest griefs and injuries had been of the same type with his. Men nerved to exposure and hardship, full of vigor and intrepidity, they had made slight account of their outward privations and sufferings, nor do we hear from them a word of complaint as to toil, or wandering, or want. Moses led his people in the desert for forty years, and that in extreme old age; yet "his eye was not dim, nor his natural force abated." But he mourned, in the deepest prostration of spirit, for the ingratitude and impiety of his nation, and in their obstinacy and frequent rebellion bore a daily burden of care and grief. Elijah encountered hunger, desolation, persecution. He was driven from city to desert, and from desert to mountain. But no peril daunted him; no opposition quenched his zeal. Yet he, too, was filled with anguish for the sins of his people, and in the solitude of the cavern poured out his complaint, that the children of Israel had forsaken Jehovah's covenant, thrown down his altars, and slain his prophets. How appropriate companions for the great Witness of the truth, at this hour, were these sufferers for righteousness' sake! Most fittingly might they have talked "of his decease which he should accomplish at Jerusalem," and communed with him of the unfailing triumph of truth and the sure victory of virtue, — of the sympathy of all heaven with sacrifices and sorrows incurred from love for the children of God. Not of death in its dreariness and dread did they talk, but of death met with faith and submission, made calm and happy by the breath of prayer, lost in victory by the near view of the crown of life that fadeth not away. In this heavenly presence, the Saviour, clothed in light, received the earnest of the reward that awaited him as death's conqueror and man's Redeemer. It was for him a scene full of refreshment, solace, and strength. It blended rays of heavenly glory with the darkest scenes of earth, the sympathy of pure and exalted spirits with the contempt and contumely of the low and vile, visions of triumph with impending torture and agony, the light of immortal life with the overhanging darkness of the grave. The heavenly forms, the voice of attestation, gave our Saviour's mission thus far the seal of the Divine acceptance, assured him that the living sacrifice of a weary and suffering pilgrimage had been well pleasing to the Father, and gave him new energy to complete the offering in agony and blood.

These purposes seem to have been the chief ends of the transfiguration. It may also suggest many important lessons for our faith and practice. To a few of these let us now direct our thoughts.

Let me first ask, In what did this miracle consist? Did it create a new state of things, or did it simply reveal a state that always exists? The latter, as seems to me. When angels and just men made perfect appear in converse with our Saviour, it is not their being among mortals, but their becoming visible to the outward eye, that constitutes the miracle. Heaven, I believe, is not afar off, but unspeakably near, compassing our homes, encircling our daily ways. As all around us, on leaves and in dew-drops on a summer's day, there are myriads of living beings too minute for the bodily eye to discern, so there is no doubt constantly about us a cloud of unseen spirits too ethereal for our gross vision, — the hosts of God encamp around our dwellings, — strains of celestial praise, such as hailed the Saviour's birth, are always borne, though unheard, on our night air, —

> "Millions of spiritual creatures walk the earth
> Unseen, both when we wake and when we sleep."

It was no rare thing, though an amazing sight, when Elisha beheld angelic hosts drawn out for his defence. Nor had the hills of Judæa grown unfamiliar to Moses and Elijah, who now "appeared in glory." The whole tenor of Scripture brings the two worlds together, makes us feel that they are as one world, — that our departed friends, and the wise and holy of all times, may be around us and with us. Could we feel this always as we do at some favored seasons, would it not be an ever-present rebuke to our negligence and sin, an unceasing stimulus to diligence and heavenly-mindedness? Would not voices no longer heard on earth be our unceasing monitors of duty, and re-echo in thrilling tones every prompting of conscience and every precept of the Divine word? Would not the venerable dead, even more than the living, be our teachers and our guides? I love to look on the transfiguration, and on similar scenes in our Saviour's pilgrimage, as but revelations, manifestations of the spiritual life, which in numberless forms perpetually surrounds us; and I feel, that, next to the presence of God and the love of Jesus, we can have no motive to duty so strong as the assurance that the most revered and the best beloved of those that have entered upon the higher life survey with intense interest the path of our pilgrimage, and that their joy is enhanced by our fidelity and devotion.

Again, the seasons when our Saviour enjoyed the nearest communion with heaven deserve our special regard. When was it that angels and glorified spirits became manifest in his society? Not when the multitudes thronged him, and children sang hosannas in the temple, — not during his few and brief seasons of ease and outward success. They first came to him after his forty days' temptation, when he had contended in lonely prayer with every allurement which could draw him aside from his appointed work. Again, in the scene now before us, came Moses and Elijah. And of what talked they with him? Not of crowns, or of applauding multitudes, but of his approaching agony and death. Again, when in Gethsemane he wrestled with the severest powers of evil, and won the victory before his hour had come, there appeared an angel from heaven strengthening him. Are not these things written that heaven may seem nearest to us when trials most abound, in loneliness and weariness, in desertion and agony, — that we may bring the unseen world into the clearest view when the power of evil is the strongest, and that, when no earthly voice gives us comfort or a God speed, we may feel that angels minister to us and glorified spirits urge us heavenward ?

Finally, the scene of the transfiguration was brief and transitory. The amazed and delighted apostles would have had it prolonged. Peter said, — "It is good for us to be here." But Jesus judged otherwise. Congenial to his spirit as were these heavenly communings, he never protracted them, but made them only his brief seasons of refreshing in the intervals of toil and conflict. On the eve of the Sabbath he had ascended the mountain ; in the morning he returns to his work of unrequited love, and from the sublime converse of glorified spirits he plunges at once into a stubborn and unbelieving multitude, and enters with the most prompt and tender sympathy into one of the most afflictive cases of disease that ever demanded his aid.

Here we have a beautiful example of what the

disciple's life ought to be. There is something fascinating in the walks of retired devotion; and many have been the saintly spirits, like Thomas à Kempis, that have been nurtured in cloisters, and have been wholly intent on heavenly contemplations. In our day, and among Protestants, we sometimes see a tendency to an æsthetic, meditative piety, which seeks the refreshments, without bearing the burdens, of the Gospel, — which would wear the crown, but shrinks from the cross, — which loves to commune with God and heaven, yet likes not to go as a messenger from heaven among the doubting, the heavy laden, the suffering, and the sinning. Not thus do we learn Christ, as we view him, first on the holy mountain, and then on the plain beneath. Not always on the mountain can his true follower be; but often in the working-day world, in the busy, active walks of life, wherever a Christian example can be felt, a Christian influence breathed, the unction of a pure and loving spirit shed abroad, — often, too, where there is misery to be relieved, sorrow to be soothed, error to be reclaimed, sin to be put away. The Christian must work as well as pray, — must bless men no less than he praises God, — must have his post of positive duty on earth no less than his conversation in heaven, — must so blend contemplation and activity, that in his retired hours he shall wear none of the features of a recluse or an ascetic, and in his busy seasons shall never forget that he is a friend of Christ and an heir of heaven. As by the reverence of the old painters our Lord was distinguished by a halo in every scene and on every occasion, so should his disciple always bear about with him rays of his Master's image.

It is only by this blending of contemplative and active piety, that the highest results of character can be reached, and the highest religious enjoyment be attained. He who is cold and selfish towards man, or neglectful of outward duty, cannot see God in prayer, or enjoy the full luxury of religious meditation. But God and Christ are always near, and heaven is ever open, to the good and faithful servant. When he prays, no shadow of self intervenes between him and the Father. When he meditates on his Saviour, he feels drawn towards him by the bonds of a close spiritual kindred. When his thoughts mount to heaven, they knock not in vain at the golden gate. And his hours of prayer, his seasons of quiet meditation, always send him back with a more trusting, hopeful, fervent spirit, to do the work of life.

These views are beautifully illustrated by an old Romish legend, with which I close. A pious monk, one day, when he had been unusually fervent in his devotions, found his darkened cell suddenly illuminated by an unearthly light, and there stood before him a vision of the Saviour, his countenance beaming with godlike love, his hand outstretched with a gesture of kind invitation. At that moment rang the convent-bell, which called the monk, in the regular course of his duty, to distribute alms to the poor at the gate. For an instant he hesitated; but the next instant found him, true to the vow of charity, on his way to the gate. The poor relieved, the work of love complete, he returned in sadness to his cell, doubting not that the heavenly vision had taken flight. But, to his surprise and joy, it was still there, and with a smile even more full than before of divine beauty and ineffable love; and there came from it the words, — "Hadst thou staid, I had fled."

SERMON X.

THE RESURRECTION.

(Preached on Easter Sunday, 1845.)

IF CHRIST BE NOT RISEN, THEN IS OUR PREACHING VAIN, AND YOUR FAITH IS ALSO VAIN. — 1 Corinthians xv. 14.

THIS is a glad day for the Church, — the second birthday of its Prince and Head, — the day when he showed himself immortal, and wrote over the gates of the grave, for the whole company of his disciples, — "Because I live, ye shall live also." "The power of his resurrection," — how must the apostles have felt it! Their only concern was that he might be decently buried, and might be laid where they could reach his lifeless body with the vain offices of bereaved affection. They go to the sepulchre to weep there; they return assured that he still lives. Their withered hopes are now renewed, — their lost Master is theirs again and for ever; and because he has risen, they now know that the mansions in the Father's house are no fable, — that death has no fatal sting, and the grave no enduring terror. As in harmony with the spirit of this anniversary, I propose this morning, first, to show you how much mankind needed express testimony from God with reference to a life to come, and then to illustrate the peculiar value of Christ's resurrection as bearing witness to man's immortality.

In order to test man's need of a revelation of eternal life, let us inquire how, without an express revelation, he could obtain the knowledge of his own immortality. Apart from special Divine communications, our sources of knowledge are consciousness, observation, experience, and human testimony. Immortality is necessarily out of the range of consciousness; for we cannot be conscious of the future. By observation and experience we can barely infer what may probably take place from what has already taken place; and if the continuance of life after the event called death has neither formed a part of our experience, nor fallen under our observation, we cannot derive our faith in immortality from these sources. Human testimony, as regards continued existence after death, cannot transcend the range of human experience; and if the veil of eternity has never been miraculously lifted, then can no man bear testimony as to what lies beyond the grave.

We often hear, indeed, of arguments for a future life drawn from the analogies of outward nature, — from the transformation of the earth-worm through death into a higher form of life, — from the forthputting of the foliage, and the upspringing of the grass and the flowers, after their winter's death. The kernel of wheat, it is said, dies and is decomposed, but reappears in the blade, the ear, the ripening sheaf. All Nature wraps herself in her burial garment, — the winter's snows are her winding sheet; but she lays aside her funeral robe and springs in fresh and beautiful life from the grave. These analogies were before the eyes of the apostles and the holy women who presided over our Lord's interment. It was in the full and gorgeous glory of an Asiatic spring that they laid him in the tomb; and his tomb was in a garden, surrounded by these boasted emblems of immortality. Why did not every green leaf and opening bud say to them, — "He whom ye bury will rise again"? Or, to make the question more comprehensive, I would ask, Why were not these analogies observed or thought out by those who, in earlier times and in pagan countries, reasoned wisely and well of the mysteries of nature and of human life? They were not. At least, I have never met with them in any classic writer. The ancient philosophers, when they reason about immortality, aim by the most flimsy sophistry to prove the pre-existence and past eternity of the human soul, and thence infer its future eternity.

I think that I can show you why these hopeful analogies were not observed, or, if observed, were not relied on, before the resurrection of Christ. Analogy proves nothing. It is merely a similarity of relations or principles between beings or objects of different classes; and to reason from analogy is to infer resemblances of which we are ignorant from those which we know to exist. And this we can never do with certainty, seldom with a high degree of probability, especially when the objects about which we reason are of widely different classes; for there must always be some point where resemblance ceases and difference begins, and there is always room to suspect that this point may lie between the resemblance which we know and that which we infer. Thus, the kernel of wheat, the caterpillar, and man, are objects of widely different classes. They resemble each other in being the creatures of God and organized existences. But they are so unlike in their modes both of life and of death, that we have no right whatever to infer, that, because something like a resurrection takes place with the kernel and the caterpillar, it also will with man.

What, then, is the true province of analogy? It is adapted to answer objections to truths of which we are assured from other sources of evidence. Here analogy is a valid ground of argument. It can remove apparent improbability from what at first sight seems strange, if true. It is no longer strange, if we can show that the same thing is true, that the same law or principle holds good, with regard to beings or objects of a different class. Thus, the doctrine of human immortality, if true, is a stupendous and amazing truth; and when the mind is first assured of it by miraculous testimony from God, it yet seems something too great and too good to be believed, and we look around through the universe in a state of partial incredulity, and ask, — "Is there anything like a resurrection in any of the departments of nature with which we are conversant?" We see that there is. We see the butterfly come forth from his rent sepulchre, — the green blade from the grave where the sower hid the seed. We see that all nature dies and lives again. Our scepticism as to what God has revealed concerning our own future life is removed, and we are prepared to receive this momentous disclosure with an earnest and loving faith. This is the use which Saint Paul makes of the argument from analogy in the chapter from which our text is taken. He first from the resurrection of Christ proves that of all men, — represents the latter as inseparable from the former, — denies the possibility of preaching or believing that man will rise, if Christ has not risen. But then comes the sceptical inquiry, "How can this be? How can the dead be raised, and with what bodies?" In reply, he exhibits in the outward universe instances of a resurrection of virtually the same being in a different form, as in the case of the kernel of wheat, which, without changing its identity, reappears in a different form from that in which it was thrown into the ground. By this analogy, he shows that there is in the annual course of nature a well-known fact, multiplied myriads of times over, in itself equally strange and encompassed by the same difficulties with the resurrection of man.

We see, then, that as to immortality nature is voiceless, and man the prey of unceasing doubt, except through Divine revelation. And does not the history of human belief and experience confirm my statement? Where, out of the pale of revealed religion, can you find an instance of firm, sufficient, satisfying faith in immortality, — of a faith strong enough to sustain the soul in its seasons of the severest need, and to give it triumph in death? I know not a single instance. The dying Socrates made the nearest approach to such a faith; but between a Christian death-scene and his, there is a heaven-wide contrast. "I have strong hope," said he, "that I am now going to the company of good men;

but on a matter encompassed with so much doubt, it becomes us not to be too confident." What term of comparison is there between such a timid, hesitating hope, and the full, clear faith of the believer in Christ, whose whole soul goes forth in the glad declaration, — "I know that my Redeemer liveth, and that his disciple cannot die"? The most striking characteristic of the Christian's death is the more than faith, the confidence that will not entertain a doubt, the almost unveiled vision of the life to come, that plays before the eyes just closing upon earthly scenes. I have spoken of the greatest and most revered of the ancient philosophers; and often has his image come up before me in the chambers of penury, and by the death-bed of the lowly, and, except in the word of God, unlettered, and constrained me to say to myself, — "Surely the least in the kingdom of heaven is greater than he."

There were others of those old philosophers who spoke fearlessly of death. But how? By bracing themselves up to look steadily and with flinty face at the dread alternative of annihilation. To prove that annihilation is no evil is the object of full half of Cicero's celebrated treatise on immortality; and Seneca, who talks more than any of the ancients about the contempt of death, manifestly leans towards the belief that death is the end of all things. Nor have I ever known or read of a happy and hopeful death anywhere in Christendom among those who could not fix the eye of faith upon the risen Redeemer. Avowed deists have sunk into their last sleep, sometimes in brutish indifference, sometimes in indescribable agony of soul. Those of our own day and country, who, though claiming to be called Christians, deny the resurrection, yet live; and may God grant them a better mind and a less icy creed, before the chill of death creeps over them!

Our need of the Saviour's resurrection as a support for our faith in immortality may yet further appear from considering the times when we most need this faith. They are not seasons when the intellectual powers are in the fullest activity, so as to permit us to take in a wide range of thought, and gather in from the expanse of nature or the phenomena of life arguments or illustrations for our faith. But a fact, an example, the mind can always apprehend; and it appeals also to the imagination, — a faculty which never slumbers, and is often most active and vivid when the reasoning powers are the least so. When the mind is overwhelmed by some sudden stroke of bereavement, or is intent on the passing death-scene of one tenderly beloved, or is distracted by the pains and infirmities of acute and fatal illness, it cannot ransack heaven and earth for assurances of immortality; and yet it needs something above and beyond itself on which to fix its steadfast regards of trust and hope. And at such a season, while even distinct self-consciousness seems suspended, and there is no ear for the myriads of voices from the outward world, or even for the tenderest human comforter who speaks of earthly things, the soul can look to the Saviour's forsaken sepulchre, can see the burial garments drop from his reanimated form, and can hear as from the very lips of the Redeemer, as the angel rolls the stone away,— "He that believeth in me shall never die."

I shall go from the sanctuary to-day to the home of a widow bereft of her only son, faithful, kind, devoted, the staff of her age, her first grief in his behalf that which rends her heart when she knows that he is dead. With what words shall I comfort the forlorn mother? Shall I babble to her of flowers and butterflies, and talk about the opening spring? Or shall I enter into a metaphysical disquisition on the nature and laws of spirit, and attempt a labored proof of immortality, on grounds which her lacerated mind can neither apprehend nor follow? Or shall I tell her to look within, in proud self-reliance, for her faith and her support, when her stricken and desolate spirit feels more than ever its neediness and its dependence, and craves the voice and the sustaining arm of the Almighty? O, no! I should seem a wanton mocker of her misery. But I can tell her of the widow of Nain, and who stopped the bier, — I can talk to her of the new tomb in Joseph's garden, and of the vision of angels on the resurrection morning; and I know that my words will not seem to her as idle tales, but as the power and wisdom of God for her relief and consolation.

Here let me remark, that, in these times of intense need, minds are to a great degree equalized. The strongest mind, undisciplined by faith, and inured to a godless self-dependence, then finds itself weak; while the loftiest and richest intellect in the school of Christ stoops to look into the place where the Lord lay, and yields itself to the guidance of humble, childlike faith. At such seasons, we all crave assurances of immortality congenial with the passing scene, covering the same ground, woven (so to speak) of the same material. We demand to see actual instances of resurrection in a body like our own, — death visibly "swallowed up in life." I am delighted to find, as I write, the testimony of one of the truly great men of our times, recently deceased, to the adaptation of our Saviour's resurrection to his own moral nature and necessities. I refer to the late Dr. Arnold, whom it would be hard to convict of weakness or superstition. Speaking of a death in his own family, he writes, — "Nothing afforded us such comfort, when shrinking from the outward accompaniments of death, the grave, the grave-clothes, the loneliness, as the thought that all these had been around our Lord himself, round him who died, and is now alive for evermore."

And now let me ask, — "Why should it be thought a thing incredible, that God should raise the dead?" What good ground is there for scepticism as to the fact of our Saviour's resurrection, if we only admit the doctrine of immortality as probable? To my mind, there is none. But, on the other hand, I should expect to find that something of the kind had taken place. I should expect to find instances of a visible resurrection somewhere in the world's history. And had they not occurred, nothing short of mathematical demonstration would suffice to convince me of a life to come. If, when the body dies, the soul lives on, it is of inestimable importance that this fact should be made known to men, to all men, to the unlettered no less than to the highly endowed; and we cannot conceive that a good God should not have made it known. But how could it be so clearly made known, and brought so near to the apprehension of minds of every class, as by an illustrious and fully attested example? If the soul lives on, was it not to be expected, that, in one instance at least, it should return to reanimate the body, — to show that the grave is not a place of eternal sleep, and that no child of God can die? To the great mass of mankind, constituted as they are, this was the most striking and satisfying proof that could have been offered. A single example is worth more than an accumulated mass of the most cogent argument; for the argument, at most, only shows that the thing may be, while the example shows that the thing is. Only take man's continued life after death for granted, and can you conceive, that, under the government of a benignant God, the curtain should not in a single instance have been lifted from that life, and no voice should ever have been sent from it to reassure those yet in bondage to the fear of death? To me the glimpses of another world which Scripture history lets in seem no less natural and truth-like than beautiful and touching. They are, to my mind, just what might have been anticipated, — enough to make us sure of a world to come, and yet not enough to make us weary of this life before our time. And most of all should I have expected to find this miracle of a visible resurrection wrought in the person of Him whose express mission it was to reveal to man his divine lineage and his immortal destiny, and to wake him from the death of sin to a life worthy of God and of heaven.

Before we part, let us put to ourselves the momentous practical inquiry, Are we partakers of our Master's resurrection? The apostle says, — "He has abolished death"; and this language is literal rather than figurative. The incident, *death*, indeed remains; but its significance is destroyed. It is not the close, or even the suspension, of being. It breaks not the continuity of life. It is simply an unclothing of the soul, — a change of its raiment. Christ's resurrection makes both worlds one, reveals to us the life on this and on the other side of the grave as one life. "I go, and come again," were his own words in relation to what we call death; and to his disciple the last earthly hour is departure, not death. Before he rose, there was a great gulf between the two worlds. There were, indeed, in the ancient writings of the covenant people, one or two instances in which mortals were said to have crossed this gulf; and Jesus had now multiplied these instances in the case of private persons, who had mingled again with the great mass of the people, and bore about with them none of the marks of death. But now the Teacher, the Saviour, he upon whom are the eyes of the whole nation, on their great feast-day, in the presence of thousands, is slain, and borne off for burial. He is taken from the prime of life and energy, and his last night has been full of stirring, constraining eloquence, so that its counsels and promises have ever since been the choicest treasury of consolation for God's afflicted children. Thus full of activity and love, he is cut off from the land of the living. And, lo! on the morning of the third day he is again walking with his friends, his wounds still open and manifest, while his enemies rage in impotent anger, that he on whose sepulchre they had stamped the seal of absolute power, and stationed a guard never known to quail before mortal arm, should have burst the seal, put the keepers to flight, and resumed his benign mission among the living. Should not the contemplation of his passage from world to world unite both worlds in our view, and open to our familiar thoughts an infinite domain of being in close connection with our present state? Let us live as if the two worlds were one, — as children of the resurrection, — as those that cannot die, but must go hence, and must carry hence the very souls that have thought, enjoyed, and suffered here.

Again, the resurrection of Jesus, with its accompanying circumstances, inspires the happiest sentiments with regard to our friends that sleep in him. Our Saviour always spoke of his resurrection as the example of that of all men. If, as some think, there is to be an oblivion of all earthly ties in the grave, and we shall know each other no more for ever, he would have intimated this by coming forth barely to manifest himself at a distance, and to live apart from those whom he had loved till death. How different the case! We see him hastening at once to show himself to those who had most regretted his departure, meeting the faithful mourners who had gone early to the grave to weep there, sending kind messages to Peter, crossing the path of the disciples on their way to Emmaus, joining the eleven as they were assembled on that same night in the large upper room, and for forty days dwelling among his friends as lovingly as before his death. Are we wrong in inferring from these things, that, among those who share his resurrection, love remains unquenched, — that, among his redeemed, every soul will attach itself to those with whom its early lot was cast and the fibres of its first being interwoven?

Finally, let the contemplation of our risen Redeemer prepare us for the time when friends shall watch in sadness by our death-pillows. May we have so walked in the light of immortality, made manifest through him, that in the last earthly hour we shall feel and fear no evil. With calm and quiet confidence may we then look to him, who has been our guide in life, as the conqueror of death and the forerunner of our freed spirits in their eternal path of duty and progress.

SERMON XI.

THE ASCENSION.

AND HE LED THEM OUT AS FAR AS TO BETHANY; AND HE LIFTED UP HIS HANDS AND BLESSED THEM. AND IT CAME TO PASS, WHILE HE BLESSED THEM, HE WAS PARTED FROM THEM, AND CARRIED UP INTO HEAVEN. — Luke xxiv. 50, 51.

THE narrative of the ascension is given by Mark and Luke in their Gospels, and again by Luke, with greater minuteness of detail, in the Acts of the Apostles. It has its prominent place in the last-named record, because from this event the apostles dated their commission as heads and lawgivers of the spiritual household. We find, accordingly, that they at once formed a Christian association, or church, of a hundred and twenty members, proceeded, after solemn deliberation and prayer, to supply the vacancy in their number created by the death of Judas, and remained in readiness for the miraculous manifestations of the Pentecost, which occurred ten days afterwards. In accordance with this view, St. Paul, quoting with reference to Christ the passage,

"He ascended up on high, he led captivity captive, and gave gifts unto men," enumerates among those gifts "apostles, prophets, evangelists, pastors, and teachers."

I now invite you, first, to consider with me the appropriateness of our Saviour's ascension, regarded as the close of his ministry, and then to draw from this event some of the heads of religious instruction which it is adapted to furnish.

Suppose the case to have been otherwise. Suppose that Jesus had remained permanently upon the earth. In that event, the church could have had no distinct and independent existence, but would have been inseparable from him. He, the heaven-born, the infallible, so far transcended all human teachers, that none would have thought the new religion adequately represented where he was not. His bodily presence would have so marked the spot where he sojourned as the radiating point of peculiar light and special privilege, that those who should have gone forth as his messengers to distant provinces and countries would have labored under the greatest disadvantages and burdens. None would have deemed themselves sufficiently instructed without listening for themselves to the great Teacher. Nor would the apostles, while he was at their head, have felt a sufficient self-confidence for their work. They would have relied on his countenance and advice from day to day, and would not have trusted themselves to draw inferences or to apply principles, without direct recourse to him. His earthly presence after a certain period would have constrained and embarrassed them, because it was a presence necessarily confined to one place, while their field of missionary labor was the world. Therefore, said he, "It is expedient for you that I go away; for, if I go not away, the Comforter will not come, — the spirit of trust, courage, and energy will not enter your souls, — but if I depart, I will send that spirit to you." By going from them, he gave them, in lieu of a revelation which they would never have deemed complete while he was among them to add to it, a finished, perfect testimony, — an example, which they could contemplate in its wholeness and symmetry, — a life, which they could regard as a fixed and unchangeable centre of light for all times and all men. He gave them, in place of an earthly presence, of which they must often have regretted the withdrawal, a spiritual presence, which they could feel always and everywhere. He assumed the only position from which he could fulfil his promise, — "Lo! I am with you always, even to the end of the world."

But why might not his body have been again laid in the tomb, and seen corruption? We answer, that his victory over death would in that case have seemed partial and temporary. There would have hung about his memory associations of frailty and decay which it would have been hard to throw off. He could not have been regarded with the full and lofty confidence with which we now look to him as the conqueror of death, and our forerunner to life eternal. It was needful that Christ, being once raised from the dead, should die no more. And it was equally needful that he should pass away from the earth in such a mode as to inspire with courage his then faint-hearted followers, and to fix indelibly in their minds the assurance that he had come from God, and gone to God.

The mode of our Saviour's ascension is in beautiful harmony with the tone of his spirit, and the whole character of his life. We have in the Old Testament a like scene (yet how unlike!) in the translation of Elijah. He was a stern, awful old man. His life was passed in open, single-handed conflict with the banded thousands of idolatry and sin. The eyrie of the mountain-bird was his resting-place, the fierce forest-winds howled about his path, and the jagged lightning was the lamp of his feet. Nurtured among the rudest scenes of nature, ever planted with iron front and lowering brow in the evil ways of men, he seemed an embodiment of the untempered justice and fearful displeasure of Heaven against sinners; and when he stood face to face with the priests of Baal on Mount Carmel, not the scathed cliffs of the mountain, or the angry sea-swell breaking over its base, presented features of rough and awful grandeur to be compared with the countenance and mien of the indignant seer. Fit was it, that, when his conflicts ceased, he should be rapt away in a whirlwind, and borne aloft in a chariot of fire.

Far otherwise did the Saviour rise to heaven; for his whole life was gentle. Of him was it written (and how truly!)—"He shall not strive, nor cry. The bruised reed shall he not break, the smoking flax shall he not quench." His walk had been by the beautiful lake and over the vine-clad hills; his lessons had been drawn from the blooming valleys and the rejoicing birds; and in the desert bread had grown beneath his touch, and the sea had become calm when it bore him on its bosom. And now, in the rosy dawn of a beautiful spring morning, he gathers his chosen ones in the streets of Jerusalem. He goes out through the same gate, and by the vine-embowered path, on which he had walked, with the same eleven, beneath the full midnight moon, from the paschal supper to the garden of Gethsemane, and talked to them, as he went, of the heavenly vine and its fruitful branches. He goes up the same hill that had borne witness to his agony, and been moistened by his bloody sweat.

Before him lies the scene of his conflict and his triumph. Hard by is the home of the faithful sisters where he had been anointed for his burial, —the tomb whence he had called forth the sleeping Lazarus, — the new sepulchre where he had been laid with weeping, and where the resurrection angel had rolled the stone away. He lifts up his hands and blesses his disciples; and while he speaks, the morning cloud parts, he rises and passes from their sight, and those hands still outstretched in blessing disappear. So calm, so glad, are all the influences of the scene, that the disciples feel not their bereavement as when he died. The blessing has sunk into their hearts, and they go back to Jerusalem with great joy; for they remember those words, — "Where I am, there ye shall be also." They realize the fulfilment of that which before they understood not, — "Whither I go ye know, and the way ye know."

> "Thus calmly, slowly, did he rise
> Into his native skies,
> His human form dissolved on high
> In its own radiancy."

He rose to heaven, we say. What, or where, heaven is, we indeed know not. We know not how far it is to be regarded as local, and how far as all-pervading, like the presence of God. But we cannot help thinking of it as in some sense away from earth, and, if so, up, — up beyond the clouds, where the sun grows not dim, where shadows gather not. Beneath, all around, there is violence, sin, and suffering, mists hang, and darkness broods; and men, in all ages and under all religions, have looked up for the dwelling of God and the home of the blessed, thus giving as it were the consent of the race in the tacit belief, that, while God is here and everywhere, and his glorified children may go wherever he dwells, there yet are up beyond our sight regions of the universe where he is beheld with clearer vision and worshipped with purer joy. We are so made, that our holiest thoughts always mount, — our best aspirations are all upward. It is an association with space, of which, reason against it as we may, we cannot divest ourselves; and to this irresistible tendency of our minds the scene before us is adapted. It connects our Saviour's translation from human sight, and his peculiar dwelling, with all that is pure, holy, and hopeful in our hearts. It lifts our desires from passing scenes and grovelling pursuits. It creates for our faith a loftier, purer, brighter atmosphere. It blends with our own prospects for eternity every elevated association that can be borrowed from the fields of space. It places heaven in direct contrast with the grave. That is down, beneath men's feet; heaven is on high. The two have nothing in common; but, in the light of the resurrection morning, death has lost his sting and the grave its victory.

Let us now give heed to some of the lessons which the ascension affords for our faith and Christian edification.

Our Saviour, though God-born and heaven-descended, is always placed before us as the pattern of suffering, sanctified, glorified humanity. As he was, so are we in the world. As he is, so shall we be, if found in his image. He is the forerunner; we, his followers. We are to follow him in death, — then to be partakers of his resurrection, — then, of his ascension; and his ascension is but the consummation of his death and resurrection. The whole is but one act, divided in his case into three separate stages, that we may contemplate each by itself, and may connect the latter stages of glory with the first of pain, agony, and decay. Calvary, Joseph's tomb, and the ascension mount lay close together, and in our faith they are one. When Jesus died, he could not but rise again; when he rose, he could not but go home to the Father. But he, when he rose, took again his own body, to show that he still lived; and he ascended in that same form to heaven, to show that the true home of the dead is not in the grave, but above. Thus is it with the disciple. Death, resurrection, ascension, are the three stages of his passage hence. The body dies and sees corruption; — the soul rises from the worn and useless tabernacle of clay, and ascends to God who gave it.

Such are the associations which our Saviour's last days ought to connect with the death of the righteous. But how prone we are to let our thoughts linger on the first stage of the passage, — on the mere outward habiliments of death, — without remembering that all these were around him who rose and went on high!

We say that we believe that our good friends have gone to heaven. But still the death-scene oppresses us, and often clothes our souls in impenetrable gloom. We must, indeed, deeply feel their absence from us, the loss of their counsel or society, of their endeared countenances and their ministries of love. But suppose that the friend whom we mourn, instead of having pressed the bed of languishing, and breathed out his life in convulsive sighs, had gone from our sight as Jesus went, and we had traced with our own eyes the bright path on which he ascended, — I can hardly conceive of oppressive sadness and bitter weeping on his behalf. Rather, because we loved our friend, should we rejoice that he had gone to the Father. We should feel thankful for him that his days of conflict and sorrow had ceased, and our surviving affection would breathe in the hope of meeting him in his radiant home, when our own summons came.

Such associations we, as Christians, ought to connect with the death of our Christian friends; for the death of the believer in Jesus is his ascension, — veiled, indeed, from the outward vision, but to be recognized by the eye of faith. But the most spiritual of us do not regard death as we should, had we our dwelling in a purely Christian community. We view it too much through the medium transmitted from pagan times and regions, and let in upon us from the unchristian portion of the world around us. Suppose, however, a community in which there was no person of mature years, who was not in heart and life a disciple of Jesus, and imagine a death in such a society. As I bring the scene before me, the death-chamber seems like the mount of the ascension, and every one says, — "It is good to be here." I see no agony of grief, no look of despair, by the bedside; but survivors unite with the dying saint in praise and thanksgiving; and their adieus are full of congratulations with him that he is counted worthy to be first summoned from the outer courts to the inner temple of his God. When the spirit has fled, I hear those that remain talking of him who has gone as no less one of the family than before, and as only having preceded them by a little way, to make ready the new mansion for them all to dwell in when the earthly house shall be dissolved. At the interment I hear no sad knell, I see no sable procession, no pomp of woe; but the dust is laid in kindred dust with solemn joy, and with hymns of gratitude to Christ, the resurrection and the life. Thus will the death of the innocent and holy seem to us now, in the precise proportion in which we borrow our views, not from the dark, cold philosophy of the irreligious world, but from the Gospel and life of our dying, risen, ascended Redeemer.

To pass to another head of instruction, we have seen that it was expedient for the disciples, that Jesus, after he had finished his testimony and wrought his work, should go away from them, in order that they might put forth energies which would have continued latent had he remained with them,—that they might be equal to duties and services beyond their daring while he visibly held the chief place and assumed the heaviest burdens. Thus is it often with those human friends through whom God gives us faithful counsels, pure examples, and holy influences. Up to a certain point, their presence educates, strengthens, and blesses us; beyond that point, it often restrains and depresses our own independent energies. We shrink into their shadows. We roll every burden upon them. We will not think ourselves adequate to any high or arduous effort, while they are with us. We assume nothing, while they have strength to do and bear everything. It is, therefore, no doubt, hard as the saying sounds, expedient for us that they should go away. Bereavement often calls out inward powers and resources previously unknown. Those who had felt, while their main earthly staff was left them, that they were weak, and lame, and unable to stand or move alone, when deprived of that whereon they leaned, often find themselves strengthened as by an unseen hand, and can forthwith "walk, and leap, and glorify God." When those who were as eyes to the blind and as feet to the lame are removed, how often are the sealed eyes opened, and the feeble feet made firm! We all have indefinitely large capacities of action, effort, and endurance, but wait to hear the call and feel the impulse before we put them forth; and they too often lie unused till the departure of those who seemed the most essential members of our domestic and social circles pushes us into the foremost rank, and, while it imposes fresh and high responsibilities, endues us at the same time with both the will and the power to discharge them. Death is thus not only the mower of sheaves ripe for the harvest, but the great ripener of character; for, by removing some plants, it is constantly exposing others to the influences needful for their maturity.

We may see numerous illustrations of these remarks in communities both secular and religious, where the very men who are the first to raise the cry, — "Help, Lord, for the faithful fail, the godly cease," — soon find themselves, to their own amazement, inspired and furnished for the places of those whom they mourn. We see the same principle often exemplified in domestic life. The mother, who, while her husband lived, had scarcely energy and self-confidence enough for her own gentle sway, when left sole parent, is enabled to fill the double office with vigor and with wisdom, through the helping spirit of the widow's God and Judge. Thus is it that from the saddest of all God's dispensations flow the highest results, mental and spiritual, in the enlargement of the capacity and sphere of duty of those whose circle is visited by a bereaving Providence.

The gospel of the ascension suggests yet another lesson. Gethsemane, the garden of agony, and Bethany, the scene of the ascension, lie close together on the Mount of Olives. The same air that had borne the sighs and groans of that night of sorrow was parted by the glorious form as it rose to heaven. Thus is it in common life. The mount of ascension is no separate spot, hallowed from the approach of grief or the conflict of doubt and fear. But the death of the righteous everywhere consecrates scenes of sadness and suffering, of privation and agony, marking them as spots nearest heaven. The spirit of Christianity here differs widely from that of all other modes of faith. They set apart, fence in, crown with splendid monuments, scenes made glorious by the victories and daring exploits of outwardly illustrious men. The Christian shrines are those of suffering or of lowly toil. The church commemorated the Saviour's death long before it kept the festival of his birth; and no scenes in his disciple's life are fraught with so intense an interest as those where he has passed through the fire-baptism of sorrow, waged decisive conflicts with the powers of evil, and risen, in the serene might of faith and trust, above outward misery and suffering. When Jesus prayed in agony, the glory that awaited him rose before his view, and gave him strength to bear and overcome; for the Scriptures tell us that he, "for the joy that was set before him, endured the cross, and despised the shame." The dark hours of the crucifixion were before him; but there played also before his vision the majesty and glory of his return to God, — of his new birth into the kingdom of heaven. Are scenes of severe or sorrowful discipline appointed to any of us? Are we depressed by penury, bowed down by infirmity, bereft of cherished kindred and bosom friends? Are we compelled to move on beneath clouds, and on a painful path? From this path we may ascend to God, — through these clouds lies the way to heaven. For us, as for our Lord, may the same scenes be those of conflict and of triumph, of agony and glory, of our bowing under earth's heaviest burdens and mounting to heaven's purest joys.

Finally, there is in the narrative of our Saviour's ascension a lesson of Christian activity and zeal for all of us who call ourselves his disciples. When he went on high, it was not the apostles alone, the official heads of the church, but the whole hundred and twenty, the entire body of believers, that came forward to assume the charge thus devolved from the Master upon his followers. And in the labors and sacrifices of the infant church all that believed bore part. All felt that they stood in a place of duty no less than of privilege, — that they were to enlarge, enrich, adorn, the sanctuary, instead of nestling idly behind its curtain-folds. Every Christian deemed himself endowed with an apostle's commission to honor in life, and to diffuse by faithful effort, the Gospel which he had found precious. Should it not be so now? The Divine Teacher is with us only through his pervading and always blessing spirit. He has left his whole work of reclaiming sinners and bringing in eternal righteousness to human instrumentality; and not to one or another order of men, but to all, his command is, — "Freely ye have received, freely give." The preaching of the Gospel belongs to you no less than to me, though in a different way. You, who profess yourselves Christians, are bound to religious zeal and effort by the law of self-consistency. In advancing your favorite secular enterprises, opinions, and measures, you never content yourselves with the services of leaders or of official persons. You sustain their hands and encourage their hearts. You tender them your efficient co-operation. You make their special work your frequent work. Yet, Christian, in the cause which you profess to regard as above all others, where are the footmarks of your activity, where the goings forth of your zeal? In what form or way have you left traces of your handiwork in the spiritual temple? Where are the religious charities which you have helped administer, — the tempted and endangered whom you have led to Christ, — the hungering souls for whom you have broken the bread of life? Are there not some in our household of faith who bear not these marks of the Lord Jesus? You indeed help employ the religious services of one for a thousand souls. But what is he, and what are his services, among so many? As the organ of public devotion, as the sympathizing friend of a limited circle of the tempted, poor, and grief-stricken, he may, indeed, do much, yet not a tithe of what demands to be done. He needs you all as fellow-workers. Every Christian should be a preacher of righteousness, a minister of the Gospel, keeping this one interest prominent through the cares and duties of daily life, remembering the high calling of Christ Jesus while engaged in the labors of his secular calling, watching for avenues of religious usefulness, and, above all, guarding with prayerful vigilance the silent outflow of his example, which, if not made holy and sanctifying, can hardly fail to wound the cause of Christ and to weaken the hold of his religion on the hearts of men. Thus consecrating ourselves to the duties as well as to the joys of piety, to the burdens no less than to the privileges of the Christian life, we may realize the fulfilment of the early recorded blessing, — "The liberal soul shall be enriched, and he that watereth shall be watered also himself."

SERMON XII.

SOURCES OF CONSOLATION.

LET NOT YOUR HEART BE TROUBLED, NEITHER LET IT BE AFRAID. — John xiv. 27.

YET said the same Teacher, — "In the world ye shall have tribulation"; and who passes or approaches the meridian of life without having felt it? How few of our long-established homes have not been darkened by the wings of the death-angel! And in those few, have there not been seasons of weary and perilous illness, of deep solicitude and agonizing suspense on account of the tenderly beloved? To this heritage of certain sorrow must our young friends look forward, if they live. We would not abate aught from the buoyancy of their hopes. Nay, we would assure them, that, if they forsake not the law and covenant of their God, they have happy lives before them, — happy, yet not cloudless. Their path will sometimes be under a darkened sky, — their rest in homes made desolate.

But in the prospect or the endurance of these sorrows, there come to us the words of Jesus,—"Let not your heart be troubled, neither let it be afraid." And he who utters these words alone can enable us fully to verify them in our experience. I now ask your attention to the Christian relief and remedy for those fears and sorrows that flow from our domestic relations and affections.

In seasons of anxiety in behalf of those whom we love, or of sorrow for their removal from us, we need most of all a firm and active faith in God as our Father and their Father, and as ordering all the events of their lives and of ours in infinite love. It is not enough that we say to ourselves,—"These sad events are a necessary part of the course of nature." We shall feel it a grievous burden to dwell where such necessity gives law. The thought that these things must needs be gives no consolation, but only clothes our sky in new gloom. Nor can yet any reasoning on general laws meet the wants of the soul at such a season. The idea of laws of nature, omnipotent, irreversible, crushing,—of a system in the main beneficent, which yet has its hard cases and its victims,—weighs down the spirit as with an iron hand. In connection with this idea, there always comes up the torturing question,—"Could not the issue that has taken place have been foreseen and averted, had we been more watchful and more wise?" The only conception which can satisfy the deep want of the soul in sorrow is that of an impartial, all-merciful Providence, under whose administration there is no wanton infliction, no aimless suffering, no event which it is not best for us to meet and bear. We need that faith in the Father which shall refer the trial to no second cause, to the uncontrolled working of no material law, but solely to the merciful purpose of one who wounds but to heal, whose very rod comforts while it chastens. True, we may not always discern at the moment the appointed ministry of sorrow. Nor yet can our children always discern the reasons and the wisdom of the measures which we take for their good. And, in the strength and pride of manhood, we must feel that in God's hands we are still children, often ignorant of our true good, craving the outward blessings which might send leanness into our souls, shrinking from the waters in which alone we can receive our true spiritual baptism.

But how are we to acquire and sustain this filial faith? I know not, except through our Saviour. It is easy, indeed, in the summer weather of health and prosperity, to take in bright views of the Creator's love from the most radiant leaves of the book of nature and of Providence; but in the hour of deep solicitude or sorrow, the eye rests upon gloomier records. As we attempt to trace the Father's countenance, clouds and darkness are round about him, — his way is in the sea, his judgments are past finding out. There come up before our minds the fearful analogies of nature, the fierce and mysterious agencies that deal desolation and death, the appalling forms of wretchedness and suffering always to be witnessed among men; and it is impossible for us so to direct our trains of thought among the mixed and clouded scenes of the outward world, as to call up the cheerful, hopeful associations which we need. Indeed, the aspects of nature and of life are so infinitely varied, that they can hardly fail to reflect the mood of the mind for the time being. Then, too, there is a prostration of spirit, which prevents our taking those large, discursive views, and indulging in those tasteful speculations, which amuse and delight our happier hours. Sorrow, while it touches to the finest issues every portion of the moral nature, leaves the mind too little elasticity and enterprise to reason out its own sources of consolation from the conflicting aspects and jarring voices of the world around.

We need, then, to be, as it were, taken by the hand, and led directly to the Father, by some elder brother, who has entered more deeply into the secret of his love, and who dwells in his bosom. This Jesus does for us. When he tells us of the loving-kindness of God, we feel that he speaks of that which he knows, and testifies of that which he has seen. We behold him moving on in a dark and ever-darkening path, yet serene and happy, because the Father was with him. While we see in his works the seal of his commission from on high, his tranquil, resigned, submissive, yet fervent and energetic spirit, conciliates our confidence,—pleads with our hearts to believe and trust him. His words seem no less divine than if uttered in our own ears by a voice from heaven. Take all else away, cloud over every outward scene, shut out every secondary source of consolation, yet leave us those last conversations and prayers of Jesus with his disciples, and leave us with and in them a vivid conception of the man of sorrows and of glory; and we have enough for comfort, support, and hope. With those divine words, with that benignant countenance, the express image of the Father's, we can go down into the valley of tribulation without doubt, murmur, or complaint, assured of the guidance and protection in which he trusted and rejoiced.

Again, in our seasons of sorrow, we need the kind of sympathy which Jesus alone can fully bestow,—the sympathy of one who has both endured and conquered, who has fathomed and surmounted the depths of earthly grief, and who, from his own experience, can say to us,—"Be of good cheer; I have overcome the world." Among our friends we cling for consolation chiefly to those who have also suffered; and no countenance beams upon us so full of comfort as that marked with the lines of deep and frequent sorrow, yet bearing the impress of religious peace, of heavenly communings, and high spiritual joy. We read our own appointed history in the face of such a friend. We see the ever-brightening path, with its glorious issues, of those who through much tribulation are to enter the kingdom of God. In Jesus we behold sorrow in its beauty and its blessedness. We learn in him that it has no harsh ministry, no vindictive purpose, but that whom the Lord loveth he chasteneth; for we know that the Father's love was no less entire and full for him, when he hung upon the cross, than when he was transfigured on the mountain. We see in him, that sorrow need not check the serene flow of holy and happy thoughts,—that the supreme good is not outward joy, but a soul at peace with God, and in harmony with heaven. And these lessons we learn from one of whose fellow-feeling with us we are all the while conscious. It is a blessed and sustaining thought, that our glorified fellow-sufferer is with us in our hour of trial, unchanged in love from the time when he wept at the tomb of Lazarus, and bore meekly the strifes, doubts, and fears of his still frail disciples. We go back in our musing to the days of his flesh. We recall that scene, when he, the conqueror of death, stands bowed in the tenderest sympathy with the sorrow which he is so soon to change into gladness. We ponder every word of that interview with the kind sisters, — a season no less memorable for the opening of the depths of a heart full of divine compassion, than for its stupendous miracle of omnipotent mercy. The words of that hour sink into our hearts, as though heard by the outward ear, and give us new strength to bear the cross in our Saviour's name and spirit.

Once more, in our seasons of sorrow, we need a clear, firm, elastic, available faith in immortality, in the eternity of our affections, and in the deathless union of those whom death has parted. This faith is not to be derived in its sufficiency and fulness from mere analogies of nature, or from that instinctive desire of life which is proof of nothing beyond itself. When everything smiles around us, it is easy to read in the swelling bud and the transfigured earth-worm the assurance that man will not wholly and for ever slumber in the grave. But those who have delighted the most in these correspondences of the outward and the spiritual find them inadequate in their hour of need. They are precious in their place and for their use. They serve to spiritualize nature, to draw voices of praise and love from her perishing forms, and to bring nearer to the heart the "incorruptible spirit" that is in all things. But when a friend goes from us and passes behind the veil, we crave something more definite. We long to see the veil parted. We long for a voice to break the eternal silence, and to assure us that the departed indeed live, — that, though dead, they live. We look upon the countless generations that have followed each other to the grave; and, if we can see no sign from the spirit-land, if none have ever returned, none brought tidings from the home to which they have been gathered, oh, it is not within the scope of a painted flower-cup or an insect's wing, nor yet of a consciousness and experience which have no future, to proclaim to us a truth so vast and world-embracing as man's immortality. From the tokens and emblems of dissolution, we turn, then, to the gates of Nain, — we listen for the voice, "Young man, arise!" — we see the cold form stirred again with the breath of life, — the sealed eyes look upon the face of the Lord, — the dead lives; and the shout of the rejoicing multitude, — "God hath visited and redeemed his people," — rings in our ears, and makes melody in our hearts, as we sit in our desolate homes, or bend at the grave-side. O, blessed be our Father, that this voice of power has been uttered upon earth, that the caverns of the grave have been unsealed and its kingdom shaken, that the omnipotent fiat has swept over the valley of death in the sight of the living, that the long procession of the dying has been met and turned back by the Lord of life!

My young friends who have not known the bitterness of sorrow, I beg you, think not lightly of these miracles. Think not with easy complacency of teachers who come in their own names, and would tell you that Jesus came in his, — who would turn the record of his mighty works into a fable, and make his resurrection a lie. This self-sustaining theology may seem good to you while your mountain stands firm. It imposes no severe restraints. It lays upon you no crushing load of duty. It flatters your self-esteem. It chimes in with the natural tendency, which none overcome without a struggle, to seek the consciousness of being good without any very earnest effort to be good. But wait till the clouds gather and the floods come. Wait till one dearer than your own life lies dead at your side, and your grief darkens for you every scene of nature and of life, and muffles into sepulchral tones every gay and hopeful voice from the outward world. I pray that you may then know the worth of your Saviour's miracles and the power of his resurrection. I more than pity you, if, at that hour, the death-awakening voice of Jesus does not kindle in your hearts a humble, thankful faith.

It is not, then, the wisdom of the wise, but the words and works, the death and resurrection, of

Christ alone, that can give us the consolation and support that we need in our seasons of sorrow. Within a few days I have reperused the correspondence of Cicero, with reference to the death of his accomplished and tenderly beloved daughter. He, in his luxurious leisure, had written eloquently about immortality. But now all his dreams of a happy future have fled, and his soul is utterly desolate. "Public employment alone," he says, "can afford resource or consolation; and the opportunity for that is cut off by the distracted state of the commonwealth." There remains for him, therefore, only hopeless grief and remediless despair. On thus seeing how absolutely nothing the accumulated wisdom of four thousand years could do towards healing the sorrows of one who had it all at his command, I felt more than ever our boundless debt of gratitude to Him who has abolished death, and brought life and immortality to light. When the bereaved parent asks, in agony, Where is my child? nature and philosophy only echo back the question with a more desponding emphasis. Jesus alone has answered it. Only the garden where they laid him yields us spring-flowers to strew upon the graves of our kindred. He shall wipe all tears from our eyes, and bring our souls, if found in his faith and spirit, unto undying communion with those whom he has taken to himself. And while we, and those who have gone from us, surround the throne with our hosannas, we shall own, with higher evidence than we can now perceive, that death is the angel of divine love, and the grave the gate of heaven.

SERMON XIII.

CONSOLING VIEWS OF DEATH.

FATHER, I WILL THAT THEY ALSO WHOM THOU HAST GIVEN ME BE WITH ME WHERE I AM. — John xvii. 24.

For many from our households has this prayer been fulfilled, and we profess no doubt that it has been. Yet does our tone of feeling with reference to the pure and good that have gone from us fully correspond with our belief? Far be it from me to chide sorrow for the departed. I, too, well know what it is, — how keen is the first agony of bereavement, — how protracted, long after all outward traces of grief have passed away, is the sense of disappointment and desolation. But, aside from all consciousness of personal privation and loss, our views of death are affected in part by the unchristian notions and feelings with regard to it entertained by many with whom we are daily conversant, and in part by the frequency with which we see removed from life persons whose characters suggest no happy or hopeful associations in connection with their immortality There are some denominations of Christians,—the Moravians and Swedenborgians, for instance,—that seem to approach much nearer than others to the true tone of feeling with regard to death. But I cannot find that on this subject they believe anything which we do not. The reason why they can the more fully realize in experience what they believe is, that they are bodies of Christians seldom joined except by sincere believers, and that they keep themselves very much within their own respective households of faith, so that their trusting and hopeful spirit for the dead is exposed to fewer counteracting influences than can be the case with us. This seclusion from the general intercourse of the world, though pleasant in some of its aspects, is not, it seems to me, to be desired or sought by the Christian. "I pray not," said our Saviour, "that thou shouldest take them out of the world, but that thou shouldest keep them from the evil." More of the luxury of faith and devotion might, no doubt, be enjoyed in these close Christian corporations; but by the discipline of the great world, and by the opportunities of religious influence which it presents, there is a much larger amount of duty to be performed, and a much higher point of spiritual attainment to be reached.

Let us, at this time, gather up some of the

views of death and eternity, which may give us consolation in the departure of those for whom the prayer of our text has been fulfilled.

In the first place, we cannot help regarding those who have been called to the heavenly society as happy in the season of their removal. It is fit, indeed, that death should be attended with circumstances of pain and dread, — else the weary and afflicted would hasten to drop the burden of life before their time. But if there be a world beyond, for each soul there must be a time of translation; and can we doubt that God's time is the right and the best time? There must be a moment when this world ceases to be the fittest scene of discipline for the improving spirit. Heaven reaps a large harvest from the most brilliant promise of early life; but is it not well that the fruit first ripe should be first gathered? The cumberer of the ground may be left year after year, so long as there remains even a germ of spiritual life; for even in autumn that germ may bud and blossom, and if it finally dies within him, it is by his own act, not by God's. He may be left, too, as a discipline for the faith, patience, and charity of others, and may not be removed till his moral desolation and penury have helped many to seek the wealth which he has despised. The good and faithful may also be spared long, not only because they are needed here, but because they may still gain and grow continually, and without check, from the means of progress here open to them. Others may early exhaust, for their own peculiar habits of mind and heart, the earthly resources designed for their culture. Being made perfect in a short time, they have fulfilled a long time. Their souls pleased the Lord, — therefore hasted he to take them away. Some shrink with too much sensitiveness from the unavoidable trials and conflicts of their earthly life, and at the same time every fibre of their moral natures is in harmony with heaven. Why, then, should the Good Shepherd leave them in bleak places, when his own green pastures by the still waters are the very rest they crave? Many are taken from the evil to come, from trials which might have crushed instead of strengthening them, from burdens which would have weighed too heavily upon their souls. Others might have been exposed to less propitious moral influences, had they lived longer. Temptations might have thickened around them, — worldly, selfish aims might have dimmed the beauty of their early promise. Of many a young man cut down, in what we call untimely death, when just leaving a religious home for unsheltered scenes of moral evil and jeopardy, may it be said, as of the patriarch Enoch, — "He pleased God and was beloved of him, so that, living among sinners, he was translated. Yea, speedily was he taken away, lest that wickedness should alter his understanding, or deceit beguile his soul." Hard as it is, when the heavenly guest is summoned from our own tables, to say, "Thy will be done!" I cannot doubt, that in the condition of mind and character of every child that God calls home, whether in infancy, youth, or age, there is something which renders the appointed time the best of all times for his translation, — that either a longer or a shorter life would have been attended with less happy results.

For us who remain, also, must not our friends be taken in the best time? Even if it be when they seem most needed here, may we not intensely need the flow of holier, more heavenward thoughts, of which sorrow unlocks the spring? No doubt, our moral progress is at times arrested by causes beyond our power, — earthward and heavenly influences are so poised against each other, that with the utmost effort we barely hold our ground, and take no onward steps. Affliction disturbs this balance, and gives our better desires freer scope and more perfect issues. There is a conscious nearness to heaven, which belongs only to those who have seen their best beloved pass within its gates. There are home feelings connected with heaven, known only by those whose families are divided between the two worlds, which gain new strength with every new translation. When from our future life we look back upon the present, I doubt not that we shall see, that, of all our experiences, our sorrows were among the most precious, — that our seasons of bereavement and darkness were those when our souls most truly grew in divine strength and wisdom, when our best resolutions were fixed, our purest sentiments made abiding, our higher natures most nourished and enriched. By God's appointment we are to be made perfect through suffering; and while the best may be rendered still better through its ministry, and the aged saint may find it in his heart even to thank God for his afflictive mercies, we who are yet midway in the path of life, and in full conflict with every unspiritual tendency and influence, must own the fitness of those events which most clearly reveal to us our true calling and our highest good.

Thoughts of heaven might, it seems to me, give us more consolation than we are wont to derive from that source. We employ with regard to death a great deal of pagan imagery, which can hardly fail to let low and unworthy ideas into our minds. We talk of the *blighting* of early promise, of the *premature* death of the young and the beautiful. We too often speak of the pure and the good that have gone from us, as if they were objects of pity. We regret for them the brief pleasures, the withering joys, of the passing days. And then our thoughts revert, oftener than a high Christian culture should permit, to the sad accompaniments of dissolution and the last lonely home of the frail tenement of clay, even as the caterpillar might look upon the torn covering of the chrysalis as all that remained of his fellow-worm, ignorant that the rent and forsaken tabernacle marked the higher birth of its tenant. But our faith tells us that to those to whom it was Christ to live, it is gain to die. Let our thoughts, then, linger not about the grave, but seek our kindred in the nearer presence of their Father and their Saviour, in the home where every holy wish is met and every pure desire fulfilled, where suffering and sorrow are no more, and life clothes itself in eternal youth and unfading beauty. What would our brief joys be to those to whom all the avenues of divine wisdom are free, the riches of infinite love unfolded, and a boundless sphere of duty and of happiness laid open?

"How happy
The holy spirits who wander there,
'Mid flowers that shall never fade or fall!
Though mine were the gardens of earth and sea,
Though the stars themselves had flowers for me,
One blossom of heaven outblooms them all.
Go, wing thy flight from star to star,
From world to luminous world, as far
As the universe spreads its flaming wall;
Take all the pleasures of all the spheres,
And multiply each through endless years,
One minute of heaven is worth them all."

We know that our innocent children, our good friends, are happy, infinitely happy. Were they of a gentle and tender spirit, pure in heart, kind, peaceful, ever seeking the things that are more excellent? Their communion now is only with the most congenial scenes and objects. Their souls shall no more hunger and thirst after righteousness, as they often did under the infirmity and depression of earthly trial. Every pure taste, every kind affection, has found its kindred nutriment and joy. It is a kingdom *prepared for them*, adapted to meet their desires, to satisfy their longings, to fill their souls with the fulness of divine love.

Immortality, in order to give us consolation, must not be looked at merely as a general truth. We must individualize it, and apply it to separate traits of character and forms of loveliness. It is not in one unvarying frame of spirit and routine of duty and joy that we must conceive of the redeemed as living on for ever; but of each as retaining his own peculiar mental and moral features, so that, while all shine as the brightness of the firmament, they differ as one star differs from another in glory. Heaven undoubtedly presents various modes of activity and avenues of progress, the tree of life bears divers kinds of fruit, corresponding to the different combinations of worthy and heavenly elements of character with which different souls pass into their higher state.

When I think of the kindred and friends who may welcome me to heaven, I want to think not of any precise number of angelic beings, alike except in their degrees of attainment, — I would bring them up in their individual forms and features, in those delicate hues and blendings of character, those traits of loveliness to be felt, yet not described, which linger always on our memories. And as their tones of voice still dwell upon our hearts, and their countenances are ever living there, why need we suppose that even these in their individuality have passed away, that is, so far as the soul gave them shape and utterance? The tongue, the face, is indeed for ever cold and dead. But in some form or way spirits must be manifest to, and hold converse with, one another. Why, then, may not some likeness to the earthly countenance and voice (at least so far as to produce sameness of impression) survive in whatever form of life the translated spirit may assume, so that, when friends meet friends in heaven, there may be something in their so widely different mode of existence to recall even the looks and tones through which they had known each other here?

These are not merely idle speculations. We want not only to know, but to feel, that our friends are in heaven and are happy; and the more vivid the conception that we can form of their present state, the stronger and more availing will be our heart-faith in their happiness. The great difficulty lies in conceiving of them as still living. Our thoughts keep running back to the time when they were with us, and to the parting scene, as if that were the end of all. But if we are permitted to take them in our thoughts, as they were in their individual traits of character, with every beautiful and lovely look and tone that we remember, and to bear them thus unchanged to their place near the eternal throne, it helps us meditate upon their present condition. We can thus bring ourselves into vivid and delightful communion with those whom the curtain of death veils from us. They come up before us, as in the days of their health and hope, when "the secret of God was upon their tabernacle, and their glory was fresh within them." They come up, the child with his innocent brow, the young and the beautiful, the revered parent with that same benignant smile, so glowing and lifelike; and as they stand before us in their redemption robes, hand seems again joined in hand, heart throbs with heart, they commune with us of happy days gone by and of gladness yet to come, and when the vision breaks, we can almost hear the rustling of their garments as they go from us, and trace the line of living light on which they mount to heaven.

Again, the feeling of entire and life-long separation from our departed friends is one of the most bitter ingredients in our cup of sorrow. We could bear, with much cheerfulness of hope, their absence, their long absence, from us. Oceans or years may intervene between them and our embrace, and still there is no settled sadness on their account; for our love bridges over time and space, — they are living, — they are happy, — the months of separation will pass rapidly away. But as for those in heaven, we are apt to feel, that, so long as we live, they are necessarily remote from our intercourse and sympathy. Far otherwise, however, is the spirit of our Saviour and of his religion, which blends the worlds that seem so far apart. We may be nearer to the dead than to the absent. Where the dead are we know not, nor need we know. But that they and we are in the house of the same Father we do know, and we doubt not that they have free range through the house, and may revisit at pleasure the apartments where they used to dwell. The scenes, the discourses, the miracles, of the New Testament bring the dead very near the abodes of the living. An old English divine, speaking of the communion of the dead and the living, says: — "Little know we how little a way a soul hath to go to heaven, when it departs from the body. Whether it must pass locally through moon and sun and firmament, or whether that soul find new light in the same room, and be not carried into any other, but that the glory of heaven be diffused over all, I know not, I dispute not, I inquire not. Without disputing or inquiring, I know, that, when Christ says that God is not the God of the dead, he says that to assure me that those whom I call dead are alive. If the dead and we be not upon one floor, nor under one story, yet we are under one roof. We think not a friend lost because he is gone into another room, nor because he is gone into another land, and into another world no man is gone; for that heaven which God created and this world is all one world. If I had fixed a son in court, or married my daughter into a plentiful fortune, I were satisfied for that son and daughter. Shall I not be so, when the King of heaven hath taken that son to himself, and married himself to that daughter for ever? This is the faith that sustains me, when I lose by the death of others, or suffer by living in misery myself, that the dead and we are all now in one church, and at the resurrection shall all be in one choir." The dead cannot be far from the living, nor can they cease to love them. Separated from us but by a thin veil, to them transparent, and almost so to our faith, they are the cloud of witnesses that compass us about, survey our path, and rejoice in our progress. Let us feel that they are with us in prayer and praise, in duty and devotion. Let the thought of their watchful love give us at once comfort and strength, — comfort for their departure, — strength that we may follow them.

The idea of the probable nearness of the departed to us now leads us naturally to speak of our reunion with them in heaven. This is to my mind inseparable from the doctrine of immortality. I cannot conceive of the continued life of the same beings that live here, without the continuance of those strong and tender affections which make so large a part of the occupation and the joy of life. I feel conscious that my love for the friends whom God has called away from me is an indestructible part of my character, and that to tear it from my soul would be to annihilate me, and substitute another being in my stead. But without this loss of my identity, I know that my happiness in heaven would be incomplete, unless I found myself consciously in the society of the pure and holy who have been taken from me. Do any stigmatize our earnest craving for the society of our friends in heaven as a selfish feeling? Whatever name it bear, I glory in it; and I know that God wrote it on my heart when he made me a child, when he made me a parent. It is an emotion that glowed in the bosom of Jesus; for was it not his prayer, — "Father, I will that they whom thou hast given me be with me where I am"? And is not the resurrection of the dead always presented in the New Testament in its social aspects? Those whom our Saviour restored to life were all given back to the bosom of their families. He raised the widow's son, and gave him to his mother.

He took the father and mother of the young maiden, and presented her to them alive. He called forth Lazarus to the embrace of his sisters. In thus doing, has he not pledged himself to do the like in the resurrection of the just? Will he not, then, bring parted friends together, and restore the long lost, yet unforgotten? In every family consecrated to his love, shall not the widow receive back her son, and the parent take his child to his embrace, and the sister her risen brother?

I can hold no sympathy with that stern, gloomy mood of theological teaching which tells us that our affection for our kindred and friends ought to be here, and will be in heaven completely merged in our love for God and for man in general. Such is not the lesson which we might learn from our own growth in piety. Our domestic affections increase in intensity and purity with the growth of our love to God. No families are so closely and tenderly united by mutual affection, as those where the spirit of heaven is shed abroad in every heart. A home where perfect love reigns is a laboratory of those kind and devout affections which go up to God, and range round the universe. Nor can we forget that he who dwelt in the bosom of the Father, and shed his reconciling blood for the whole family of man, was a son, a brother, and a friend, — that he wept at the grave of Lazarus, — that he had a favorite disciple,—that his dying eyes sought out his mother. The soul has, indeed, an indefinite capacity of loving; but it has not an infinite range of knowledge or power of acquaintance. In heaven we shall, no doubt, love every child of God; but we cannot know all alike, or be equally intimate with all. From the very finiteness of our natures, we must have our peculiar associates and friends; and who so likely to stand in that relation as those who were nurtured at the same family altar? Doubt not, then, that in heaven we shall be united as we are now,—that as our love for God and for his universe of being grows, so will those elective affinities which embrace individual friends grow in equal proportion, so that we of the same household shall become more and more one family, our aims and pursuits, our tastes and aspirations, more and more intimately blended, so long as God shall exist.

SERMON XIV.

COME UP HITHER.

THEY HEARD A GREAT VOICE FROM HEAVEN, SAYING UNTO THEM, COME UP HITHER. — Revelation xi. 12.

I HAVE stood in a narrow valley, shut out by gigantic mountains from all the world beside. The grass and flowers were drenched with dew. The sun had not risen high enough to shine upon them. The cliffs, with bare, craggy brows and bald summits, frowned on either side, and the whole landscape was insufferably dreary and desolate. I have stood on the peak of one of those cliffs, and thence, as far as the eye could reach, have seen only verdure, beauty, and grandeur, — the thin mist steaming up from winding rivulets, dew-drops sparkling, hill-tops beaming with crystal light, flakes of fleecy cloud flitting across the sky, and their blue shadows dancing up and down the mountain-sides, and all nature bathed in the Creator's blessing. And that little valley then smiled far beneath me, and looked like a very Eden. Thus do all earthly scenes depend upon the point of view from which they are beheld. The dwellers in the valley often get, for many days, no cheerful view. But to him who dwells aloft and looks down, all things are bright and good. We, for the most part, live below, where the mists are all around us, and the dew lies late upon our path. But a great voice from heaven has reached us, saying, — "Come up hither." Jesus invites us to lead with him a higher life in the bosom of the Father. He lifts us where we can look down upon the world, with all its strivings and its sorrows, and see it as it lies beneath the smile of divine love, its clouds spanned with the bow of peace, its tears the dew-drops of a happy morning. This is the Christian's point of view, for which he should aim and strive continually. Let us, my friends, now obey the call, — "Come up hither." Let us ascend the mount of clear vision. Let us view the elements of our earthly lot, as they would be viewed by an inhabitant of heaven.

What, then, would be the aspect presented by our world to one who, from a lofty eminence, could take it in at a single glance? It would seem to him an eminently happy world, full of bountiful provisions for the enjoyment of its living occupants. He would see every department of nature teeming with glad existences, — the air and the ocean depths, the pathless forests and sunless caverns, all crowded with life and joy. Man would look happy, and seem highly favored. Rich harvest-fields, affluent homes, scenes of domestic love and social enjoyment, would fill the foreground of the picture. On a bright autumnal Sabbath like this, he would look far and wide, and see men everywhere resting in plenty from their harvest-tasks, and going up with their families in gladness (would to Heaven that it were in equal gratitude!) to the sanctuary of their God. No house would seem without its special blessings, — its joys wherewith the stranger meddleth not. Here and there, indeed, he would see some one in depression or suffering. But in many of these cases, he would find, on closer inspection, that habit had worn off the sting of chronic troubles, — that many a poor man was rich in the unbought blessings of health, peace, and love, — that many a sufferer owned, with a gratitude too full for utterance, the tenderest human sympathy, the light of a heaven-born faith, and the daily visitings of the Saviour's mercy. Only in the tabernacles of sin would he behold traces of forlorn misery; and even there he would see that God had not left himself without a witness, but that wayward man was striving with infinite love, darkening his own dwelling, purposely shutting out the light of God's countenance, and, with fiendish art, over the fire of guilty passion distilling curses from what God had ordained for good.

But the eye of our heavenly witness would discern some homes of deep affliction. While there was light and gladness all around, over these dwellings would hang a thick and heavy cloud. But how would this cloud appear to him? Big with inundating rains, or charged with the angry thunderbolt? O, no! but freighted with fertilizing showers, shed in due season, where the soil craved them, where the plants of God's husbandry needed them, — shed, perhaps, at the very moment when the sun had risen with a withering heat, and the germs of virtue and piety were ready to perish. Griefs from the hand of Providence would seem to him to drop as the rain, and distil as the dew; and often would he see them changing the wilderness into a garden, and bringing up, "instead of the thorn, the fir-tree, and instead of the brier, the myrtle." Often, too, where faith and patience had been severely disciplined, and the field seemed to human eye white for the harvest, he would see one more shower needed before the reaper put in his sickle, and bound his choice, ripe sheaves. As he beheld worldliness and selfishness purged away, and the soil of man's flinty heart thus softened and fertilized by sorrow, his eye would rest with a solemn gladness on the house of affliction, as best showing forth the Father's love, and he would say with Jesus, — "Blessed are they that mourn."

But he who thus took his point of view from

heaven would see not earthly things alone. He would be surrounded by celestial beings and objects, — would be let into the counsels of the Almighty, — would discern the harmonies between heaven and earth, the dispositions with which man was regarded from above, the treasures laid up, the joys reserved, for him at the right hand of God. And what would he see? Weak, short-lived man constantly recognized in the great plan of universal Providence, — love, tender care, minute watchfulness over every human soul, on the part of Him who balances the sun and speeds the stars on their circuit. He would see nature, in all her vastness and beauty, but the means, man the end, — nature but the nurse of his infancy, her laws ordained, her harmonies attuned, for his happiness and progress. He would see all the happy spirits about the throne looking upon man with brotherly interest and sympathy, ready to move on errands of love for him, rejoicing in every prodigal's return, welcoming to the shores of eternity every new pilgrim. But over what scenes of earth would he discern most joy in heaven? Would it be over scenes of gladness, where the song and the laugh rang merrily, over unbroken families, over mansions of luxury, over the bright eye, the buoyant step, the full soul? No. He would see angel visitants most frequent and most happy in scenes of sorrow, where the stricken spirit was learning to submit, and trust, and love, — where the plants of heavenly grace, deep-rooted in well-watered furrows, were springing up into everlasting life. And as soul after soul passed through this ordeal with firmer faith and warmer piety, they of heaven would mark such spirits as of their own lineage and kindred, saying, — "These are they that have come out of great tribulation, and have washed their robes, and made them white in the blood of the Lamb."

He who thus stood in the assembly above would see around him many earth-born angels, translated from desolate homes below to their Father's house. He would behold the lost and wept of human families enthroned in unfading glory. He would marvel at the grief of those left behind; for how, he would ask, can they that love their friends lament so hopelessly their entrance upon unspeakable joy? Nor would he appreciate that sundering of the bonds of kindred and intimacy, which we so keenly feel; for he would see that the ransomed spirit forgot not the house of clay and the companions of its pilgrimage. He would see the love of kindred and friends only made purer and stronger by the touch of death, and the redeemed above still bound by indissoluble ties as one family with those below. He would hear from the translated infant warm intercessions for sorrowing parents, — from the ransomed mother the prayer of an unslumbering love, that her orphan little ones might be kept from the snares of sin, and safely and purely led home to her embrace. He would behold the dead the guardian angels of the living, deeming it more than heaven to be charged with ministries of mercy to the family below, — to inspire sweet dreams, happy thoughts, and sustaining hopes. He would see every pious house overshadowed by the seraph wings of those who had been trained for glory within its walls. To his eye, death would be swallowed up in life, the walls of sense would disappear, and heaven and earth would seem the universal house of God, in which all that dwelt in him dwelt also in one another.

Thus, no doubt, does it seem to those of our innocent and pious kindred that have gone before us. Such are the views which they take from the walls of the new Jerusalem. Nor need we wait for death, in order to take these views. Jesus, through the parted heavens, says to us, — "Come up hither." My afflicted friends, he bids you look up from your darkened homes to the house not made with hands. You have, indeed, consigned the outward forms, which were the delight of your eyes, to a sleep from which there is no awaking. But that which knew, and loved, and hoped, is with God, not a bright trait of character dimmed, not a pure desire ungratified, not a bud of promise blighted, no change passing over them but that from stage to stage of progress and joy.

Some of you mourn those taken away in infancy, ere the blight of sin or grief had fallen upon their young spirits. Such as they are near the Good Shepherd's heart. Yield them up to him, my friends, as trustingly as if he were on earth, and asked you for them, and proffered them his teaching and his guidance. How gladly would you welcome him, were he here, into your families, and carry forth your little ones as he passed by the way, that his shadow might rest upon them, and that his words of love, once heard and unforgotten, might sink deep into their hearts! Were he gathering, as once in Galilee, his little company of faithful followers, and did he enter your homes, and say of those that cluster around your family altars, — "Suffer them to come unto me," — could you keep them back? Would you not thankfully surrender them to his care, and let him guide and bless them in his own way, and in his own unceasing presence? He has done yet more for those who have been gathered into his heavenly flock. He has taught them to bear part in the anthem of the redeemed. He has filled their minds with truth and their hearts with love. He has led them in the spotless robe of infancy to the God that gave them, and they are without fault before his throne. If you love them, will you not rejoice for them? Would you crave them back, yet more to suffer and again to die, — perhaps still worse, to be living and yet dead, to stumble into the pitfalls of sin, and at length to carry to the judgment-seat, marred and blackened, those spirits which they have now rendered back pure as they came into being?

My Christian friends, it is not only to those that wear the weeds of recent sorrow that it has been said, — "Come up hither." The invitation comes to us equally in our brightest and happiest days. As disciples of Christ, our true dwelling-place is with him before the throne. It is only as our life is hid with Christ in God, that we spiritually live. If we are truly his, our heaven will be literally begun here, — not, indeed, the heaven of outward circumstance, but the heaven of the soul, that of unruffled peace, joy in God, calm submission, and implicit trust. We shall walk by faith, and not by sight. We shall dwell in God, the centre of all harmonies; and then the course of earthly events will not seem to us irregular and fragmentary, but we shall trace through all its hidings and its windings the plan of infinite mercy, — nature and Providence, joy and sorrow, life and death, all will be to us "the varied God." Storms may, indeed, come; but we shall be above them, and, as from the pavilion of the Most High, we shall see the lightnings flash and hear the thunders roll beneath us.

Brethren, we need this heavenly frame of mind, this lofty point of view, not only with reference to the severer trials of life, but no less for our daily conflicts with the lust of power, gain, or pleasure, with petty temptations, with easily besetting sins. We need, above the mists of earth, above the false beacon-fires of policy or selfishness, a position from which we can survey the path of life with a calm, unbiased eye. We need a stand-point from which we can view duty as God views it, and as we shall be content to have viewed it when life's last sands are running. Satan perpetually plants himself in our way with an angel's stolen garment; and nothing can deliver us from his wiles but our diligent heed to the great voice from heaven, saying to us,—"Come up hither." This voice, if we hear it in our days of joy, will reach us in sorrow and bereavement; and God will call us up into the ark prepared for his chosen ones, when the storm is abroad, and the floods lift up their voice.

While here, we must, indeed, lead a divided life, bearing the image both of the earthly and the heavenly. The spirit will sometimes be willing, but the flesh weak. Sight will sometimes get the better of faith, and we shall then remain in the valley, instead of climbing the mount of God. At times our horizon will seem all shut in. Mysteries, deep and unfathomable, will hang over the course of Providence. Our way will lie through gathering clouds. But in death will the great voice from heaven say to us, once and for ever,—"Come up hither"; and with angels and ransomed men, with patriarchs, prophets, and apostles, with our sainted parents, our bosom friends, and the lambs without spot or blemish, translated from our flocks to the service of the heavenly altar, we shall stand on the sea of glass, having the harps of God, and chanting the praises of Him who hath abolished death, and brought life and immortality to light.

SERMON XV.

THE VANITY OF LIFE.

THEN I LOOKED ON ALL THE WORKS THAT MY HANDS HAD WROUGHT, AND ON THE LABOR THAT I HAD LABORED TO DO; AND, BEHOLD, ALL WAS VANITY AND VEXATION OF SPIRIT, AND THERE WAS NO PROFIT UNDER THE SUN. — Ecclesiastes ii. 11.

I KNOW of no more genuine record of human experience than the book of Ecclesiastes affords. It is testimony wrung from the heart of one who had tried the whole round of earthly pursuits and pleasures, who had fathomed the resources of knowledge and fame, wealth and power, the feast and the dance, laughter and mirth, lust and wine, and who sums up the whole as mere vanity and vexation of spirit. The author professes to have reached the decline of a life of pre-eminent lustre, luxury, and prosperity; and yet there was in the retrospect nothing on which his eye could repose with satisfaction, — nothing that had filled his soul, or left a fragrance behind. He pronounces the dead far happier than the living, and those who died before they had tasted the cup of life the happiest of all; and yet to him death is an endless sleep, the dust mingling with kindred dust, the soul reabsorbed into the divine essence from which it came. Far be it from me, though I now come to you in sadness, to present such dark views of life. In such views no Christian can rest. To every believing heart Jesus repeats the primeval blessing of the Almighty on the works of his hands; and still, as in the morning of creation, all things are very good. Yet the view of life which our text suggests must have distinctly presented itself to every one who has borne the burdens and bowed under the sorrows of mortality; and it is the only view which remains possible for one destitute of Christian faith, — it represents the true state of things with one who is living without God and without hope in the world. In order for the worldly and self-indulgent to arrive at this view, it is only needful for them to pause and reflect. And I would that they oftener reached it; for if they did, they would not rest till they had come to Jesus, and learned of him. Let us now consider the vanity of the present state of being, considered as our only state.

Suppose, in the first place, that a decree were to go forth, perpetuating your present condition, — pronouncing that you should remain eternally just as you are now. How would you receive such a decree? There are, indeed, many of you who seem happy, prosperous, rich, surrounded by favorable circumstances. But is there one of you who would be willing to stop the wheel of fortune now and for ever? Should this take place, everything would seem to you dark, narrow, insufficient, and unpropitious. Where is the man who has climbed as high, or won as much, or established himself as firmly, as he means and desires? Where is the soul that has not still in embryo some darling plan which it would be misery to drop? Where is the family which lives not to a greater or less degree broken by the absence or death of its members, and which depends not for much of its comfort and joy on the return of the long absent, or reunion with the holy dead? Who would be willing that the divided family should remain so for ever? If you will look into your own hearts, my friends, you will find that you are living more in the future than in the present, more in your plans than in your possessions, — that you depend more on what you think that you are laying up for time to come, than on any means of enjoyment actually in hand. What, then, have you attained as to this world? Flowers without fruit, golden promises, flattering hopes, a rich expectancy of happiness; but could you see nothing beyond the passing moment, you would at once pronounce all to be vanity and vexation of spirit, and would exclaim in bitterness, —

"What have I of all the works that my hands have wrought, and of all the labor that I have labored to do?"

But what will this future on which you are building bring to you? Incompleteness, vexation, disappointment, bereavement, sorrow. Few of your blossoms will ripen into fruit; few of your plans will be realized; very little of what you now clearly see in the future will shape itself as you see it. Many of the visions that now beguile you will pass away as a dream. Never will come the time upon earth when you will say,—"I have attained,—I am ready to enjoy,—now let the wheel stop rolling, and I will be content." The farther you go on in life, the more blighted hopes will lie behind you, the more vacant places will there be in the circle of your kindred and friendship, the more will there be in your outward condition to make you feel that there is no rest or home for you on this side of the grave. But you will still toil and strive on, till age creeps upon you; and then you may, perhaps, seat yourself down to the calm enjoyment of the fruits of your labors. But if you then look within and around you, what will you find your condition to be? You will see the instruments of enjoyment fled, when its means are at length attained. Your perceptions will be languid, your elasticity of spirit gone, your taste for every form and object of luxury paralyzed. Those with whom you had hoped to walk in the quiet of life's evening will have departed hence, no more to be seen on earth. The children whom you had thought to see clustering like tendrils, fresh and green, about the aged vine, will be either scattered abroad in the world, surrounded with cares and hopes of their own, or numbered among the early dead. And in looking back from the close of the most prosperous life, you will find that your whole course might be likened to the drawing of water in a vessel full of holes and pouring it into a broken cistern, — that, of the results of all your labor and sore travail upon earth, you will have lost most by the way, and kept none to the end.

Again, if you would look into your hearts, in the gayest and most gladsome moments of earthly enjoyment, you will perceive much of this same emptiness and vanity. Who has not at such times been conscious, as it were, of a double self, of an uneasiness in the midst of gratification, of a restless feeling in the very fulness of seeming joy, of a voice that whispers, "Up and be doing," while many voices bid us stay, and drown all other thoughts in the scene before us? When, except in early youth, have we found the time when we could throw ourselves wholly into any such scene, and say with an undivided heart, — "It is good for us to be here"? It seems to me that there is no season when melancholy is more apt to steal over us, and the feeling that all is vanity to rise up within us, than when gay voices are around us, and the insignia of mirth are spread before us. The mind cannot help turning to that reverse of the picture, so near to some, so sure to all, when sorrow will darken the happy dwelling, — when that head so full of glad thoughts will toss upon the fevered couch, — when that heart throbbing so quick with young hopes will beat slow and sad its passage to the grave, — when, instead of the song and the dance, will be the coffin and the dirge.

But though at these seasons such thoughts will come over us, we crowd them out. There are, however, times when they are forced upon us, and we cannot expel them. There are times of sudden and overwhelming grief, when calamity breaks in upon us like a swift flood, and seems to wash away the very ground on which we stand. As, amazed and dizzy, we witness the withering in an hour of that on which we had reposed the trust of many years, as we bend over the lifeless forms of one after another of those with whom every fibre of our own being was bound up, we feel that there is nothing permanent or trustworthy here, — that at our best estate we are altogether vanity, — that earth's fairest mansions are but whited sepulchres, her choicest fruit but dust and ashes. We are then conscious of the frailty of what remains to us, no less than of what has been taken from us, and can say from the heart, that there is nothing here below on which we can place the least dependence, — nothing which we dare to love as we have loved, or to trust as we have trusted. Then, were it not for the words of eternal life, we could say in intense anguish, — "All is vanity and vexation of spirit, and there is no profit under the sun."

But after all, though we walk in a vain show, there is enjoyment in life, — in our mere earthly life. Yet from what does it flow? Not from the ever-changing scene, not from the winter-frozen and summer-dried fountains around us, but from the unchanging love of God, the bow of whose promise remains fixed over the stream of time and the waves of unceasing vicissitude. Not by these time-shadows, but by their eternal substance, by the immutable I AM, are we blessed; and the bright gleams from the current of earthly events, that make us glad, are but the reflection of his smile. He who gives the ravens their food feeds also his human children, and by filling all things with his love makes us happy. We ask why we are glad. We analyze life and its resources, and can find no reason for our happiness. All seems so unsubstantial and evanescent, we wonder that we should ever have felt an emotion of joy; and all the while, it may be, we forget to look to Him who alone has made us happy, — whose ever-flowing love has imparted a continuity to change, has breathed life into a world of death, has made things in themselves vain — yea, and things which are not — the sources of enduring good. But if this be so, then is God our chief good and our highest joy, and in proportion as we approach him do we quit the vain for the real, the shadow for the substance.

And, blessed be God, there is that in life which is not vanity or vexation. Though favor be deceitful and beauty vain, though the grass wither and the flower fade, the word of God abideth for ever, — even that word which in Jesus was made flesh, and which is anew incarnate in every regenerate heart. The outer man may perish, the desire of the eyes and the pride of life may fail; but the signature of God's spirit on the inner man time cannot efface, or the waves of death wash away. The soul, character, virtue, piety, remain, amidst the reverses of fortune, the desolation of our households, the wasting of disease, and the thunder-blast of death. And if on the theatre of life the soul may clothe herself in garments of righteousness that shall never wax old, then is life precious and holy and full of dignity; and if, from the wreck of all things earthly, the soul may gather the trophies of a purer faith and a more fervent love, then may we bid a welcome, — solemn and tearful though it be, — a welcome to the storms and billows of adversity, believing that they can work only for our progress and our highest good.

There have, I trust, my friends, been seasons of your lives, when, had you analyzed what made you blessed, you would have found it not vanity, but a holy and eternal reality. You have, it may be, at some time encountered strong temptation. Sin was near. Opportunity favored. The tempter whispered, — "Thou shalt not surely die." Passion or appetite earnestly craved the guilty compliance, and you felt your faith wavering. But you summoned God to your help. You arose in the majesty of inward might, and said, — "Tempter, depart; Father, I am thine." You came off conqueror, and beheld Satan, like lightning, falling from the heavens. This victory has not ceased to make you happy. There was no delusion in the joy of such an hour. It will bear the closest scrutiny. It was a joy which earth could not have given, and which time cannot take away. You feel that your soul grew in this conflict, — that you took a new onward step in your eternal career, — that you gained treasure that will endure while God lives.

You have gone forth, it may be, at some time, on an errand of love, alone, without sympathy, without sounding a trumpet before you, in the spirit of true Christian benevolence. You were made a blessing to some desolate and forsaken one. Your compassion dropped as the dew of heaven upon some withered spirit. You were eyes to the blind, or as a father to the poor. You were made the minister of hope to the despairing or of life to the spiritually dead. Years may have rolled by, and there perhaps remains not an earthly sign of the good that you wrought; and yet you feel that it has not passed away,—that it could not perish,—that, though no longer seen, it is eternal. That outgoing of the soul towards a fellow-being, that lengthening of the chain of sympathy, that development of godlike love, is a good which time cannot take from you, or immortality exhaust.

Again, you have been in deep affliction. It was at the tenderest point that the arrow of a mysterious Providence pierced your soul. It was where you most hoped and expected to be spared, that God's hand was heaviest upon you. Yet you had faith to look up through the clouds and darkness, and to say in full sincerity,—"Father, thy will be done!" You brought the sacrifice to the altar, with a consenting, though bursting heart, saying,—"Lord, here thou hast that is thine." That act of faith has not passed away. It remains the indestructible property of your soul. You believed in God, and he counted it for righteousness. It stands recorded in his book of eternal remembrance,—it stands indelibly engraven on the tablets of your own heart. The sorrow can endure but for a season, perhaps has already given place to brighter skies; but the trust in God, which, when your soul was dark, filled it with submission and praise, is still the strength of your heart, and will be your portion for ever.

None of the soul's religious exercises are lost. Your penitence, your seeking after God, your prayers of faith, your labors of love, you cannot look upon as vanity. In contemplating duty wrought, temptation resisted, sin subdued, you feel no vexation of spirit. In looking at the results of your religious culture, you have no disposition to say, — "There is no profit under the sun."

These thoughts open to us the true value of life, and show us wherein the author of our text looked upon it from a false point of view. He thought of it as a final home, — as an end, not a means, — as the sum, not the cradle, of man's being. He deemed the supreme purpose of existence to be the attainment of the highest point of worldly joy and greatness, and no wonder that he found all to be vanity and vexation of spirit; for he sought full satisfaction for the immortal in the perishing, for the unseen spirit in things seen. We, as Christians, regard the present state less as life than as a passage from death to life. We take the good things of earth as types and pledges of unseen and satisfying joys, as the revelation of God and the earnest of heaven. We look to earthly pleasures, not as the end of our being, but as refreshments on our pilgrim way. We receive and enjoy them with gratitude, yet dare not trust them, or set our hearts upon them. We see the sentence of change and death written upon them, nor would we have it otherwise; for we ourselves desire to be changed, and we would have changes going on around us, to keep us on the alert, and to have our spirits disenthralled when our own change shall come.

But while there is nothing in these views to embitter life, how much is there in them to make us look forward to death with composure and cheerfulness! We speak, indeed, of being attached to the world, of clinging to life; but this is entirely indefinite language. The world about us, the complexion of life, is continually changing. Those aspects of nature which most charm us pass away almost as soon as they appear. In our earthly lot, how often does the day give no token of what shall be on the morrow!—how seldom do the elements of our domestic and social life remain unchanged from year to year! New faces surround us, new intimacies encircle us, new careers of effort call us away from the old. Our parents are gathered to their fathers. Our children follow them. Our earthly house is dissolved. There is silence where there were glad voices,—desolation, where there was thrilling joy. Our life becomes a bundle of broken fibres,—our condition on earth constantly grows more indefinite and fragmentary. Still we adhere to this idea of life, as if it were something fixed and tangible. The truth is (and it is a truth that should call forth an unceasing flow of gratitude), that one and the same God lives in all this change, and through a vast diversity of operations conducts the same work of love, so that what is definite and permanent is not life, but the God of our lives. These constantly varying forms, in which God blesses us, are but so many ways in which he seeks to make himself known to us, and solicits our trust and love. It is not, then, to life, but to God, that we should cling, and thus seek the true life, which waits for its consummation, till the corruptible shall clothe itself in incorruption, and the mortal shall put on immortality.

SERMON XVI.

THE LIFE OF THE AFFECTIONS.

THOUGH I UNDERSTAND ALL MYSTERIES, AND ALL KNOWLEDGE, AND HAVE NOT CHARITY, I AM NOTHING. — 1 Corinthians xiii. 2.

In choosing this passage for a text, I can hardly need tell you that charity here denotes not mere almsgiving or mere kindness of heart, but that expansive, comprehensive love which embraces God and every child of God.

Ours is an age of great intellectual activity. Mental attainments, skill, power, and achievements were never estimated so highly as now. In former times, and under different degrees of culture, first, mere physical strength, then, the mere accident of birth or hereditary rank, then, and almost till now, wealth, have successively been the measures of greatness, and the prime objects of ambition, desire, and envy. But now the aristocracy of the world is an aristocracy of intellect. The gifts of mind are everywhere deemed the best gifts. Every one wishes to be known as a person of large, or sound, or well-furnished intellect, and the reproach of ignorance or folly is dreaded as the deepest possible stigma. Now this state of things is to be rejoiced in as beyond measure better than that in which mere external advantages were the supreme objects of esteem and desire. We are right in looking down, as from a superior point of view, upon times when strength, or rank, or wealth, was worshipped for its own sake. But there is danger, that, while we look down, we fail to look up, — that, while we rejoice in having found something better than men used to seek and strive for, we may not recognize that which alone is supremely good. Religion is the life of the affections; and, in the reverence now paid to intellect, there is danger that religion be undervalued, and that the affections, which are its throne, receive much less than their due regard and cultivation. I fear that religious institutions and observances are looked upon with a great degree of superciliousness and indifference by many who think that they are seeking the best gifts. I apprehend that many young people, now pressing forward into life, regard it as the sole aim and end of being to obtain intellectual character, reputation, and influence, to be wise and prudent, and to leave the impress of their own minds, according to their measure, on the few or the many, on their community, their country, or their race. I see many youth of promise, just entering upon active life, who cherish generous and lofty sentiments, are raised above all mean or degrading tastes, and intend to act their part well and nobly, who yet evidently do not take a religious character and influence into their plan of life, or look forward to a place in the Church of Christ as an essential post of duty, or anticipate the blessing of the fatherless and the widow among their crowns of rejoicing. My present object is to set before you the religious life, the life of the affections, the life of God in the soul and of the soul in God, as the highest and most desirable style of character.

Permit me, at the outset, to define the religious life. I mean by it a life, not of mere decencies and proprieties, but of warm and active love. It includes, first, the habitual and thankful recognition of a present God and a watchful Providence, and the exercise of the religious affections in prayer, praise, and grateful obedience, — then and thence, the cherishing of sincere brotherly love towards our fellow-men, the cultivation of meekness, gentleness, and kindness towards all, and a cordial interest in every cause of human progress and well-being. In fine, the religious life implies a heart which constantly breathes for itself and for all men the prayer, — "Thy kingdom come." And it is this which I would now set forth as of incomparably greater worth than a merely intellectual life, and as alone giving the patent of true nobility to a mind, however large, active, and powerful.

I first remark, that the life of the affections is essential to the full development and healthy working of the intellect. The affections are our highest faculties. They have the nearest view of truth, and the strongest hold upon it, often by direct intuition apprehending portions of it, to which reason and judgment must work a weary way of analysis and proof. Of the men who have enlarged the bounds of human knowledge, and have essentially connected their names with the progress of the race, there has been hardly one whose mind was not trained by religious faith and reverence. By this you will not understand me as saying that no great men have been unbelievers or irreligious. Far from it. There have been many men void of religious belief and principle, who have been brilliant, profound, learned, eloquent, — who have left great names and a luminous track where they disappeared. But what I mean to say is this. Prepare as complete a list as you can of the various departments of human knowledge, — take up those departments one by one, and call over in each the creative minds, — those that have given to each its existence and its laws, — those whose labors were you to expunge from their respective departments, you must tear out large and solid portions from the learning and science of a race,—you will find that the men on this catalogue have, with hardly an exception, had their minds nurtured and strengthened by the religious affections,—that they have revered and worshipped God, have felt and owned the power of Christian truth, and have often been warm, generous, and devoted philanthropists. Diligent study of the history of science for the purpose of testing this view has given me a conviction which has no room to grow stronger, that there exists an essential connection of cause and effect between the life of the heart and that of the mind, and that the highest walks of intellectual greatness cannot be reached without the keenness, breadth, and loftiness of vision, and the great fundamental ideas and principles, which religious belief and consciousness alone can supply.

You and I, indeed, may not aspire to the first rank of intellectual eminence. But if we desire to fill respectably and usefully an humbler place, it is well that we know how great minds have become great; for by the same instrumentality smaller minds may be enlarged and elevated. And, in truth, there are many minds that need moral culture alone in order to make themselves extensively felt and highly respected. There are many men who exert no intellectual influence, simply because they have no moral power. They are keen, shrewd, well-informed, of sound discretion, of admirable executive capacity; and yet you cannot render them the confidence or deference that they seem to claim, simply because their views are all sordid, narrow, and selfish. They are never stirred by fresh and generous impulses. There always hangs about them a sceptical, distrustful atmosphere, which makes their presence like a very iceberg to the hopeful, earnest, and sanguine. But give them faith in God and man, — thaw out the ice around their hearts, — once start in their souls the flow of devout and charitable feeling, and their minds would grow apace, would acquire new depth and largeness of view on every class of subjects, and would be felt and owned as leading and controlling minds in their respective circles. Their influence, too, would in that case be worthy of being confided and rejoiced in; for they would then recognize in all their reasonings and decisions those foundation-truths in the moral universe which they now ignore, but which, from the very necessity of the case, must lie at the basis of all practical wisdom.

I would next compare the life of the affections and that of the intellect as to the promise of success and attainment. In every path of intellectual effort, the saying of the Apostle with regard to the ancient games, — "All run, but only one receives the prize," — is almost literally applicable. The prizes are but for few. What many seek, here and there one can win; and for every grade of intellectual rank and influence, many aspirants fail where few succeed. But the high places of moral excellence are within the reach of all. In our Father's house are many mansions, and an equal welcome for all who strive to enter.

Then, too, how much nearer absolute perfection can we approach in the moral than in the intellectual life! Our growth in knowledge is growth in conscious ignorance. The dimensions of truth enlarge before us faster than our conceptions of it. Perfect knowledge and perfect wisdom are unknown terms this side of heaven. But of the life of the affections, of that love which mounts in prayer to the throne of God, and excludes none of his children from its embrace, the Divine Teacher has said,—"Be ye perfect, even as your Father in heaven is perfect." In piety and charity we may measure our spirits with that of the perfect Redeemer,—may look with despair on no trait of his character,—may make absolute perfection our constant aim, our ever nearer goal. These thoughts are strikingly illustrated in the history of our race. The wisest men have always been outgrown in a few generations, and the ignorance of men who filled the world with their renown is the laughing-stock of modern schoolboys. We look down on all ancient wisdom as men used to look up to it; and future generations of children will learn in their infant schools truths that have but just dawned upon the greatest minds of the present day. But a good man the world never outgrows, never looks down upon. Elijah and Daniel, Stephen and Paul, fill as large and high a place in the world's eye as if they had lived in the last century. Fénelon and Oberlin will seem to the end of time to have reached as lofty a summit of perfection as that on which they stand to our view. The stars in the galaxy of moral excellence never grow dim, and can never be outshone. And these stars shoot up into the firmament from the lowliest homes and the humblest walks of duty; for no obscurity of earthly place can cut off one who lives in love, and labors for man in the strength of God, from the early recorded blessing, — "They that turn many to righteousness shall shine as stars for ever and ever."

We might again compare the life of mere intellect with that of the affections, as to the power of resisting severe temptation and blighting evil. It is a common idea among the young and sanguine, that a clear mind, sound sense, and an accurate perception of the qualities and tendencies of actions, are enough to save one from moral degradation and ruin. Many strong-minded and well-disposed young people deem it impossible that they should ever blacken their characters by vice, they have such very just and clear views of the path of life, and are so well aware of all its snares and pitfalls. But none can estimate in advance the subtleness of moral evil, or the over-mastering power of passion. Opportunity may urge, desire may wax strong, outward safeguards may be removed, and corrupt example may be witnessed on every side; and the merely intellectual life has no element that can allay desire, subdue appetite, or stem the current of custom or example. I have known men, second to none of our day in mental power and culture, but sceptical as to religious truth, ensnared in palpable and gross meanness, arrested in an honorable career by a shameful exposure, and condemned ever after to toil wearily up the ascent on which they were rapidly climbing, with the burden of a suspicious character and a damaged reputation. I have known, and so have you, others absolutely cut down, on the career opening before them with peculiar promise, by those vices which, once indulged in, leave not the victim the freedom of which he previously made his boast. Many such, of the highest mental endowments, sleep in early graves, dug by their own profligacy. Many more still cumber the earth, of which they were the destined ornaments. But the affections, fixed on a present God, and filling the life with words and deeds of charity and mercy, have power over every meaner element and propensity of our nature.

The soul that prays has ever at hand a name in which it can bid the tempter depart. The soul that owns the all-seeing Father, and lives consciously in his presence, draws ever new strength from its heavenly communings, and cherishes elements of thought and feeling with which guilty reveries, plans, and purposes cannot co-exist. God's omnipotent spirit dwelling in the soul of man, and that alone, can say to appetite, — "Thus far shalt thou go, and no farther"; and to passion, — "Peace, be still."

There is another view, which strikingly illustrates the superiority of the life of the affections. To take it, we must follow life to those latter days, which a part only reach, but to which all look forward, and for which all make provision. The life of intellectual vigor, reputation, and influence has its meridian, and then its decline. High moral culture and attainments alone modify the operation of this law, and that not invariably. Beyond a certain point, one must expect to see more recent wisdom preferred to his own, and to yield place to younger aspirants for the rewards which mere acumen and activity of mind can command. And he who is thus set aside or thrown back, to make room for those of a succeeding generation, if possessed of no moral resources, grows almost uniformly unhappy and misanthropic. You can think of those whose early career was brilliant and eminent, but of whom the world has evidently made all the use that it ever will make, and has left them, with the consciousness of being thrown aside, to expiate the moral and religious unthrift of earlier years by a vacant, weary, and wretched old age. Not so with him who has lived in piety and love. Moral qualities fade not with declining years, wither not with the frosts of age. The plants of our Heavenly Father's planting are all evergreens. Nor yet is the good man, in his old age, readily thrust aside, or willingly spared from his post of duty. Veneration and love for him only grow the more intense and tender, as his steps tremble on the margin of eternity. We never feel ready to miss him from the scenes hallowed by his devotion and enriched by his charity. Blessings follow him to his home, when he can leave it no more; and the grateful intercessions of those who honored him in life waft his dying spirit to the presence of his Father and his Saviour, while he, to his last moment, so far from feeling that his work is done, deems it but just begun when he emerges from the contracted routine of earthly duty into the larger, loftier sphere of activity offered him in heaven. But look around you, in low places and in high, and say if there be an old age that you would willingly make your own, among those whose youth and prime were unconsecrated by the covenant of God, and unblessed by the joys of religious faith and trust. Yet can you not find in every walk of life aged Christians, in whose places you would gladly stand, and for the peace and joy of whose declining years you would earnestly pray, should God spare you long and late, and suffer you to linger upon earth after the heat and burden of the day are over? If so, enter young, enter now, on that life of faith, reverence, and love, on which the dew of eternal youth still rests, when desire fails, and the weary pilgrim approaches his long home.

In speaking of old age, I ought to recur to the discipline of severe trial and desolating sorrow, through which alone we can reach declining years. For this discipline, the merely intellectual life has no resource. Its route must lie by many graves; but it leads not by the Redeemer's broken sepulchre. Its path is through much tribulation; but it points not the troubled spirit to the mansions in the Father's house. These severe sorrows bow down the strong man, yea, the strongest, and may bow him in hopeless despondency, and make him drag through the residue of his days a burden of incessant pain and weariness. And are you willing to encounter the withering of early hopes, the sore bereavements, the intense sufferings, which lie more or less in the path of all, without anything higher or better to sustain you than the cold philosophy of the irreligious world, which can only bid you bear and throw off as you can, by your own unaided strength, evils, in themselves unrelieved and unmitigated, which you cannot avert and cannot remedy? Are you willing to move on through these gloomy passages of your pilgrimage, without having them lighted and cheered by rays of hope, love, and promise? The life of the affections leads through these gloomy passages; but they are not wholly dark. It has faith in a fatherly Providence, which can inflict no useless evil. It is sustained by the consciousness of an omnipotent presence and support. It enjoys the felt companionship and sympathy of the suffering, glorified Saviour, and the communion of those who through faith and patience inherit the promises. It beholds the reconciled countenance of God, and commands, high above clouds and darkness, an ever nearer view of heaven. Its way leads by tombs; but they are all open, — the resurrection angel has rolled the great stone away, and sits upon it. Its path is through much tribulation; but the glory of the eternal kingdom rests upon it. With reference to these trials, then, which you cannot shun, let me entreat you to enter on that life of piety and love which can sanctify them for you and you by them, — which will mark each sorrow by a new stage heavenward, — which will make every season of affliction a time of peaceful trust in God, and deep, fervent joy in the holy spirit.

Finally, it becomes every prudent man and woman, every discreet youth, to take some account of that only event, death, which is sure to all. You all believe, I doubt not, in God and in immortality. You cannot help believing, in some form, in the certainty of a righteous retribution. —in the consequences of this earthly life as reaching out, for joy or woe to every soul, into the boundless future. You cannot help feeling yourselves accountable to the Author of your life and the God of eternity. And can you omit all recognition of him in prayer, praise, and duty, and yet feel safe? Did you know death to be close at hand, as it may be, is there anything in the mere attainments and exercise of a vigorous and cultivated intellect, which would nerve you to meet the last hour with serenity, confidence, and hope? Would not the deepest self-reproach fasten upon your soul, because you had not owned God in all your ways, and offered your mind and heart a living sacrifice to him? And would not the pungency of this self-reproach be in precise proportion to the talents which you had kept unconsecrated? Many live as if they occupied a position which exempted them from the cultivation and exercise of the religious affections, excused them from allegiance to their Saviour, and absolved them from every law but that of judicious and dignified self-love. But no man, consciously on his death-bed, ever felt himself an exempt. There is for the dying but one style of character by which they can ever be persuaded to measure their spirits; and that is the life of piety and love, which I have now sought to set before you. This, and this only, can give peace in death. But this fears no evil, as the valley of the shadow opens. The life of mere intellect death breaks off abruptly. Those paths, which it can pursue with grovelling steps and earth-bound vision, have no issues beyond the grave. The life of the affections death suspends not; but only merges it in the unchanging friendship and undying love of heaven. Its path is that on which the Saviour passed from mortal conflict and agony home to the throne of God. Tongues shall indeed fail, and knowledge in its earthly uses cease; but love, born of God, and heir of heaven, — love never faileth.

SERMON XVII.

TRUE LIFE.

MAN DOTH NOT LIVE BY BREAD ONLY; BUT BY EVERY WORD THAT PROCEEDETH OUT OF THE MOUTH OF THE LORD DOTH MAN LIVE. — Deuteronomy viii. 3.

WHAT is the life for which we seek and hope? Mere existence? No. But conscious happiness, — an existence which we feel to be a blessing, — a large preponderance of success over disappointment, and joy over sorrow. This is what all desire; but they seek it in different ways. On the memorable occasion on which our Saviour quoted these words, he had sought it by a fast of forty days in the wilderness. And those were days of peace, joy, and victory; for they were passed in the bosom of the Father, in communion with God and heaven, in the girding of the spirit for those mighty and incessant labors, for that living and dying sacrifice, by which man, the wanderer and the sinner, was to be redeemed, reconciled, and brought home to God. The tempter came. Bread in the desert might have grown from the very stones. Jewelled crowns and sceptres were laid at his feet. It was by these things that men sought to live. But to Christ they were not life. The word of God was his only life; to do the will of the Father, his meat and drink; to finish the work of toil and blood, his crown and kingdom.

Our text suggests two theories of life; — the one, the living by bread alone; the other, by obedience, duty, and love, by angels' food, by the manna that comes down from heaven. Let us consider both; and may God grant us grace to make the choice which was made by Him who for our sakes was tempted without sin, and who will strengthen us, as we are partakers in his temptation, to bear part also in his victory.

Man doth not live by bread only. Yet multitudes think thus to live, — by things outward and earthly, by the accumulation of material, perishable objects of enjoyment, or of wealth, which can represent and command them all. The general sentiment of society most manifestly is, — "Money, wealth, is the great end of life, the one thing needful for happiness, the chief criterion and measure of success and attainment. Money answereth all things. Give us this, — give us the means of living as we please, and a constantly growing surplus fund beyond our immediate wants, and we have the supreme good. With this, whatever mental or moral endowments we can get without trouble and keep without care, we will not reject; but, without money, no intellectual treasure, no eminence of moral worth, can suffice for our happiness. Let us first seek that which is outward; and let the kingdom within take thought for itself, — at least, we will waste upon it no superfluous care or effort." If such be not the common language of society, what means this tumultuous striving, this trepidation, eagerness, and anxiety in the pursuit of every form of outward good, this earnest struggle to get and to keep what is earthly and perishing? Yet few have made the trial for any length of time, without experiences adapted to re-echo the voice of holy writ, — "Man doth not live by bread only." There are chambers of the soul which nothing earthly can fill. There are in the region of the affections waste places which remain always desolate in the worldly heart. There is in the spirit of man a home which the Infinite God made for himself, which no inferior tenant can occupy, and which, when he dwells not within, feels the painful void. There are, in the native constitution of the soul, niches for all the kindly social affections; and where these affections are not cherished, there must needs be a sense of vacuity and loneliness, even in the most prosperous earthly condition. There must be all the while a latent consciousness that the soul is not fed or satisfied,

— that it has acquiesced in something far below its birthright. There cannot fail to be heard at times, from objects of the fondest pursuit and confidence, a voice saying, — "We cannot meet and fill the cravings of the immortal spirit." And it is to this voice, ill understood, misinterpreted, that we are, as I suppose, to impute the effort of so many for an amount of earthly good beyond all possible power of enjoyment. Their first visions of happiness are of a mere competence. That attained, but happiness still beyond their grasp, they aim at wealth, and are led on in the blind chase, always supposing that the prize, which has hitherto eluded their grasp, lies at the goal next in sight.

Apart from the unsatisfying nature of this grovelling mode of life at all times, there are peculiar seasons when its barrenness must be most keenly felt. When that on which one has reposed his whole confidence is threatened or withdrawn, how rayless must be his every prospect and retrospect! His gods are taken, and what has he more? The mad-house or the suicide's grave has too often been the resting-place of those whose only trust was in outward possessions. Nor is there any form of affliction so devoid of resource or of consolation as the hopeless loss of earthly good to him who has desired and sought nothing higher or better.

In those other, and, to a true heart, incomparably keener, sorrows reserved for almost every man, what agency of relief or consolation can be expected from that which the multitude so earnestly seek and so dearly prize? Can wealth sustain or comfort the bereaved husband or father? When the strong ties of natural affection are sundered, is it a solace to know that they had been gilded and jewelled? If they were not strengthened and sanctified by Christian communion, by the fellowship of heaven-seeking souls, — if the only common interests have been sordid and grovelling, then has the prosperity enjoyed together left the survivor only the heavier burden of remembrances not again to be realized, and of joys for ever fled.

For him, who has sought to live for and by mere outward and earthly good, it is also appointed to die; and it seems to me that the most inveterate worshipper of Mammon might be converted to spiritual desires, longings, and efforts, if he would only stand by a coffin, gaze on the clay-cold features of the dead, hearken with the spirit's ear to their teachings, and remain, eyes and heart intent on that most eloquent of scenes, till its voices had all been uttered. Was he who lies there fortunate, prosperous, rich? Did he fare sumptuously, and surround himself, in the world's heartless phrase, with all that heart could desire? If so, what did all this avail him on the death-bed or at the judgment-seat? Has aught that he had gone with him to purchase special immunities or privileges in heaven? Has his inventory been registered on the Lamb's book of life, and have the harps of the redeemed rung in louder notes of welcome for him? If he was a follower of Christ, did any added consolation flow in upon his departing spirit from what he was going to leave behind him? Or rather, was not his sole repose, in dying, on that Rock of Ages which proffers equal shelter for the homeless and friendless saint? But did he trust in riches? Then, in death and at the judgment was that wherein he trusted transformed, from a talent which he might have used for God's glory and man's good, into a millstone about his neck, weighing him down to the depths of despair.

Such are the leading features of the life which sustains itself by bread alone, and which is outward and earthly in all its resources, aims, plans, and hopes. But such is not the life which God has ordained for us. "Man doth not live by bread only; but by every word that proceedeth out of the mouth of God, by that doth he live." As this is no less true of our outward life than it was of that of the manna-fed Israelites, it is emphatically true of the life of the soul. Its only happiness is in the word of God, in his law of duty, holiness, and love. We, who have always lived in comfort and affluence, and have known no sharp suffering or severe privation, find it hard to divest ourselves of the feeling, that very many outward things are absolutely essential to our happiness, and that our peace is in some measure in the keeping of that which passing events may give or take away. Yet there are in our congregation those who could teach us a different lesson. Some of the happiest persons that we know have no earthly inheritance save the kindness and charity of their Christian friends. I have never witnessed greater elasticity of spirit, a fuller flow of gladness, or a warmer interest in the prosperity of others, than among those whom a careless observer would have registered among the forsaken and the wretched.

What, then, are the elements of this higher life? Since man, spiritually speaking, cannot live by bread only, by what is he to live?

First, by faith, — faith in an all-seeing Father, whose sceptre ruleth over all, and who, if our hearts are his, will cause all things outward to work together for our good, — faith in a Redeemer, who has loved us and given himself for us as our Saviour from sin, and our Guide to duty and heaven. What a priceless privilege, in a life of unceasing change, to look beyond manifest good and seeming evil to the throne of love, whence both are sent in equal mercy to our souls, — and to feel assured, that, in a world not man's, but God's, our lot is ordered and our path directed by one who loves us better than we can love ourselves! Deprive me of this faith, and the burden even of a prosperous life would seem insupportable; for I should apprehend that I might have been lifted on high, and spared long, only for some more appalling doom. But give me this faith, firm and constant, in a fatherly Providence, in the minute and incessant care of the Almighty; and my heart, thus strengthened, could not lose its cheerfulness under trials, however intense or desolating. How inestimably rich, also, is the solace that we may derive from looking to Jesus, our divine fellow-sufferer, and remembering, as the waves of sorrow break over us, or as the valley of death opens before us, that his crown of thorns has become the diadem of his truest glory, and his cross the sceptre of his universal sway!

Again, man, by the appointment of God, is to live by hope, — by the hope of heaven, which alone can anchor the soul amidst the fitful fortunes of our earthly pilgrimage. It is this hope that equalizes human conditions as to their capacity for happiness, and enables us to cast aside doubt and fear as to what lies before us on the path of life. Travellers to a better country, sure as faith can make us of a safe conveyance thither, why need we be over-anxious as to the mere incidents of our journey? I know not what earthly lot we might not thankfully welcome, for the experience which it might afford of our Father's presence, and the advantages which it might furnish for a consecrated walk to heaven; for every lot, nay, each seeming extreme of good and evil, has its own stern discipline, its blessed baptism, as it may prove, of severe trial, and each has its peculiar seasons of refreshing from the Divine presence, and its foreshinings of heavenly joy.

By God's appointment, we are also to nourish our souls by charity, by sympathy with our brethren, by bearing their burdens and helping their joys. There can be no life worth living without brotherly love, — without a ready heart and hand for the needy, the suffering, and the erring. What a vast power of happiness, what a treasury of glad experiences, lies locked up all around us, in the talents which we will not use, the time which we will not spare, the money which we will not bestow, for our poor and afflicted fellow-mortals! We act too often as if we were afraid to be happy. We linger on the brink of a new charity, as we would on the verge of a precipice, and frequently draw back and contract ourselves into a narrower sphere of being than was ours before. What more pitiful sight than a man, with abundant leisure, with large capacities of usefulness, with ample wealth, vastly beyond the possibility of need, yet as much afraid of doing good as he ought to be of selling his soul, shrinking with a cold sneer from every mode of religious or moral activity or benevolence, contentedly leaving the wretched and degraded in their sin and suffering, and, when forced for decency's sake to render some little aid to a fellow-being, doling it out as he would measure drop by drop his own heart's blood? And yet this very man, if he would only look into his own heart, would find that the paltry sums thus bestowed, pitiful as they were in proportion to his wealth, had purchased him his happiest moments, and thus yielded him an interest which the untouched bulk of his estate can never pay.

But I would not speak of charity as the privilege of the rich alone, but as the right and duty, nay, as the essential nourishment, of every soul that truly lives. Nor does it imply abundant means, leisure, or capacity. Its law is, — "Be merciful after thy power. If thou hast much, give plenteously. If thou hast little, do thy diligence gladly to give of that little. And whatever else thou hast or hast not, give thy heart." Let there be no barrier of indifference, coldness, or selfishness between you and any child of God. Account every man as your brother. Feel that you are one of the universal family, bound to all its members in indissoluble kindred. Say, with the heathen poet, — "I am a man, and I account nothing that concerns man as indifferent to me." Thus will your own sphere of being be indefinitely enlarged, and your fountain of life kept full.

Finally, our true life must be connected with, and flow from, the testimony of a good conscience, which, if merited, no outward condition can suppress or pervert. Were we in the habit of looking within as constantly as we ought, how full and sufficient a source of gladness might this be! Suppose that every morning and evening there came to us the audible voice of God, saying, — "I have chosen thee, — I have loved thee, — thou art mine, — I will guide thee by my counsel on earth, and afterward receive thee to glory," — would not this voice make us supremely happy, let the world smile or frown, let the current of our affairs roll with a smooth or a turbid stream? And what but this voice, more than audible, pervading every chamber and recess of the inner man, is the testimony which conscience bears to the good and faithful servant? Why should it not breathe perfect joy? To know, that, with all our infirmities and sins, it has yet been our endeavor to walk before God in a prayerful and trusting spirit, — to look around among our fellow-men, and see not one towards whom we have knowingly and willingly violated the law of equity and love, — to be conscious also of an inward desire and longing after the things that are true and excellent, — this is indeed the shining of heaven into the soul of man.

Of the spirit which bears these traits it may well be said, — "The glory of God doth lighten it, and the Lamb is the light thereof."

This testimony of a good conscience is a treasure which evil times and untrustworthy men not only have no power to take from us, but may even render more sure and availing as a source of contentment and joy. By it I have known men made far happier in a reduced fortune than they had been in affluence. In what were called their better days, though they lived at peace with God and man, they did not give themselves time to enter into intimate communion with their own souls, and to feed on the heavenly manna, which falls only when the world is calm and still. But when reverses came, they found unspeakable solace in the reflection, that God had taken only what they had honestly gained and generously used, that they had made duty the soul of business, and had not been driven by the love of lucre to forsake the law of God or to violate the covenant of their Redeemer.

Faith, hope, charity, their gifts sealed by a conscience void of offence, — it is by these things that men live, — in these alone is the life of the soul. Be faithful, sincere, upright, beneficent. Honor God and bless man with heart and soul, with mind and strength. And then commit the outward affairs of life, in calm faith, to the guidance and disposal of a kind Providence, assured that the soul at peace with God is above them all, sufficient through divine support for its own well-being and happiness in time and through eternity.

Such are the heaven-appointed means of life and growth within the reach of all of us. It is these that our Saviour proffers to us. They were his peace and joy. They are the fountain still flowing at the foot of his cross. Other streams there are, sparkling, attractive, rolling over golden sands and beneath a brilliant sky; yet there is a voice in their murmur, ever saying, — "He that drinks of us shall thirst again, and thirst as often as he comes to draw." But from the mountain of the beatitudes, and again from the olive-shade of Gethsemane, and from the darkness and agony of Calvary, I hear the voice, — "If any man thirst let him come unto me and drink, and the water that I will give him shall be in him a well of water springing up unto everlasting life."

SERMON XVIII.

THE KINGDOM OF GOD.

THE KINGDOM OF GOD COMETH NOT WITH OBSERVATION. — Luke xvii. 20.

In the hallowed calm of a summer Sabbath, there is much to remind us of the gentle, noiseless, yet all-powerful influence of our religion. There are striking and attractive analogies between the outward and the spiritual universe. The reign of summer, in which we now rejoice, came not with observation; but it has quietly stolen upon us, has grown while we were sleeping, has derived its nutriment from alternate sunbeams, dews, and showers, each beautiful in its season, but at no one moment suggesting associations of intense power. And yet they have made the desert blossom, have gladdened the forest, and replaced the late sterile, frost-bound landscape by gorgeous bloom and rich promise; and they remind us of Him of whom it was said, — "He shall come like rain upon the grass, and

20 *

as showers that water the earth"; and at the same time, — "He shall have dominion from sea to sea, and from the river to the ends of the earth."

In the realms both of nature and of mind, man works with observation, — God, in silence; man, in abrupt, fragmentary efforts, — God, in continuous and progressive plans, in which are at once the hidings and the vast results of omnipotence. As in harmony with the voices and impressions of the season, let us consider the idea of our text, as illustrated in the establishment of our Saviour's kingdom on the earth, in its re-establishment in the individual soul, and in the healing and sanctifying influences that go forth for society from every true subject of his kingdom.

1. Our Saviour's kingdom, as founded by him personally, came "not with observation." How quiet, gentle, unobtrusive, was his passage through life! None could say when his kingdom came. There was no sounding of trumpets before him, — no ostentatious announcement of the beginning of his reign. No series of events could have been less conspicuous, no discourses less pretending, than those of his ministry. Even his most stupendous miracles were wrought in comparative retirement, by the death-bed and at the grave-side. His days were chiefly spent among the lowly, the stricken, and the suffering. When he spoke, it was by the way-side or in the fishing-boat, and the

passing shower or the opening blossom gave him his text. Sometimes his hearers were attracted by a story full of stirring imagery and striking incident, — they listened intently, and the graphic words sank into their inmost souls; yet they knew not for months afterwards, that in those words were wrapped the deepest mysteries of the kingdom of heaven. Then, again, with reference to some engrossing event or question of the day, he uttered a few simple, pertinent sayings, so perfectly well-timed, that they seemed adapted to no other place or moment; yet those who heard them could not forget them, but found that they suited other times and occasions, that they had an exhaustless depth and fulness of meaning, and at length that they were the very mind and will of the Eternal for all lands and ages. His least formal utterances could not fade from men's memories, but were cherished as gems of heaven. There was no show of a system either in his preaching or his life. His ministry lasted but little more than a year; and of that a very few days only were passed in other company than that of unlettered fishermen, and most of the time in the desert, on the lake, or in rural hamlets, then obscure and despised, though now illustrious, because they bore his footprints. He was perpetually harassed by the importunity and waywardness of his friends, or the captiousness and malice of his enemies. He left no written record behind him; and his words and deeds were preserved in the most miscellaneous form by a few of his illiterate followers, whom no impulse short of the most affectionate and zealous interest in his memory could have induced to become authors. Yet when we look at his gospel as a whole, we can say, "It is finished." We find nothing that needed to be said or done left unsaid or undone. And as his disciples, who, on the morning of the ascension, had inquired about his reign as if it were yet to begin, looked back upon his works of power, his words of love, the agony of the garden, and the victory of the cross, they saw that the kingdom of God had fully come. The isolated threads and colors of his doctrine and his life grouped themselves in beautiful symmetry and harmony; and on the canvas where they would have thought to see only a few bright, but vague and disconnected touches, they beheld a finished picture, with the inscription, to which their hearts thankfully responded, — "Surely this was the Son of God."

Before unbelieving Jews, and Gentiles too, how strikingly true was it that his kingdom came not with observation! The Jews saw in Jesus and his followers only a score or two of ignorant fanatics, and thought that they had merely to smite the shepherd in order to scatter the flock; but hardly had they smitten him, before his name was publicly proclaimed within their temple-walls, and won thousands in a day to its profession and baptism. The Gentiles supposed the conflict between the new religion and the guardians of the ancient law to be only a paltry quarrel between rival Jewish sects, deemed the leader of the new heresy not worth crucifying, and advised the Jews to chastise him and let him go. But while the generation that saw him die yet lived, his cross had been made the revered emblem of the faith of thousands in every part of the vast Roman empire, and corrupt rulers and avaricious priests saw that a more than rival power had been roused against them, and that the kingdom was passing irrevocably from their grasp. To my mind, this quiet establishment of Christianity, without any of the usual apparatus of great revolutions, is a conclusive token of the immediate agency of God in the fortunes of the infant Church. No other hand could thus have marshalled and put in motion the perfect and divine array of means, motives, and influences for human salvation, and held forth in the eyes of the astonished world the finished work, before in the ears of friends or foes had resounded the startling declaration, — "Behold, I make all things new."

2. The sentiment of our text is verified in individual religious experience. Yet it is often overlooked or denied. I apprehend that many depend for their evidence of the Christian character on their being able to mark the precise

moment when the kingdom came, rather than on tracing the certain proofs of its establishment within. But in the New Testament we are nowhere bidden to look to any past epoch for the proof that we belong to the family of Christ. Our self-searching is constantly directed to the present state of the motives, affections, and principles. "Examine yourselves whether ye be in the faith." "If any man have not the spirit of Christ, he is none of his." "He that hath my commandments and keepeth them, he it is that loveth me." In many, the growth of the religious character has been so silent and gradual, that they can point to no decisive moment of change. Some have never been destitute of serious impressions. When they ceased to repeat a prayer from a mother's lips, they commenced praying for themselves, and have perhaps never passed a day of their lives since infancy without thoughts of God and duty. Now, though in such persons there has been a new and spiritual birth, — a transition from the state in which they were the passive recipients of religious thoughts from their parents to that in which, with full understanding and deep emotion, they made choice for themselves of the better part, — it is a transition of which they cannot be expected to mark the stages, as they could, had they ever led an utterly vicious or irreligious life. Such persons, born and brought up as within temple-gates, and self-consecrated from early childhood, have never known the thraldom of the world's yoke, or the bitterness of its unrequited service, and have therefore escaped those agonizing experiences by which others can mark their entrance into the kingdom of God.

Among those, also, who were formerly negligent of religious duty, and worldly in their prevalent tastes, desires, and feelings, yet free from those expressly sinful habits of speech and conduct which need an abrupt and sudden change, there are, no doubt, many who have been awakened and drawn heavenward so gradually, that they can define no season when regeneration took place. All that they can say is, — "Once I was blind; now I see. Once my heart was a stranger to the religious affections; now I love to pray, my heart promptly turns to God, and I delight to seek out and follow my Saviour's footmarks." In such a case, the kingdom of God has no doubt come; but it came not with observation. There has been godly sorrow for sin; but it was gentle in its flow, was blended with the hope of pardon, and cheered by the promises of God. There has been an entire change of character; but it was wrought step by step. The change commenced with prayer; and the soul had begun to pray before it was fully conscious of it. First came the momentary appeal, the silent upbreathing of the spirit to God. This soon prolonged itself into musings on the concerns of eternity. It next took form and words, and sought fit places and seasons for communion with the Father. Then it gradually spread itself through the life into a daily walk with God. And this spirit of prayer has subdued, one by one, the unspiritual traits and habits of the soul, has sanctified its once worldly tastes, has carried on and up into the boundless future its desires and aspirations, has rayed itself out in the every-day life and conversation, and established a new law, and breathed a new spirit, for common scenes, cares, and duties, so that the very habits which were mere outward decencies have become Christian virtues, and the very acts which used to be performed for the praise of men are now wrought with a single eye to the Divine approval. Thus, in the passage of many of the sincerest Christians from darkness into God's marvellous light, has the dawn broken so gradually upon their vision, that they could not say when night gave place to day.

It seems to me that the religious experience of the faithful eleven among our Lord's apostles must have been of this stamp. When they were called, they appear to have been decent, sober, thoughtful men, but exceedingly unspiritual, and with an immense change to be wrought before they reached the full Christian stature. But we read in their history of no precise moment when either of them passed from darkness to light. Their growth in grace was very gradual. Even at the Last Supper, worldly ambition had not wholly yielded to the hope of a heavenly inheritance; and after the resurrection, we find them still slow of heart. But from the seed of the kingdom, sown in tears and watered with blood by the Man of Sorrows, there sprang up at length in their souls a fervor, spirituality, and self-consecration, which the world has not yet seen equalled, and can never see surpassed.

For a different class of the regenerate, I well know that the coming of the kingdom of God is preceded by a violent inward convulsion, and an agony of intense sorrow. The conflict is a death-struggle; and in contrast with its gloom and terror, the quietness that succeeds it seems more than the peace of heaven. This violent form of religious experience, when not directly flowing from harsh and repulsive views of the Divine character, is most apt to take place when the previous life has been one either of confirmed obduracy or of open and manifest guilt. And in these cases it is not the reign of God that comes with violence, but the kingdom of sin that passes away as in a whirlwind. The fierce convulsion and agony of soul are the casting down of the thrones, that the Ancient of Days may sit, — that the gentle and peaceful Jesus may come in and reign. Satan falls like lightning; the spirit of God descends like a dove. The old heavens may be rolled together as a scroll, and pass away with a great noise; but the new heavens and earth, wherein dwelleth righteousness, are swept by no stormy breath.

Let it not be inferred from what I have said, that I would establish a low or lax standard of Christian character. The contrary is my desire and aim. I not only think, but know, that the occurrence of pungent religious experiences at some past time is a delusive and dangerous test of character. I know avowed infidels, who in their earlier days passed through the agony of contrition, and the ecstasy of relief and imagined pardon. I know those who, relying on such remembrances, have grown remiss in duty, and relapsed into utter worldliness of spirit and character. I have known those who have carried to the very borders of the grave the assurance that they were Christians, on the ground that they had once been converted, who yet, in the judgment of the broadest charity, had lived for many years without any apparent sense of religious obligation and duty. Nay, I have known this whole convulsive process passed through in a time of violent sickness, without leaving any distinct traces on the memory when health returned. But there are questions which would to God I might induce each of you to ask himself before he sleeps, and to feel that his position in the spiritual universe, his lot in the event of death, depends upon the answer. They are these. What is my present frame of heart and character? Am I living as a child of God and an immortal being? Do I sincerely pray, and that daily and habitually? Is God much in my thoughts, and does the consciousness of his presence enter into my daily life, and form an element in my thoughts, plans, and purposes? Is his will, as such, my law? Do I sincerely love my Saviour, and is his example my rule and measure of duty? Are my thoughts much in heaven, and does the power of the world to come govern my heart and breathe in my daily walk and conversation? These are momentous questions; for they relate to the fundamental laws of the kingdom of God. If you can answer them in the affirmative, the kingdom has come in your soul, though it may not have been with observation. Otherwise, whatever may be your remembered experience, the work of repentance and regeneration remains for you; and through no other gate can the kingdom be entered.

There is yet another error to which we are liable, in judging whether the kingdom of God has come in the heart. It is that of substituting outward mechanical activity for vital piety. Showy, ostentatious forms of duty and benevolence are frequently demanded as a test of character. Men vie with each other in the cry, — "Come, see my zeal for the Lord!" and often are the domestic altar, and those walks of quiet duty on which no trumpet sounds before one's steps and no applauding multitude shouts behind, forsaken and neglected for such works as are to be wrought with shout and song. These last works must, indeed, be wrought, though it would be well to dispense with the shout and song. But let none imagine that an engagedness and ardor, which crave the excitement of sympathy and crowds, indicate the establishment of the kingdom of God in the heart. God reigns in the stillness of home, in the silent night-watches, in the lonely path of duty, in those unostentatious charities in which one hand knows not what the other does, in patience, forbearance, and long-suffering, in rigid, minute conscientiousness, in the thousand nameless thoughts and words of which man can take no note, but which have their record on high.

The sentiment of our text is beautifully illustrated in many of the instrumentalities which God employs to bring men into his kingdom. I have time now to speak, in this connection, only of his afflictive Providence, in which we cannot but admire the analogy between the natural and the spiritual harvest-field. The sower sows his seed, and early drought checks its upspringing. Day after day rises in vernal glory and sets in beauty; yet the husbandman waits in vain for the hope of the year. At length, the sky is overcast, the heavy rain falls, and the whole landscape looks more dreary and desolate than winter. But when the sun reappears, every seed has germinated, and every furrow presents its rank of green blades, which have drawn vital nutriment from the drenching showers, and will in due time attest in rich, ripe harvest the blessing of the early rain. Thus do seeds of Heaven's planting often lie dormant in the soul of man. Life's happy days rise and set without a cloud, — scenes of gladness and hope pass before the soul; and yet there is no spiritual growth, no heavenward movement or aspiration. Thick, unbroken clods of earth press down the heavenly seed. Affliction comes, blighting, desolating. Cherished joys are withered; the fondest hopes disappointed; the idols of earthly love laid low. The soul for a season lies prostrate and in darkness, and neither sun nor stars appear for many days. But as the cloud passes away, the soul finds itself enriched and blessed. The seed which had long been choked has found room to grow. There spring up better thoughts, higher purposes, desires, and affections, that lay hold on heaven. The kingdom of God comes, though not with observation, not recognized at first in the atmosphere of sadness that encircles the home and heart, but soon shedding over the desolate home and the grief-stricken heart a peace more profound and a higher joy than had been felt or conceived before.

3. But I must pass to the last topic proposed for our consideration,— the sentiment of our text as illustrated in the influence of Christian char-

acter; and of this I can speak but briefly. The Christian is indeed bound to exert himself in express modes of benevolent activity; and, in these days of abounding iniquity and of earnest striving against sin, it is a mystery to me how any Christian can answer to his conscience or his God, if he lets not his voice be heard and his example distinctly witnessed and felt on the right side, in the great conflict now going on against the various forms of self-degradation and social wrong, — in the cause of temperance, freedom, and humanity. But the true disciple, when he has said and done all that he can in these causes, has exhausted but a small part of his influence. Most of it is silent and unobserved, — quiet as the dew on a midsummer night, but like the dew fructifying. It is impossible to estimate the good that may flow from the simple, unpretending discharge of common duties, — from the application of a Christian conscience to the little daily details of business and social and domestic intercourse. There are numberless things in ordinary life, which will be said and done in an indescribably different way and spirit by the Christian and the mere man of the world; and the difference, though it could not be defined, will be distinctly felt, and will make the Christian life a perpetual benediction to all who come within its influence. Conversance with such consistent exemplars of the religious character is among the choicest means of grace that God ever uses; and in the day when the secrets of all hearts shall be revealed, and when the zealous mover of benevolent machinery, who yet has neglected to keep his own heart, and the unostentatious Christian, who thinks that he has done nothing great, shall stand side by side in the judgment, it will no doubt be in favor of the latter that the sentence will go forth, — "Take ye the talent from the unprofitable servant, and give it to him that hath ten talents." Many souls, that knew not whence they first derived their better impulses and principles, so gentle was the influence of the good man's example, will see in the light of eternity that it was the outflow of his spirit, the calm and quiet beauty of holiness in his life, that won their hearts to the love of Christ, and awoke in them the germs of penitence, faith, and prayer. Thus in the kingdom of heaven will many that are least be made greatest; and no soul that has sincerely loved the Saviour will be left without the blessing promised to those who turn sinners to righteousness, and the disobedient to the wisdom of the just.

SERMON XIX.

THE MYSTERIES OF PROVIDENCE.

IF THE LORD WERE PLEASED TO KILL US, HE WOULD NOT HAVE RECEIVED A BURNT-OFFERING AND A MEAT-OFFERING AT OUR HANDS, NEITHER WOULD HE HAVE SHOWED US ALL THESE THINGS, NOR WOULD AS AT THIS TIME HAVE TOLD US SUCH THINGS AS THESE. — Judges xiii. 23.

MANOAH feared that he and his wife were going to be destroyed, because they had been visited by an angel of God. Our text is his wife's reply to him. The heavenly messenger had come and departed in fearful splendor, and there was much in the scenes that they had witnessed adapted to inspire them with awe and terror. But he had accepted their offerings, had conversed with them familiarly and kindly, and had made disclosures of God's merciful purposes to them and their household; and, setting these things over against the terrific appearances that had alarmed Manoah, his wife rightly inferred that the angel had come on an errand of unmingled love.

We often need to apply a similar train of reasoning to the mysteries of Providence. God's angels come to us in fearful forms, — the angels of disease, desolation, and death. Their wings brood long over our dwellings. For some of us, their ministries come with appalling frequency. They often inflict what seems at first sight unmingled evil. They palsy the strength which had wrought only in the service of God and man. They unnerve the arm which was the sole support of helpless infancy or age. They take large portions of his stewardship from the faithful steward. They remove from our keeping children whom we had vowed to train for heaven. They destroy lives that seemed most essential to the dearest interests of religion and humanity. At such times the murmuring heart will say in distrust, — "Why hast thou done thus?" The one calamitous event often stands out by itself. Nothing has gone before it to interpret it, or to lighten its severity; nothing has accompanied it for our special relief or solace; and nothing has as yet followed it in the world without, or in our own experience, to justify the ways of God, and to sustain submission by reason. Were there only room to suppose so, the infliction would seem arbitrary and wanton; and, if considered by itself, might be thought to proceed from a God who laughed at our calamity and mocked when our fear came, — from a capricious and malignant tyrant, and not from our Father.

I say, that, in individual cases, there might be room for the suspicion of malevolence and vindictiveness on the part of the Supreme Arbiter of our destinies. In point of fact, this has been the prevalent belief everywhere save under Christian culture. A large share of divine caprice and malignity has entered into every form of polytheism; and the idea of revenge and needless, wanton mischief on the part of the gods has led to the most inhuman and revolting forms of propitiation and sacrifice. And the Jews, forbidden to attach such ideas to their God, and yet unable to account for these isolated instances of dire calamity and suffering in a world full of divine mercy, imputed many of the most appalling forms of physical evil to the agency of demons, thus cutting off for themselves the sources of consolation which they might have derived from the religious views presented in their sacred writings. Under these mysterious visitations of Providence, we are driven, or rather we gladly have recourse, to reasoning like that in our text. We appeal to other and more frequent experiences, in which the Divine mercy has been manifest, — to sorrows which have been sanctified to our growth in grace, and to our long seasons of unmingled and unclouded happiness. We survey the leading features of the plan of Providence, and then say, If, by the present sorrow, God meant to crush us to the earth, if it came even on an errand of doubtful mercy, the past could not have been what it has been. Divine love could not thus have followed us step by step, and hour by hour, only to prepare for us a severer fall and a deeper gloom. In tracing out this thought, let us follow the order suggested by our text.

"If the Lord were pleased to kill us, he would not have received a *burnt-offering* at our hands." Burnt-offerings, under the Jewish law, were pure and spotless victims, wholly consumed without reservation. They were ordained as an expression of trust and gratitude, and, when offered in sincerity, brought the Divine blessing upon the home and heart of the worshipper. Have not burnt-offerings from our households gone up to God, — lambs without fault or stain, not indeed selected by ourselves, but chosen by the Most High, — taken wholly from us, consumed, lost to the outward sight, — their unseen spirits mounting to the upper heaven, as the smoke from the ancient altars rose to the sky? These utter, entire sacrifices many of us have been constrained to make, and have made them in unspeakable agony; yet have afterwards confessed that they were not so much taken from us, as accepted at our hands. These bereavements have left blessings in their train. When met and borne in faith, they have given us new experience of spiritual joy. They have opened new fountains of inward life. They have bound us by new and stronger ties to the unseen world. The hearts to which our own so closely clung have borne us with them heavenward. They have led us to a nearness and familiarity of feeling with reference to heaven, which can subsist in no soul that has not near kindred there. These events have weakened the power of temptation and the yoke of sin. They have made our growth of character more sure and rapid. They have enlarged our circle of sympathy and our power of usefulness. They have borne for us "the peaceable fruits of righteousness." As, in the rude form of worship permitted by God till Jesus offered himself on Calvary, the Israelite bore to the altar the fairest of his flock, the pet lamb that knew his voice and fed from his hand, with many regretful thoughts, and yet in coming months felt that for his act of piety a double blessing rested on field and fold, basket and store, — so from the most unwilling sacrifice that we have been strengthened to offer submissively at our Father's bidding, there has grown the richest spiritual increase. Our sorrows have cut short our sins, nurtured our faith, given vividness to our hope, and made our love more and more like that of the Universal Father. In new sorrows, then, from which we have not had time to gather in and count the happy fruits, we will hear from like scenes that are past the call to trust and gratitude. Did it please God to destroy us, he would not have accepted our burnt-offerings.

Nor yet our *meat-offerings*. Of the meat-offerings, only a small portion was consumed, as typical of the consecration of the whole, while the residue was enjoyed by the priests, or by the worshipper himself, with his household and friends. Of these offerings the greater part were in acknowledgment of the common or peculiar favors of Providence connected with the homes, possessions, and families of those who brought them. Has our meat-offering, my friends, been duly rendered, — our tribute, as God has prospered us, for his church, his kingdom, and his poor? Have those alms gone forth which may sanctify all the rest? If offered, God has accepted and blessed them. And whether we have rendered or withholden them, how many are the favors, the deliverances, the peculiar mercies of our homes, to which we should look back, when in any hour of doubt or sorrow a murmuring spirit would arraign the Divine goodness! What a talismanic power there is in that one word, — *home!* What a cluster of tender and endearing associations does it suggest! It is the most complex of all words, and every fold that we open in its meaning discloses new depth and richness of infinite mercy. The careful husband and fond father, the assiduous and loving wife and mother, the prattle of infancy, the glee of childhood, the harmonious circle of brothers and sisters, the blending of heart with heart and soul with soul, the gentle repose of weakness and fear on bolder counsel and a stronger arm, the kindly division of cares and burdens, the mutually helping hand along every steep and rough passage in life, — these are but a few of the merciful appointments of Him who has set the solitary in families, and turned the hearts of parents to children, and of children to parents. These home blessings in all their fulness we have many of us enjoyed for years; and when some of them have been suspended, the greater part have still been spared us, and have been made even doubly precious through the power of sorrow to refine and ennoble the affections. To these mercies, new every morning, fresh every evening, borne on the wings of every moment, let us look, and learn that God is good, when we bow under those sudden and agonizing afflictions that might seem sent to crush, and not to heal. Let the calm and quiet scenes of home enjoyment, which have borne unceasing witness to a protecting Providence, shed their light of divine love upon our hours of doubt and darkness. True, to our half-sealed ears, these desolating sorrows blend only notes of wailing and despair with the hymn of life; but they accord with the songs of angels and the hosannas of glorified spirits, and in the melody of our own hearts, if believing and devout, they will flow on from sadness to submission, from submission to trust, from trust to holy joy, till we enter the golden gates, and join the worship of the redeemed.

To pursue the order of the text, — "If the Lord were pleased to kill us, neither would he have *showed us all these things*." What has he showed us? What is he daily showing us? How much is there in every scene and form of outward nature to rebuke distrust, to quell fear, and to make us feel that the world we live in is indeed our Father's! Especially in the summer world now around us, so rich in bountiful provisions, so laden with sights, sounds, and flavors designed solely for gratification, how is the truth that God is love poured in upon the soul of man through every sense and every avenue of enjoyment! From the first song of the birds to the last ray of mellow twilight, whether in sunshine, beneath sheltering clouds, or fresh from the baptism of the midday shower, the whole scene is full of the present and the loving God. He sustains the wayfaring sparrow. He gives the raven his food. He clothes the frail field-flower with beauty. He pours gladness into the unnumbered insect tribes,—nay, into that minute microscopic creation made to fill with sentient life and joy the least crannies and crevices of the universe, that no grain of sand or drop of water may fail to reflect the image of the All-merciful. In our seasons of doubt, darkness, and sorrow, have not these miracles of Divine care and love a message from God for us? Should they not echo to our stricken hearts the words of the Redeemer,— "If God so clothe the grass of the field, and feed the fowls of the air, shall he not much more care for you?"

Manoah's wife added,—"If the Lord were pleased to kill us, he would not have *told us such things as* these." She referred to promised temporal mercies in her own household. God has told us yet more, infinitely more. In the revelation by Jesus Christ he has revealed to us truths and given us promises, which, received in faith, must put to flight all hopeless despondency and gloom. In Jesus we learn our Father's perfect providence and all-embracing love, the kind ministry of earthly disappointment and sorrow, and the blessings ordained for those that mourn. He tells us of the mansions in the Father's house, where our best earthly treasures, when taken from us, are garnered for us. He points out his own path of trial and suffering as blessed and happy, —as full of peace, and light, and joy. He tells us of tribulation, but of victory too. We go with him to Gethsemane and to Calvary; but we stand with him also on the transfiguration and the ascension mount. He tells us that in this world we shall have sorrow, but says, — "They that suffer with me shall reign with me; be thou faithful unto death, and I will give thee a crown of life." In his teachings and in the record of his pilgrimage, we learn all that we can need to know of the mysterious dealings of Providence. To interpret them fully we cannot expect or hope. But we do learn, and are left without a remaining doubt, that, when the most severe, they are sent in love, — are hidden mercies, designed to discipline our faith, to spiritualize our affections, and to draw us into closer fellowship with our Saviour's sufferings, that we may afterwards become partakers of his glory. Here, then, let our refuge ever be, when sudden and desolating calamity falls upon us or ours. Let us go to our Saviour's own words on the night of his sorrow. Let us stand in faith by his broken sepulchre, and hear from the lips of him who was dead and is alive again, — "I am the resurrection and the life." O, could we take in anything like an adequate view of the gospel revelation, how brief, how unworthy of comparison with joy boundless and eternal, would seem the severest trials of the present state! Here are pardon, salvation, heaven, immortality, offered us, — scenes surpassing all imagination spread before us, with but a few days of clouded joy and bereaved affection at the threshold of our being, and then all beyond, if we bear our Saviour's image, union, peace, gladness, without limit and without end. Surely, did it please God to destroy us, he would not have told us such things as these. Only let the soul be filled with these truths, and then let sorrows rain down like rattling thunderbolts, — they could not crush or shake it; but it would breathe itself forth in those noble words of him who had been caught up into the third heaven, — "None of these things move me, neither count I my life dear unto myself, so that I might finish my course with joy; — in all these things I am more than conqueror through Him that hath loved me."

These are some of the considerations which may sustain us under such mysterious dispensations of Providence as lie, no doubt, in the future path of most of us. Why these dark events occur, it is idle to ask. Were there no mysteries in the Divine administration, it would be either because we were omniscient, or because God was not so. In a beneficent system, embracing all worlds and beings, and spanning twin eternities, there must needs be events to which a finite mind cannot assign their true place and office. Did we see and know all, where would be faith, with its sisterhood of Christian graces, — faith, which makes us children of God and heirs of heaven, — faith, which must precede sight and knowledge, as in a higher state of being we learn ever more and more of the plan of universal Providence, and yet must ever pause and worship before mysteries still unrevealed? Let us thankfully take whatever discipline the Father sends, and, if it disclose not at once its meaning and its ministry, let us wait, in humble trust, till a more mature Christian experience on earth, or the light of heaven, shall solve the doubt and dispel the mystery.

SERMON XX.

THE GADARENE DEMONIAC.

GO HOME TO THY FRIENDS, AND TELL THEM HOW GREAT THINGS THE LORD HATH DONE FOR THEE, AND HATH HAD COMPASSION ON THEE. — Mark v. 19.

We lose much of the impression which our Saviour's miracles ought to produce upon us, when we look at them simply as isolated and amazing dispensations of Divine power, aside from the common course of human life. Some of the most interesting and touching views of these miracles are those which we take in connection with the homes which they made glad, with the withered hopes which they revived, and the departed joys which they restored. I have often dwelt in fancy on the return home of the poor demoniac, whose history gives us our text this morning. The whole scene paints itself with peculiar vividness on my mental retina. I may not succeed in transferring it to yours; but if I do, I know that I can in no better way prepare your thoughts for the festival of redeeming love which many of us are to celebrate before we part.

The subject of this miracle has long been a victim of the most mysterious and appalling form of disease with which God has seen fit to afflict his human family. His insanity is not of that mitigated type which suffers control, lets in rays of sober thought, and remains within reach of the endearments and charities of home. He is a maniac of the wildest and most fearful stamp. He cannot be kept, even in chains, at his own dwelling; but, with the preternatural strength of madness, he makes his fetters and handcuffs as mere withs of tow. He breaks from all restraint. He wears no clothing. His chief abiding-place is among the tombs, where, in darkness, amidst putrid exhalations and the tokens of loathsome decay, he nurses every wild and wayward fancy, and revels, like a very fiend, in all that is gloomy and terrific. He is reckless even of intense personal suffering. In his paroxysms, he rolls himself and lacerates his body upon the sharp rocks, and is covered with the scars of self-inflicted wounds. He perhaps had been a kind and happy husband and father; and now, as he wanders among the tombs, a vague remembrance of the pleasant home he once had will ever and anon dance before his hot brain, and with an unearthly laugh and shout he rushes homeward. But his wife, as she sees him approaching, must bar her doors against the maniac, and hide from his sight the children, whom, in a sudden flash of irresponsible anger, he may dash against the stones. And while he lingers for a moment at the closed doors, and prepares to force an entrance, the place grows unfamiliar, the recollection of former scenes fades away, and the blind instinct of his awful malady hurries him back to his dwelling among the tombs. Thus has he been for years a terror to the whole country round, — so fierce and violent, that no man dares pass where he is known to be near. He is dead to all worth living for; his children are fatherless; his wife, a widow.

There passes near him one morning a little company of travellers, who have just crossed the lake and are on their way to the neighboring city. He rushes from his lurking-place to attack them. But, as he approaches them, there is a face in the group that arrests the torrent of his mad fantasies, and calls back some gleam of consistency to his chaotic thoughts. That eye has a power which he cannot resist. There beam from that countenance rays of love, which fall upon his darkened soul, and draw him nearer to the stranger. It flashes across his memory, that, when he dwelt among men, all hoped that the Messiah would soon appear. He perhaps had been a devout man, waiting for the consolation of Israel; and, with the rapid reasoning of a madman, he says to himself, — "None but the Christ of God can wear that face, which both awes and attracts me, who for years have shunned all and put all to flight." He enters for a moment into conversation with the stranger, and every word betokens a wildly disordered intellect. But that eye still rests upon him. That face still beams upon him; and there shines through it the same spirit which in the morning of creation brought light from darkness, and order out of chaos. It is the glory of God in the face of Jesus; and it is pouring ray upon ray on the maniac's soul. The clouds part. The gloom is scattered. The phantasms of a bewildered brain flit away. The lurid flashing of that eye gives place to a look of calm intelligence. The tidings spread. The people flock from the city. They find him sitting at the divine Redeemer's feet, clothed, and in his right mind. Full of pious gratitude, he is unwilling to leave his Saviour. But Jesus has not forgotten the maniac's household. He, in whom all the families of the earth are blessed, lost during his earthly sojourn no opportunity of sending comfort and gladness to men's homes. "Go home to thy friends," says he, "and tell them how great things the Lord hath done for thee, and hath had compassion upon thee."

His family have not yet heard of the miracle

of mercy. The father is seen at a distance approaching his former dwelling. All is trepidation and alarm. The doors are barred. The mother bids her children conceal themselves from their father's sight. But,—"Look," says one of them, "he is clothed like any other man." "Yes," says another, "and he is walking calmly and quietly, not with the rude gestures and hideous outcries with which he is in the habit of coming." "And, mother," says a third, "he looks as he did when he lived at home, and we used to watch for him, and run out to meet him, and strive with each other for his first kiss." And the desolate mother sees, with a heart too full for utterance, that it is indeed the long lost given back,—the dead alive again. As the doors are thrown open, and the husband and father is clasped in the tearful embrace of those who deemed him lost to them for ever, what vows of gratitude to God, what blessings on the heavenly Teacher, go up from those happy hearts, from that restored home! As the father talks to his children of the power and love of the Son of God, whose look had healed him,—as he recounts every word of the kind Redeemer in that touching interview, how fervent must have been the thankfulness, how warm the vows of consecration, to him whom disease obeyed, and who yet (the father tells them) was so meek, lowly, and gentle in his aspect, that the youngest child would not fear to approach him! In what sweet peace did that family rest on that memorable night! And, as the Saviour passed its sleepless watches on the mountain or the lake, think you not that his spirit was with the household that he had made so glad, and that his intercessions went up for them especially, that to their outward joy might be added the blessings of a living faith and an enduring love?

All through our Saviour's weary and homeless sojourn, were there not welling up for him sources of gladness in families which he had thus blessed, in homes which he had thus lighted with unexpected deliverance and joy? For this is but one picture out of many. All along the shores of that beautiful lake, and through the whole region of Galilee, were dwellings where the healing touch of the incarnate love of God had rested. Here was the leper, whom he had given back from his banishment as a loathsome outcast. There was the paralytic, whom he had raised from his deathbed. In this family, that lovely maiden, the life and joy of the whole household, was made ready for the grave; but he had stood by her lifeless form, and borne it from the embrace of death. There, too, was that widow, — "the reed on which she leaned was broken; the oil was dried up in her cruse." Her only son was carried forth for burial; but the Lord saw her, and had compassion on her, and the young man awoke at his bidding. Now number up the miracles of Jesus that are on record, take each of them as the representative of a family raised from sadness and desolation to joy and overflowing thankfulness; and you may form some faint idea of the amount of mercy of which he was the immediate source, — of the multitudes to whom he was personally endeared as the medium through which they had received God's best earthly gifts. You may thence learn who composed the crowd of Galileans that accompanied him with hosannas to the temple, — why the cowardly chief priests dared not apprehend him publicly while there were such multitudes from Galilee in the city, — who those people were that smote their breasts in agony, when they saw him dead upon the cross.

These miracles, apart from their worth as credentials of our Lord's Divine commission, are of infinite value from their compassionate character. They are all of them works of signal mercy. They unfold to us a love unwearied and inexhaustible, — a compassion that can let no suffering go unrelieved. They reveal to us the High-Priest who is touched with the feeling of our infirmities, — who bears the griefs and carries the sorrows of his brethren upon earth. They give us an implicit trust in the surviving sympathy and love of our ascended Redeemer. They bring him near us in every season of trial or sorrow. And, by looking through the Son to the Father whose image he bore, we are brought by these miracles into face-to-face communion with God. His glory and his goodness pass before us. From the demoniac's dwelling, from the gate of Nain, from the tomb of Bethany, there come to us assurances, which admit not of being made stronger, that God is love. When clouds and darkness are about him, we can go back to that year of his right hand, and learn that mercy is the foundation of his throne.

These miracles are of peculiar value as revealing the providence of God. Had what we call the order of nature never been broken, we might have imagined it something real and constraining. We might have looked upon the universe as a vast piece of mechanism, rolled on in its revolutions with no reference to human weal or woe. We should have yearned for miracles to show us that the world was not governed by chance, or fate, or combinations of brute matter. But now the wonderful works of Jesus have laid bare the springs of nature, and uncovered her foundations. Its mechanism, though perfect, is seen to be not absolute. Its laws bend to man's necessities. The wheels are indeed there; but, as in Ezekiel's vision, there is a living spirit in the wheels, and whithersoever the spirit goes, there the wheels go. We thus learn that the established order of events is a means, not an end, — varied in former times for the welfare of the spiritual universe, and therefore in itself flexible, subservient to spiritual laws and uses, and ordained for the nurture and progress of the souls subjected to its discipline. The same hand, that through Jesus visibly arrested the common course of events, must still govern and modify that course by the invisible shaping of remoter causes. Miracles at any one time imply a discretionary providence at all times, and thus they come to our hearts with an unspeakable power of consolation in our seasons of deepest gloom and greatest need. The sick have been raised by a word from the couch of hopeless suffering; a look has restored the maniac to perfect soundness; the dead have heard the voice of the Son of Man, and come forth. These darker ways of Providence are then dark no longer. There is for us, no less than there was for the men of Galilee, a power mightier than disease, — a love stronger than death. The arm that then raised the sick and dying, still mighty to save, is laid beneath every sufferer. He who bore back the prey from the grave watches the sleeping dust, and receives the ascending spirit.

I have spoken of the gladness sent to so many homes and hearts by the miracles of Jesus. Has he ceased to exert this benign agency? Or have outward miracles, having discharged their ministry, yielded place to still "greater works"?

Would you answer this question, go with me to the dwelling of as happy a family as you may find among a thousand. On the lips of the parents is the law of love; tenderness and reverence are blended in every look and tone of the children. An unkind word is never heard, a morose countenance never seen there. The father daily stands as priest at his own household altar, and his overflowing gratitude hardly leaves room for supplication. On the Lord's day, they go up to the sanctuary together, and not one of them retires when the table of redeeming love is spread. Their whole lives adorn the doctrine of their Saviour; and their home is a radiating place for pious example and holy influence. But go back a few years, and what was that family? The father a self-made maniac, — the slave of brutal appetite. His chief haunt was where they dig graves for men's souls; and when he came to his own house, it was but to curse his family, and to make his home a hell. The children were growing up in ignorance, waywardness, and squalidness, promising only to add to the mass of pauperism and crime. The mother alone trusted in God; and her heart would long ago have broken, had she not looked for a rest where the wicked cease from troubling. But the divine Redeemer visited that family. The mother's prayers were at length heard. The father's heart was touched. The Lord looked upon him, and he wept. His tears flowed from a repentance not to be repented of. His Saviour's face shone in upon his darkened and perverted soul, and left its image there. And then father and mother together bore their children to the Redeemer for his blessing, and in united prayer and effort consecrated them to his altar and his kingdom. He has accepted the offering, and set his seal on all their hearts. Nor is this a scene by itself. Such are the blessings which Jesus has shed and is shedding abroad in thousands of families all over Christendom. Such are the fountains of compassion that still flow from him whose love we this morning commemorate. There this day meet in his temple and surround his altar multitudes whom he has ransomed from the lowest degradation and the foulest guilt, cleansed from the most loathsome leprosy, and brought from the most God-defying madness, to sit at his feet, clothed and in their right mind.

But while we contemplate with adoring love the miracles which Jesus wrought in the days of his flesh, and the blessing which he now dispenses over the wide world from his mediatorial throne, shall we not prepare for our approaching altar-service ascriptions of gratitude for the great things that he has done for us, and for the compassion that he has had upon us individually? With what portion of our well-being and happiness is not his image blended? What is there that renders our life here blessed, or that lights up the future with promise, which he has not either bestowed, or made more precious and availing? Do we behold with a safe and glad feeling the majesty and beauty of the outward creation, and joyfully listen to the anthem of universal nature, as, like the voice of many waters, her blended tones rise in praise and gratitude to her Author? Jesus has opened our eyes to the beauty, our ears to the harmony, of creation. To him do we owe it, that we see not wrath in the storm-cloud and meet not the glance of a malignant deity in the lightning's flash. To him do we owe it, that we are not dwelling as orphans in a world without a God. Are we bound by close and happy ties of kindred and family? To him do we owe the permanence, purity, and sacredness of these relations, — to him those domestic virtues which are the defence and joy of our households, — to him the affections, which we call natural, but which flow from the new consecration that he has given to the family union. Do we think of departed members of our circle as not lost, but gone before, — as treasures laid up for us in heaven, — as friends, with whom we shall take sweet counsel and walk in unbroken communion through unknown ages? It is Jesus that sealed these hopes for us, when his voice broke the slumber of the grave, and when he himself, having tasted death for every man, walked again among the living. Have we the consciousness of Divine pardon, and, with all our unworthiness, can we welcome the thought of our Father's presence? It is because we have heard the voice and trusted in the reconciling blood of him who alone had power upon earth to forgive sin. Have we principles of duty, with which we have withstood, and hope still to withstand, the assult of fierce temptation, — principles which we can obey with joy, and which their trial only makes the dearer to us? They have come to us from the Mount of the Beatitudes, and from the lips of the Man of Sorrows. They have been fastened upon our souls by his example, — sealed for our salvation by his death. If there be in us any virtue or any praise, we owe it to him who trod before us the path of duty, and with his own bleeding feet wore its rough places smooth, — who has made goodness amiable by his own loveliness, piety attractive by his own winning spirit, heaven inviting by the thought that he is there. Do we look forward into eternity without fear, and think of the grave as but the portal to a more ample, glorious, and happy sphere of being? It is Jesus that has taken for us the sting from death, and the terror from the grave. His mercies, like his Father's, beset us behind and before, — compass our path and our lying down. There is not a bright scene of life that is not lighted by his smile, — not a pure joy that is not kindled by his breath.

I say not these things to heap unmeaning praises upon the Redeemer's head. The more I meditate on all of blessing and of hope that is given us upon earth, the more do I feel that human life is but an extended commentary on our Saviour's words, "I and the Father are one," — that the Father and the Son work together in all that gladdens this life, and in all that fits us for a higher and better home; so that he, who by his own negligence or guilt "hath not the Son, hath not the Father." I feel that no department of the Father's goodness is complete, till rays from Tabor and from Calvary have rested upon it, — that no cup which the Father designs for us is mingled as he would have it, till Jesus has poured into it those waters of which he that drinketh shall thirst no more. Let us, then, approach the holy table with the liveliest gratitude to him whom God hath ordained to be our Prince and our Saviour; and may he so become known to us in the breaking of bread, that we may fervently renew and never more violate that fellowship with him, which is our peace on earth, and our eternal life in heaven.

SERMON XXI.

BEAUTY.

HE HATH MADE EVERYTHING BEAUTIFUL IN HIS TIME.— Ecclesiastes iii. 11.

How rich are the traits and manifestations of man's creative genius! Think of the vast number and diversity of gorgeous and attractive forms, with which descriptive and imaginative talent has enriched the literature of all ages. One might revel in the works of genius for a whole millennium, and still its transmitted treasures would be unexhausted. And the fruits of mental toil, in all times, from the rude lyric of the savage to the rounded and polished productions of the most advanced culture, how redolent of beauty,—how thickly studded with gems of the purest lustre and transcending magnificence! Yet new sources of inspiration are still continually opening, and for thousands of years to come original genius will find fields not preoccupied, so that the stimulus of novelty will stir and reward the literary artificer to the end, no less than in the infancy, of time. Art, too, how endlessly varied in its embodiments of all that is fair, and grand, and glorious! Even the same simple theme, like the Madonna, may pass down from generation to generation, and every new pencil may make the theme its own by some added or varied line of beauty, some new shading or mellowing of the features, some bolder stroke or softer touch. How numberless, also, are the combinations of blended or interchanging majesty and beauty which rise and are yet to rise in the simple and the complex, the lowly and the lofty forms of architecture, — in column, tower, and dome, — in cottage, temple, and cathedral! Who can say to the creative spirit of man, "Thus far shalt thou go, and no farther"? Who does not feel that human capacity, in whatever form it may seek to embody its conceptions, is absolutely limitless and inexhaustible?

But whence this power in man? What are his creations but copies of the thoughts of God? That they are nothing else is implied in the fundamental canons of literature, art, and taste. Truth to nature is the sole test of beauty. That which has no counterpart in God's actual world has no honor in man's ideal world. That which departs from the plan of the Supreme Architect does violence to human taste, and is rejected as monstrous and repulsive. Man, the creator as he vainly styles himself, is but the copyist; and it is because nature is infinite in its varieties and combinations of beauty, that we feel that genius has no limit, and can never have fully uttered and embodied itself. There is always more to delight the eye and ear in the works of God, than man has ever recorded, sung, or pencilled. More of beauty has been over, around, and beneath us, on our walks to the sanctuary this day, than it ever entered or will enter the heart of man to conceive. The glad heavens, the rejoicing earth,—the numberless forms of life that burst into being with each summer morning,—the light that glimmers from dewdrops, glows in flowers, in gaudier or chaster radiance shines from the vast complexity, the sublime unity of nature,—the rolling around and up of gleams of glory from all creation,—the smile of God reflected from all beneath and all above,—does it not infinitely transcend all power of thought or imagining, and make us feel that the combined intellect of humanity for centuries of centuries could write out but here and there a single leaf of the immeasurable volume, which bears the Creator's imprint? Do we admire the partial copies that man has made? Do we bow down to the genius that can see and hear a little portion of the Divine idea? Shall not, then, our thoughts go up with unspeakably loftier reverence and more fervent adoration to Him who "has made everything beautiful"?

Reflect for a moment on beauty as an attribute of the Supreme Intelligence. Reflect on God as the Originator of all that delights the eye and charms the fancy. What an inconceivable wealth of beauty must reside in the mind, which, without a copy, first called forth these numberless hues and shades that relieve each other and melt into each other in the vast whole of nature, — which devised these countless forms of vegetable life, from the way-side flower that blooms to-day and withers to-morrow, to the forest giant that outlasts the rise and fall of nations and of empires, — which meted out the heavens, measured the courses and arranged the harmonies of the stars, spread the ocean, poured the river, torrent, and waterfall! What an infinity of resources do we behold in the alternate phases of the outward universe, each of which seems too beautiful to be replaced by one of equal loveliness, and yet yields at once its fancied pre-eminence to its successor! Thus, who can say which is the more replete with beauty, day with its all-revealing light, or night with its countless centres of fainter radiance; — spring, with its outgushing from every fountain of life, its promise half hidden, half disclosed, its fresh, thin field and forest drapery; summer, with its richer, deeper verdure, its gayer forms, and more festive aspect; autumn, with its harvest wealth, its party-colored foliage, and its piles of gold and crimson in the western sky; or hoary winter, in its simpler, purer robe, with its delicate frostwork and its icy stalactites? Go where you will, you escape not the reign of beauty. During the long polar night, the northern fires bathe heaven and earth in splendor more gorgeous than day. The torrid sand-waste still lies beneath a glorious sky, and is studded with oases rich in all the tokens of creative love. Wreaths and fillets of azure mist belt the bare mountain crags, while about their summits the

> "Signs and wonders of the element
> Utter forth God, and fill the hills with praise."

Even in mid-ocean, the phosphorescent fires by night, the dance and swell of majestic billows, the gorgeous clouds that float or rest over the surface of the deep, the leap, flight, and play of numberless forms of life above and beneath, sustain the unwearied interest of him who views the works of God with open eye, and bear concurrent testimony with the voice of holy writ, that "He hath made everything beautiful."

Now do not these manifestations of beauty throughout the visible universe reveal a corresponding attribute of the Almighty, — an attribute for which technical theology perhaps has no name, but the true heart can coin one? It is more than power, and more than wisdom; for these perfections of the Deity would have found an adequate expression in the vast proportions of the faultless harmony of creation. It is something else than love, which might have wrought its ends by means less diversified, and in a less attractive universe. It is something which bears the same relation to taste in man, which giving bears to receiving, devising to enjoying, or artistical invention to susceptibility. Its source in the Divine mind must be the human idea of beauty refined, exalted, carried out into infinity.

The depths of the Divine Intelligence we indeed cannot fathom; but there are some views of practical interest to be derived from the thoughts which I have very imperfectly expressed, yet which have, I trust, awakened in your minds a fuller echo of your own experience than has fallen upon your ears.

First, they suggest one mode of worship, which must always make us better, — that of the devout contemplation of the visible works of God. I apprehend that, while almost all enjoy change of place, the exhilaration of travelling, and the rest and recreation which free air and pleasant scenes bring with them, the chief associations connected, even in serious minds, with scenery of peculiar magnificence are too often those of amusement rather than devotion, and that the thoughts are prone to rest on the society and the casual sources of enjoyment in the proximity of mountain, cataract, or ocean, rather than on the salient features of the Creator's handiwork. I deem it a duty for all who can to cultivate conversance with these scenes, not for recreation alone, but for the sake of the heart and the character. It enlarges and expands the affections, it ennobles the moral nature, it imparts new tenderness and refinement to the whole inner man, thus to commune with God in his own forms of beauty, thus to enter more fully into his thoughts as they are embodied by himself, unmarred by human agency.

But let me not be understood to imply, that close and high communion with God in nature is a luxury reserved for wealth or leisure. The beauty which we would seek lies at every man's door. Our heavens, our fields, our gardens, are full of it. Only the eye, the heart, is wanting; and he who cannot enjoy such scenes as have met his eye this very day may range the world over, and names, prices, and statistics will be all that his mind will gather up and bring home. The clover-blossom, the midday or the evening cloud, the morning red, the glistening dew, the sparrow's flight, or the swallow's nest, may bring the Creator as near, — may suffuse the heart as richly with the divine spirit of beauty, — may prepare it to enjoy in a future life its range from world to world, as now from thought to thought, as surely and as effectually, — as those scenes where only the favored few can go to worship. With regard to nature it has been said, (and, it seems to me, with literal truth,) "To enjoy is to adore." There can be no full and true enjoyment of nature, except by those who see the hand and hear the voice of the Eternal in his works. I never heard of an atheist's enjoying the outward universe, nor do I believe it possible. The soul that begins to perceive the beauty of the creation yearns for communion in its solitude, for the living spirit in its stillness. To enter into the heart of nature is to talk face to face with its Author.

The thoughts which I have suggested lend, also, a motive to our conversance with the monuments of human art, taste, and genius. As we resort to sages raised up and inspired by God for the interpretation of religious truth, so may we fittingly look to those whose eyes and ears he has made peculiarly sensitive to the beauty and harmony of nature for the interpretation of her laws and mysteries, for conceptions often truer than our own, for transcripts more faithful than our duller inward vision can take for itself. The genuine poet or artist stands between us and God's world of beauty, in the same relation in which the seer or the evangelist stands between us and his realm of truth. The former has from him a mission to the imagination, as truly as the latter to the judgment or the will. The latter, indeed, occupies the most important place; for matters of faith and duty are concerns of life or death to the soul. Yet the former may impart aid of inestimable value to the mission of the latter; for truth and beauty are in sacred harmony, and the mind possessed by the spirit of beauty can the more readily perceive the proportions, relations, and evidences of truth, — the soul in which the beauty of creation finds a ready response, being at that point in communion with the Divine mind, can the more easily and cordially enter into that spiritual oneness with God, which is the perfection of character. But most of all does the devout mind love to commune with truth and beauty in those forms of literature, in which they have been blended by Divine inspiration. It finds no poetry so sublime as that of psalmist, prophet, and apostle, — that which connects the image of the heavenly Shepherd with the green pastures and still waters, draws lessons of a paternal Providence from the courses of Orion and Arcturus, names for the rain and for the drops of dew their Father, and resorts to every kingdom of nature, and gathers in materials from every portion of the visible universe, to portray the New Jerusalem, the golden city of our God, the gates within which the sun goes not down, for "the glory of God doth lighten it, and the Lamb is the light thereof."

Again, beauty, though distinct from love, is the minister of love. Though, without creating it in nature, or making man susceptible of its influences, God might have been good and our Father, it immeasurably enhances our sense of his goodness, and renders him much more our Father. Its every ray is edged and fringed with mercy. Its every form bears the inscription, "God is love." When it beams upon us from the heavens, it reveals his benignity. When it glows on the earth, or gleams from the ocean, it reflects his smile. When it stretches its many-colored bow on the cloud or the waterfall, it utters his thoughts of peace. Who can watch the course of one of these bright summer days, from the song that ushers in the gray, misty dawn, till twilight broods and the stars come out over slumbering nature, without feeling that eyes of God are all around him,—that the Divine presence is, on every hand, reflected into his soul from field and sky, from cloud and star?

Have not all these scenes a voice of tender sympathy and consolation for the grief-stricken? Was it not for this, that our Saviour directed the anxious and desponding to the fields in blossom, and the rejoicing birds, and said, "If your Father thus feed and clothe them, shall he not much more care for you?" In a world thus full of beauty, thus suffused by the smile of the

Universal Father, there can be no sorrow sent as sorrow. It can be only those whom God loves that he chastens. The griefs that flow at his bidding, severe and desolating as they seem, can be to the soul only what dreary vernal rains are to the upspringing grass and the unfolding blossoms,—what the cloud big with thunder is to the sultry atmosphere of summer. Not to blight the harvest of human hope and joy, but to bring forth in fresh luxuriance every plant of our Heavenly Father's planting, do the rains descend and the floods come upon the afflicted heart. Not to destroy or hopelessly bow down the soul, but to dispel the suffocating mist of worldliness, to open a clearer, higher range of vision for the inward eye, to make the upper heavens look serene and beautiful, falls the bolt that sends alarm and agony to our homes and hearts. Let us, then, in our sorrows, welcome the revelation of Divine love, with which the heavens are dropping and the earth teeming, which day utters to day and night rehearses to night. It is because new heavens and a new earth are made ready for us, that we must sometimes suffer here. It is because our affections and hopes should be elsewhere, that change, blight, and death must pass upon their dearest objects. It is to train the earthly vine about the tree of eternal life, that the heavenly husbandman cuts its lower tendrils, so that it may cling ever closer, and climb ever higher, till in his own good time he unearths its root, and transplants it to

> "Those everlasting gardens,
> Where angels walk, and seraphs are the wardens,
> Where every flower brought safe through death's dark portal
> Becomes immortal."

SERMON XXII.

CONTINGENT EVENTS AND PROVIDENCE.

LORD, IF THOU HADST BEEN HERE, MY BROTHER HAD NOT DIED. — John xi. 21.

IT was with these words that the two sisters of Lazarus successively accosted our Saviour, when he visited them four days after their brother's death. And they said the truth. Many had been the dying whom his touch, his word, had given back to life; and, had he stood by the bedside of his expiring friend, the tomb would have remained unopened. But he had purposely brought about the contingency named by the sisters. He knew that Lazarus was ill, and for that very reason lingered on his way to Bethany, — waited for him to die. Yet Lazarus and his sisters were the objects of Christ's peculiar love; and his strong sympathy with their distress and dread would have prompted him to walk day and night that he might avert the fatal stroke. But it was essential for the higher ends of the Divine administration, essential for the religious nurture and elevation of that very family, that Lazarus should die. And when, with their restored brother, they had too a more living faith, a more fervent hope of immortality, a richer experience of the power and love of Christ, than they had ever imagined before, they undoubtedly thanked God that Lazarus had been left to die.

There is a very close analogy between the state of feeling expressed in our text, and that experienced by the greater part of the bereaved in our own day. *If* is the emphatic word in the complaint of the sisters. "*If* thou hadst been here, my brother had not died." How few bereavements there are, which are not made doubly afflictive by an *if*, — by a past contingency, which, had it occurred, would have turned aside the sword of the death-angel! If our friend had not incurred this or that exposure, — if he had done this instead of doing that, — if we had been early enough alarmed on his account, — if we had foreseen such and such results from what was well considered and rightly meant, — a life so much valued and desired would have been spared. Many of you can bear me witness, that such thoughts have arisen in your minds during seasons of sorrow; and with some of you I know that they have occasioned absolute agony of spirit, and formed the most bitter ingredient in the cup of affliction. So long as these thoughts are present, perfect resignation is impossible. They come in between you and God, prevent your minds from resting on him as the sole author of the afflictive event, and bewilder you in that endless maze of second causes, which no mortal can thread, and in which no soul of man ever found repose. I feel, therefore, that I shall confer a lasting benefit on many of you, as regards both past and future griefs, if I can suppress that *if*, discourage your uneasy reflections on what might have been, and lead your minds up to Him, whose wise and kind purpose remains unaffected by these contingencies that give us so much pain.

Let me first remind you, that, if there is room for these painful reflections in any one case, there is equally room for them in almost every case. Take any instance of death, except by constitutional decay, trace back the last hours, days, weeks, or months of the departed, and you can always fix upon some circumstance which seemed the turning-point of his destiny, and of which you can say, "Only let that have been otherwise, he would have been still living." Only let danger be foreseen, and, humanly speaking, in nine cases out of ten death would be prevented. Thus, was toil or fatigue the reputed cause of fatal disease? It may, indeed, have been no more than others incur, or than the deceased himself has often incurred with impunity. Yet, with death visibly impending, he would have suspended the perilous labor, have left the wearisome task undone. Or has our friend fallen the victim of infectious or epidemic illness? Had he been aware of his peculiar peril, he would have passed beyond the infected region. Or would earlier medical treatment have arrested the disorder? Could its severity have been foreknown, those earlier measures would not have been deemed superfluous. Or has our friend perished by what we most irreligiously term accident? Had the fatal conjuncture of circumstances only cast its shadow before, he would have taken warning and escaped. Did we see early enough the train of second causes which issues in death, hardly any but the very aged would die. Nor is it death alone which we should thus avert. Calamities and misfortunes of every class flow immediately from the shortness of human foresight. Did we know of the impending conflagration, its first kindling might be smothered by the hand. Could the ocean storms be calculated, and the shifting currents of the sea be mapped for every voyage, there would be no shipwrecks. Did we foreknow, in almost every case we could provide. In fact, it is chiefly in this short-sightedness that human weakness consists. It is at this very point that the Divine Providence overrules man's counsels, executes those thoughts, and moves in those ways, that are higher than ours. When, therefore, you say, "Had it been thus or so, my husband, my brother, my child, had not died," your complaint in reality concerns, not the circumstances of that one case, but the ordinance of Divine wisdom, by which man is kept in so great a degree ignorant of the future.

Let me next remind you that this principle applies not merely to the calamitous, but equally to the happy, portions of our earthly experience. Recovery, preservation, prosperity, wealth, single instances or occasions of success or high enjoyment, depend equally on contingencies, which, when we look back, we see might have been far otherwise. Two courses are before you, my friend, and the motives for taking them are evenly balanced. You make your choice, and are led on step by step to success or happiness. You retrace the series of causes, and find that the prosperous event flowed from that first choice. You can now also trace the results of the other alternative which you almost chose, and can see that it would have been utterly disastrous. Yet your choice was determined, not by foresight of the end, but seemingly by the most casual circumstances. Thus there is room for the perpetually recurring *if* in our joys which we cannot number, no less than in our sorrows which we can count. The doubt which rests on our decisions is big with more hope than fear, brings in its train more gladness than grief.

Now, with reference to afflictive events, the great mistake to which we are prone consists in imagining that it was in our power to foreknow all that events in their progress make known to us. The child of a watchful and experienced mother is taken away by acute disease. The attack was sudden; yet the seeds of the disorder must have been lurking in the system for days or weeks previously, and there were preventive measures by which the danger might have been warded off. The mother's memory, sharpened by her grief, can now recall symptoms that might have indicated disease, — a drooping of the eyelids, or a flush of the cheek, or an unusual drowsiness, wakefulness, or peevishness; and, in remembrance of these unheeded indications, her sorrow is drugged with intense bitterness, as she reproaches herself that she had not taken alarm at the tokens of incipient illness, and administered such remedies as might then have proved effectual. I would say to that mother, — "These symptoms, my friend, needed the event to interpret them. They have occured thousands of times when they denoted nothing fatal. They were such that even science and skill could have drawn no certain conclusions from them. They were so slight and indefinite, that they would not have justified fear, or warranted your resort to special means of relief. Providence did not see fit to reveal to you your child's peril, till death was at the door; and you have no more ground for painful reflection and self-reproach, than if the child had been slain by a thunderbolt from a cloudless sky." In unnumbered instances, the event reveals to us facts that existed long prior to the event, but which in the nature of things it was impossible for us to know; and, where knowledge could not be, there can have been no responsibility. No matter what light we subsequently gain as to the past, — while Providence withheld that light, there was nothing for us to do, and there can be no ground on which we should cast censure upon ourselves.

These remarks indicate the point on which we chiefly need to practise Christian submission, namely, as to the necessary limits of human foresight. We need to be resigned to our ignorance of coming events, and to our consequent inability to avert them. This ignorance is a part of the Divine plan; and we can hardly conceive how essentially it ministers to our happiness. A single calamitous event occurs, my friend, to you or your household, and you half murmur that you could not have discerned its approach in season to prevent it. Suppose that you were endowed with keen foresight as to all the possibilities and remoter causes of disease and calamity for yourself and your family, — think you that there would be a moment when some such possibility would not be present? Would not incessant, anxious watchfulness paralyze your power of enjoyment, fill the day with weariness, and drive sleep from your pillow by night? Such knowledge would make you a sort of secondary providence in your own circle, and would impose upon you a weight of care and supervision such as no being less than the Omnipotent could sustain. Could you lead such a life for a single day, you would pray to drop it before nightfall. Except as God keeps us, we are in incessant peril. We all constantly pass through hidden danger, and the death-angel daily brushes our skirts. We never lie down to our rest, or leave our beds, without owing our life for another day or night, humanly speaking, to a multitude of contingent events, which might all have happened otherwise, and which Providence has adjusted for us, but each of which in prospect would have given us the most intense anxiety. We should suffer more in a single day from a clear view of all that we and our friends are liable to encounter, than from all the bereavements and sorrows that the most afflicted of us have been called to bear. Blessed be God that we know not what a day may bring forth! When he mingles for us the cup of grief, it overflows with consolation and with hope. Could we snatch it from his hand before he has prepared it for us, we should drink only a potion of dread and agony.

In fine, we may sum up the condition of our mortal life in this wise. There are two systems at work together in human affairs. The one is that of man's duty; the other, that of God's Providence. There is a world of practical wisdom in the adage so old and trite, — "Duty is ours, events are God's." In the hour of bereavement, the question as to our fidelity to duty in the relation now suspended will come up, and ought to come up. Have I been faithful to the temporal, the spiritual interests of the friend taken from me? Have I been unselfish, even-tempered, frank, sincere, munificent to the full measure of his rights and my ability? Have I habitually acted towards him as my certain knowledge or my best judgment dictated? With regard to the apparent causes of his removal, have I been innocent of wanton carelessness, so that I have neither done nor sanctioned what was in itself injudicious or inconsiderate, — what would have been so, even if no untoward consequences had flowed from it? When you can answer these questions to your satisfaction, you have no ground for uneasiness. You did what you could. You had not Divine foresight. Much which you know now was indeed hidden from you; and, had you known it earlier, you would have done differently. But God meant that you should not know it. He had higher purposes of his own to serve by your ignorance.

Had he seen fit to spare your friend, he would have indicated the danger in season for you to ward it off, or the certain remedy in season for you to apply it. Do not, then, harass and torment yourself, because you were not in God's stead, — because you were a short-sighted mortal as to events so nearly affecting your peace and happiness.

Such is the system of human duty. Do your duty; and in the vast majority of instances it will lead to the outward results that you desire. Obey the laws of your physical nature, and.health will be the rule, disease the exception. Use wise precautions in seasons of peculiar peril; and the shaft that smites down the unwary will, in most cases, fall harmless at your feet. Be assiduous, watchful, and judicious in the care of your children; and, in most of your households, death will be infrequent. Above all, do your duty to yourselves, to one another, to your children, as immortals, fellow-pilgrims on earth, fellow-candidates for heaven; and, however numerous may be the partings by the way, they will be relieved by the hope of immortality, and you shall all meet again where you will never say farewell.

But with all your care, watchfulness, and fidelity, there is yet another system, that of Divine Providence, which has no law but the eternal love of God. His decree has gone forth, "In the world ye shall have tribulation." For wise reasons, which are in part revealed to us now, and which we may fully know hereafter, he sees fit to discipline us by disease, calamity, and bereavement. We need this discipline as sinners, to bring us to repentance. We need it as aspirants for goodness, to make our aims more steadfast, our desires purer, our faith stronger, our trust firmer. We need it as pilgrims here and citizens of a better country, to detach us from the attractions by the way-side, and to fix our thoughts and affections on things above. When God sees that we need this discipline, vain is our care and skill, vain our anxious thoughts, our wisest precautions. Disease at his bidding will seize the most robust frame, and elude the most wakeful prudence. Calamity will thwart our best-laid plans, and disappoint our best-founded hopes. Death will enter the fold the most carefully fenced, will take the child the most vigilantly guarded, the youth whose life and health are the parent's chief solicitude, the maiden on whom no rough blast from without has ever breathed. In these mysterious events, the experience of every year and month proves over and over again that "the race is not to the swift, nor the battle to the strong; neither yet bread to the wise, nor yet riches to men of understanding, nor yet favor to men of skill." All that remains for us is to bow in trustful submission, and to say, "It is the Lord, — let him do what seemeth to him good." These afflictions are in no sense of our own procuring, nor should they be rendered one whit more sad by the momentary thought that we could have prevented them. They are a burden beyond our strength ; and we should give heed to the exhortation, "Cast thy burden upon the Lord."

Among the most mysterious and appalling events that occur under the Divine government is the death of those who are called away in opening life, and with endowments of mind and character which give the best promise of usefulness and happiness in this world.* Yet how essential it is that the young should sometimes die! Were any age or condition exempt from the frequent visitings of death, it would be divorced to a lamentable degree from the sense of accountability, and would be made almost accursed because the powers of the world to come no longer rested upon it. Unutterably sad is the death, the burial-scene, of the young wife and mother. But by means of the one that dies, may not a multitude of the living be kept near heaven while surrounded with earthly joy and hope, led to "use the world as not abusing it," and to make duty the supreme end of life? Yes. The shadow of death sanctifies hundreds of young homes which the death-angel may not enter for

* This and the following paragraph were written with reference to individual instances of death then recent.

many years, shields the guardians of their peace and purity from youthful giddiness and frivolity, and sustains them in patient, cheerful duty by the consciousness that, in an hour when they think not, the Son of Man may come. And who need the admonishing voice from early graves, as do the young men of this busy, distracting, tempted generation? They are hard by the quicksands on which thousands make shipwreck. For them the pestilence walks in darkness. Among them destruction wastes at noonday. Appetite allures them. If they escape it, gain holds out its gilded bait. Evil examples beset them. Sin, its deformity covered up by its stolen mask of joy, encounters them at every street's turn. Gates of spiritual death open at almost every step of their way. Gulfs of perdition yawn for them beneath almost every footfall. Well is it for them that the grave should sometimes open near them, eternity utter its voices, and the cry come from the death-bed of those as young and as sanguine as themselves, "Prepare to meet your God.—Know ye that for all these things God will bring you into judgment."

With this most essential ministry to the living, there are many aspects in which the death of the young may seem a peculiarly merciful appointment. How often do we witness the early removal of those, whose tender sensibilities would have made the necessary exposures and conflicts of life intensely severe! God calls into the fold those who could not have borne the bleak winds of the mountain pasture. They are taken from certain sorrow which they may have been ill fitted to sustain, — from cares and responsibilities from which they would have shrunk in unconquerable timidity, — from a world which always has its crown of thorns for the gentle, retiring, sensitive spirit. When we see how easy the death-struggle is often made for those early summoned hence, how cheerfully and hopefully they sink to rest, how readily they resign the cup of earthly joy for the well-spring in the heavenly garden, we cannot but feel that there is Divine benignity in the mandate that calls them home.

SERMON XXIII.

HEAVEN.

IT DOTH NOT YET APPEAR WHAT WE SHALL BE: BUT WE KNOW THAT, WHEN HE SHALL APPEAR, WE SHALL BE LIKE HIM; FOR WE SHALL SEE HIM AS HE IS. AND EVERY MAN THAT HATH THIS HOPE IN HIM PURIFIETH HIMSELF, EVEN AS HE IS PURE. — 1 John iii. 2, 3.

COMPARATIVELY little is made known to us through the Scriptures concerning the life of heaven; and that little is given us chiefly by material imagery, — by symbols which we know not how to interpret. It is often asked, If the great object of the Gospel be to fit us for heaven, why is not a fuller revelation of its joys made to us? Why are we not enlightened as to the mode and laws of its being? Why have we not a map of the celestial city, so that we may survey beforehand the mansions in the Father's house made ready for us? It is my present design to answer this question, and to show the consistency of the kind and degree of knowledge vouchsafed to us on this subject with the Divine wisdom and love.

In the first place, were the future life fully laid

open to us, its brightness would throw the present state into utter eclipse, and make our earthly pilgrimage irksome and grievous. It is God's will that we should be happy here, that we should love life, husband it, prolong it, and yield it up only at the manifest demand of higher duty; and the dimness that rests on the future makes the best men willing to stay here, though sure of happiness hereafter. But were heaven within their clear view, their longing to depart would paralyze their power of active service here, render them impatient for the final change, and turn this fair world into a prison-house. Now there is enough revealed to feed desire, and to make the faithful soul willing to obey the summons hence; while, in the idea of a change, and in the uncertainty of its degree and circumstances, the Christian is contented to await his time, and to remain on a post of duty where he can see and know what makes him happy. The natural shrinking from an unknown condition of being sustains an interest in the present life in the hearts of those best fitted to die, while, when that unknown state is at hand, their confidence in the Divine mercy enables them to enter upon it without doubt or fear.

Again, the representations of heaven in the Bible are such as to adapt the inspired record to the needs of all classes of minds. *We* doubt not that the life of heaven is spiritual. We expect there pleasures, not of sense, but of soul. But the Gospel was first preached, and is still preached every year, to multitudes who occupy the lowest plane of intelligence and culture. It goes to them in their coarseness and degradation; and in that state how could they take in a picture of spiritual joy? With their undeveloped moral natures, how could they feel alarm at the opposite representations of spiritual suffering and agony? But they can appreciate the material imagery, — on the one hand, the golden streets, the never-setting sun, the freedom from pain, sickness, and sorrow, — on the other, the darkness, the undying worm, the unquenched fire. By these symbols their fears and hopes are aroused. They are led to make experiment of the teachings of Jesus. They learn his lessons of love and duty. They are born into the spiritual life. Then, with their heart-experience of sorrow for sin, and of peace and joy in believing, they gradually enter into the meaning of these symbols, and identify heaven with the purest thoughts and best affections that they can cherish. Their conceptions of heaven grow with their characters. While they could appreciate only outward joy, heaven was to them merely a glorious place. As they increase in spirituality, it becomes less a place and more a state. It represents to them at every stage the highest point that they have reached, the utmost of blessedness that they can apprehend.

To pass to another topic, I would ask, Would not any detailed description of the life to come raise more questions than it answered, — excite more curiosity than it gratified? For a full description of life in this world, what countless volumes must be written to portray the various professions, tastes, habits, and enjoyments of different ages, classes, and nations! And can the life of heaven be less rich in its resources, less various in its pursuits and its joys? I love to think of it as infinitely diversified, as, though the same, yet different to every soul. I believe that every direction which the mind can take, every bent which the character can assume under the guidance of religion, reaches out into eternity. There are here many devout inquirers into the springs of nature and the mysteries of science. Will not the broad universe be open to their survey, so that they may track the footprints of creative wisdom from world to world, and from system to system? There are those who linger with pious reverence on the records of Providence in long past ages and vanished generations. May not the archives of a past eternity be spread for their research, and feed their adoration and love? There have been prophets to whom the distant future was made present; there are still prophetic spirits that reverently lift the veil to contemplate developments of the Divine glory in ages to come. In heaven may they not be prophets still, watching the dawn, and to less far-sighted spirits heralding the progress of new dispensations of almighty love? There are those in whom the imaginative element predominates in the religious life, — poets by the gift of God, — capable of tracing the more recondite beauties and harmonies of creation, and of combining its scattered rays of benignity and glory. May not a creative fancy in heaven, as here, be the faculty through which they will apprehend the Divine perfections, pour their own thank-offerings, and lead troops of kindred spirits in the chorus of praise? There are still others, whose piety takes the direction of active, energetic philanthropy, — men whom the love of souls inspires for the most arduous services and sacrifices. May not they be training themselves for swift angelic ministries to the suffering and the sinning? May it not be their mission to repeat the message of the Redeemer's birth-song till the last wanderer is gathered into the fold, and there is glory to God, and peace, and good-will throughout the earth and universe? There are, again, saintly men, addicted to a quiet, contemplative devotion, who, while they cannot utter the awakening word, or speed the winged arrow of truth, bless their race by the example of a heavenly spirit, holy, harmless, undefiled, and faithful. Will not heaven give them the repose they love, — the rest of pious confidence, and calm, blissful adoration?

Thus may heaven provide for the cultivation of every pure taste and worthy pursuit, for the unrestricted exercise of every class of spiritual endowments. If this be the case, how could the whole be written out in a volume designed for the instruction of the ignorant, the solace of humble toil, the wayfarer's companion, the manual of childhood, the staff of the aged, and the hope of the dying? Or, had some portions of this blessed life been revealed, and some threads of our earthly existence shown us as they are woven into the web of eternity, it could only have awakened doubt and despondency in those minds on whose favorite departments of thought and duty no light from heaven was shed. The silence of the record would have seemed to put a ban upon tastes which they could not help cherishing, and pursuits which they could not help loving.

But while for these reasons a specific revelation with regard to the heavenly life was not to be expected, does not the very idea of immortality include the answers to many of the questions which we might ask the most anxiously? We are too little familiar with the import of the seeming truism, that it is we ourselves that are to be immortal. Heaven is too much thought of as an arbitrary conferment, by which we become at once entirely different beings, only an angel in place of every soul redeemed from among men, like the troop of blessed spirits that came, one for every corpse on shipboard, in Coleridge's "Ancient Mariner." It is this idea that underlies the doctrine of immediate heavenly happiness for the abandoned sinner, who certainly, in his own person, is not a possible subject for such happiness, and all that Omnipotence could do would be to annihilate him, and create a pure spirit in his stead. The same idea appears in all our scepticism as to the continuance in heaven of anything worthy of heaven that we have loved and enjoyed in this world. If we are the same beings there as here, we must carry with us the tastes, affections, and habits of thinking and feeling, with which we depart this life, and those of them which can find scope for exercise and space for growth in heaven must unfold and ripen there. Thus is it asked, Will friends know and love each other there? I find in Scripture many hints toward an affirmative answer; but, were it not so, I should need an express revelation in order to make me believe or imagine the negative. These earthly affections are not only an essential part of our nature, but are indissolubly interwoven with our religious characters. Every element of faith and piety, every act of prayer and praise, is associated with the parents, teachers, and exemplars, who have helped to form our characters, — with those who have joined us in worship, sustained us in our conflicts, consoled us in our sorrows, united with us in the commemoration of redeeming love. To tear them from our hearts would be to lacerate every fibre of the spiritual life. These affections grow, too, with our growth in piety. I feel assured, therefore, that the change which brings us into more intimate union with our God and our Saviour must also render our social affections purer and more fervent. In like manner, I would say of every trait of mind and heart, which can grow with the growth of character, which at once ministers to the religious sentiment and is cherished by it, that it must needs be indestructible. The perpetuity of whatever can live and find appropriate nourishment in heaven is involved in the doctrine of immortality, and, so far from needing express revelation to prove it, I should demand for its disproof the clearest Scriptural testimony.

In addition to what has been said, I would suggest, that much may have been left unrevealed with regard to heaven, in order to furnish room for the highest exercise of the imagination. Imagination is not among the faculties which religion aims to suppress; but under the auspices of faith, it only assumes a broader range, and wings a loftier flight. Yet its realm is always that of the dimly seen and partially known. It shuns the region of definite outline and circumstantial detail. Were heaven all revealed, heaven would proffer no room for its creations, and it would remain, in the devout as in the irreligious, an earth-bounded faculty, tempting the soul to grovel below, instead of bearing it aloft. It seems to me that the Scriptural representations of the life to come are precisely adapted to make fancy the handmaid of devotion. Enough is revealed to give fixedness and certainty to the idea of heaven. We have the great outlines of its life, the staple of its duties and its joys. But the sacred writers hardly begin to fill in these outlines. Their specifications are few and meagre. They tell us of the sea of glass, the great white throne, the marriage-supper of the Lamb, the white robes, the golden harps, — imagery that brings over the soul multitudinous and transporting thoughts of splendor, glory, joy, purity, and praise. But who can map with literal exactness the blissful scene to which these symbols point? or to what two independent minds can they suggest the same combination of the elements of joy? We are supplied, as it were, with the unshaped materials, with which fancy may rear and furnish its own heavenly mansion. We are to take the pencil into our own hands, and to create the future of our hope from the colors which inspiration has thrown in resplendent masses upon the palette. "It doth not yet appear what we shall be"; but no pure and lofty imagining need droop in doubt, nor need we fear to let the future grow more and more definite under successive touches; for, however bold the reach of fancy, we are assured that God has reserved for us more and better than it has entered into the heart of man to conceive. Here, then, we have a boundless field for contemplations, through which our faith may be kept constantly on the increase; for none believe in heaven so firmly as those whose imaginations are the most aspiring, within the outlines, yet beyond the details, of positive revelation. Burning curiosity with regard to the future, the longing to know more and to feel more of its unrevealed realities, detaches the soul from earthly vanities, shields it against temptation, sheds over it in its conflicts and its trials more and more of the atmosphere of heaven. And when a dear friend is passing or has passed behind the veil, what a solemn interest attaches itself to the thought of his personal experience of what we still behold so faintly! How near we come to heaven, as we strive to lift the veil, as we imagine his welcome to the society of the blessed, his glad amazement at the disclosures of eternity, his strains of adoration, his shining path of duty, his beatific vision of the Redeemer, his all-pervading consciousness of the Divine presence, the merging of his dying prayer in praise, of his parting sigh in joy unutterable and eternal! I have been deeply impressed with the beauty and power of these contemplations of heaven in reading the Life and Letters of John Foster, the English essayist, one of the most saintly men that ever lived, the records of whose years of decline and infirmity make me feel as if he stood already on the delectable mountains, saw across the river of death the gates of the celestial city, and heard the "harpers harping with their harps." I must indulge myself in quoting from one of his letters to a friend of nearly half a century's standing, then at the point of death in a distant city.

"To me a little stage farther remains under the darkness; you, my dear friend, have a clear sight almost to the concluding point. And while I feel the deepest pensiveness in beholding where you stand, with but a step between you and death, I cannot but emphatically congratulate you. . . . . .

"But, O my dear friend, whither is it that you are going? Where is it that you will be a few short weeks or days hence? I have affecting cause to think and to wonder concerning that unseen world; to desire, were it permitted to mortals, one glimpse of that mysterious economy, to ask innumerable questions to which there is no answer, — what is the manner of existence, — of employment, — of society, — of remembrance, — of anticipation, — of all the surrounding revelations to our departed friends? How striking to think that *she*,* so long and

---

* Referring to his wife recently deceased.

so recently with me here, so beloved, but now so totally withdrawn and absent, — that she experimentally knows all that I am in vain inquiring!

"And a little while hence, you, my friend, will be an object of the same solemn meditations and wondering inquiries. It is most striking to consider, — to realize the idea, — that *you*, to whom I am writing these lines, who continue yet among mortals, who are on this side of the awful and mysterious veil, — that you will be in the midst of these grand realities, beholding the marvellous manifestations, amazed and transported at your new and happy condition of existence, while your friends are feeling the pensiveness of your absolute and final absence, and thinking how, but just now, as it were, you were with them.

"But we must ourselves follow you to see what it is that the emancipated spirits who have obtained their triumph over death and evil through the blood of the Lamb, find awaiting them in that nobler and happier realm of the great Master's empire. . . . . .

"It is a delightful thing to be assured, on the authority of revelation, of the perfect consciousness, the intensely awakened faculties, and all the capacities and causes of felicity in that mysterious, separate state; and on the same evidence, together with every other rational probability, to be confident of the reunion of those who have loved one another and their Lord on earth......

"I know that I shall partake of your kindest wishes and remembrance in your prayers, — the few more prayers you have yet to offer before you go. *When* I may follow you, and, I earnestly hope, to rejoin you in a far better world, must be left to a decision that cannot at the most be very remote; for yesterday completed my sixty-third year......

"But you, my friend, have accomplished your business, — your Lord's business on earth. Go, then, willing and delighted at his call.

"Here I conclude, with an affecting and solemn consciousness that I am speaking to you for the last time in this world. Adieu! then, my ever dear and faithful friend. Adieu — for a while! May I meet you erelong where we shall never more say farewell!"

In view of such a parting, we might well ask, What more can we need? Could the clearest vision of heaven inspire a more elastic faith, a more sublime confidence? Nay, does not the very dimness that rests upon the future world impart added grandeur to the spectacle of these two old men interchanging their greetings on its confines, with entire certainty that they will soon be renewed in the house not made with hands?

There may be yet another reason why we have so little detailed information with regard to heaven. There is no doubt much which we could not know, — for which human speech furnishes no words. Language is the daughter of experience. It speaks of what we know, testifies of what we have seen, and can convey to us nothing, the elements of which have not in some form entered into our experience. It can give the blind no idea of colors, or the deaf of sounds. Now there can be no doubt that in the future life our mode of being, of perception, of recognition, of communication, will be essentially different from what it is here, and perhaps so different that nothing within our earthly experience could furnish terms for its description. St. Paul's phrase with reference to it, "a spiritual body," is still uninterpreted, and involves a mystery, which "the great teacher, Death," alone can solve. All that we can say is, that it may denote some freer, more ethereal embodiment of the soul, — some mode of existence midway between that of Him, who is emphatically a Spirit, and our present gross material forms; but of such a state of being we can have no conception prior to experience. St. Paul says that in his vision of heaven he "heard unspeakable words, which it is not lawful [or rather, is not possible] for a man to utter," undoubtedly referring, not to any express prohibition, but to the essential poverty and inadequacy of language, which forbade the disclosure.

27

But, with all our ignorance, we have full assurance on one point, and that the most essential to our present improvement and happiness. "When God shall appear," shall draw near the soul in death and judgment, "we shall be like him." And if like him, like Jesus, his express image, whose heart is all laid open to us, whose traits of spiritual beauty and excellence are within our clear view. To be like Christ, — need we know, could we ask more? Were we fully like him now, it would be heaven here, — heaven under burdens, trials, crosses numberless, — heaven, though the world around us were filled with violence. This one idea outweighs all the material imagery, which St. John has heaped up like a mountain of gold and precious stones on which we may climb to get a glimpse of heaven. It did so in his view; for the form of the Redeemer is foremost in every scene of his vision. He is the light of the golden city, the object of homage to the adoring host. They sing his song on the sea of glass. It is he who leads them by living fountains of waters, and they "follow the Lamb whithersoever he goeth."

Our text gives us yet another trait of the life of heaven. "We shall see God as he is," — shall see him as Jesus ever saw him, — shall enter into the depth of significance that lay in his heart when he said, "My Father." Here we behold God chiefly through outward forms of his creation and agents of his Providence; and, though in our seasons of highest devotion clearer and fuller views of his character dawn upon our souls, we find it hard to retain or recall them. There, through what mode of manifestation we know not, but undoubtedly through the more intimate connection which unembodied spirits may have with the Infinite Spirit, we shall be brought into a communion with him, corresponding in its clearness and continuity to our face-to-face converse with one another.

Our text adds, — "Every man that hath this hope in him purifieth himself, even as God is pure." The heaven of the New Testament demands prepared and congenial spirits. What element of happiness does it offer to the impure, the resentful, the worldly, the sensual, the frivolous? What has it that can attract the heart which loves not God, and seeks not to be like him? Every thought of heaven impresses upon us the need of a closer walk with God on earth. If there we are to be like him, we must have grown like him here. If there we are to see him as he is, we must have already drawn nigh to him in prayer and praise, and lived near him in daily obedience and devotion. Then may we greet death in tones of solemn welcome, and say, "Thou comest not to destroy, but to crown my hopes. Thy dark wing shall waft my spirit to Him whom not having seen I love, and in whose nearer presence is joy unspeakable and full of glory."

SERMON XXIV.

THE HEAVENLY VINE-DRESSER.

EVERY BRANCH THAT BEARETH FRUIT HE PURGETH [i. e. PRUNETH] IT, THAT IT MAY BRING FORTH MORE FRUIT.— John xv. 2.

JESUS and his Apostles were walking at midnight on the vine-embowered path that led to the Mount of Olives. The full moon shone on rich clusters of grapes loading every tendril, and already far advanced toward maturity. What a contrast between the verdure and fruitfulness that overhung their steps, and the vanished, withered hopes that made the hearts of the disciples sad and desolate! Not thus, however, had the vines on the hill and by the road-side looked a few weeks before. Under the vine-dresser's hand, in the very infancy of that year's life, they had sustained seemingly rude and merciless mutilation. The lower shoots had been lopped off; the luxuriance of the last year's growth had been pruned; and amputated stocks, bald, bare branches, had projected their unsightly outlines against the rocks and the sky. Had the pruning been less thorough, the clusters would not have hung so thick or so rich; and the neglected vines, yielding grapes worthy neither of the table nor the vintage, would have been fit only to be trampled under foot or cast into the fire. The sap, that would have flowed to waste through the lower tendrils, had sought the topmost branches. The vital energy, that would have been exhausted in useless foliage, had elaborated the bud, the blossom, and the grape. "Thus," says our Saviour in the beautiful parable which gives us our text, "thus will it be with you, as the heavenly vine-dresser applies the pruning-knife of bereavement and desolation to your fearful and anxious spirits. You have clung to my earthly presence. You dread desertion, contempt, and persecution. You cannot brook the thought of what awaits you on the morrow. But did I remain at your side to anticipate your wants, to meet danger in your stead, and to confine to my local and material presence the thoughts, affections, and aspirations that ought to mount heavenward, the Comforter would not come, your higher natures would lack their full development, your lives would bear little of the fruit which I have chosen and ordained you that ye should bear. But if I go home to the Father, and leave you to a straitened and afflicted lot upon earth, the tendrils of your nature that cling to earthly supports being lopped away, your souls, like the noble vine, will send out their shoots heavenward, laden with the ripening fruits of trust, love, and self-denying virtue. The knife indeed cuts to the quick; but it is in the hand of my Father and your Father, who, because the vine has begun to bear fruit, prunes it that it may bring forth more fruit."

It seems to me, my friends, that there is no text in the Bible richer in beautiful significance, in comfort and encouragement, than that which I have chosen this morning. It presents one of those perfect analogies between the outward and the spiritual universe, which could have been drawn only by him whose prerogative it was to "take the things of God and show them unto men," but which, when suggested, we can all appreciate and feel. My text has of late been brought forcibly to my mind by conversations with some of you, with whom I could see that it had been verified in the quickening impulses given to pious feeling and holy resolution by severe domestic bereavement. Yet it has its significance and fulfilment not only at distinctly marked epochs of sorrow, but equally in the common experience of life, as we pass from youth to manhood or womanhood, and thence to the meridian or the decline of our earthly pilgrimage.

1. The principle of our text is verified in the gradual contraction of our earthly horizon as we

advance in life. The youth sees the whole world before him. The fruit of all the trees in the garden hangs in his sight, and he seems to hear the voice, "Of every tree thou mayest eat." His whole future is dim indeed, but hopeful. He forms large plans, cherishes large desires. His purposes, his efforts, reach out in a thousand different directions. Pleasure, business, honor, prosperity, domestic joy, social advantages, all seem within his grasp. With vast longings, and with the direction of his life still undetermined, his spiritual industry, however sincere, is liable to be dissipated; and, did this condition last long, his character would remain unformed, his principles feeble, his moral attainments low and unsatisfying. But, even without the consciousness of disappointment on his part, Providence early applies the pruning-knife. He is confined within some single walk of industry, — has one established home, sphere of duty, circle of friends, and round of enjoyments. His place in the social scale, the modicum of success and honor within his reach, is determined. Bounds, over which he cannot pass, are set to his earthly life. Yet within those bounds his desires and active powers are not only strong as ever, but have supplanted the spasmodic, impulsive energy of youth by a maturer and more sustained vigor. And has he the principle of duty, the love of God, in his heart? Then must the life, limited in every earthward direction, mount heavenward. The stream pent up must rise toward its source. The desires must gravitate toward objects that promise them satisfaction; and, if they have begun to seek God and heaven, the epoch when they are made to feel the finiteness and insufficiency of all lower good must be the time when they seize on the divine and infinite, with a grasp too tenacious ever to be relaxed. The active powers crave an unlimited field for their activity; and, if they have learned to labor for the soul's well-being, then the experience of their earthly limitation must direct their whole energy to the sphere where they can never be cramped or baffled.

In point of fact, it is precisely at this period of life that we often witness the most rapid growth of character, — its growth in evil no less than in good. The dispositions and traits of character, which one manifests at his very entrance upon the cares and duties of active business or of domestic life, soon and fast acquire a fixedness and depth which render essential change exceedingly improbable. And where a right direction has been taken in childhood or youth, it is amazing with what sudden maturity we often see a young man or woman clothed, so that the person, who out of the immediate home circle had seemed a mere cipher, becomes at once, on assuming an independent position in life, a centre of beneficent influence, a burning and shining light, an ornament to society, a pillar in the Church of Christ. All this takes place, indeed, not without vigorous and devout self-discipline, yet through the instrumentality of that Providence which pruned the already fruitful branch that it might bring forth more fruit.

2. Our text is equally verified in connection with the inevitable disappointments of maturer years. I refer not now to such disappointments as attract the notice and sympathy of others, and go by the name of trials and sorrows, but to a much larger class, concealed from general observation, and even from the most friendly eye. Of the buds on the tree of life, many more drop than blossom. But few of our expectations are realized, and those few but partially; or, if they keep their promise to the sense, they break it to the heart, and success or joy in fruition falls far short of what it had seemed in prospect. Even after the day-dreams of youth have ceased, we almost all set for ourselves a much higher mark than we reach. We aim at wealth, and secure a bare competence. We look for eminence, and rise not above mediocrity. We lay well-matured plans, and they are defeated we hardly know how. We strive for influence, and find wills that refuse to yield to our argument or persuasion. We depend on co-operation, and our helpers drop away in the hour of need. We look forward to

this or that epoch of felicity, — it comes, but brings as much care as joy. We say to ourselves, "Let me only attain this or that stage of success, and I am content," — we reach it, and find that it has not advanced our happiness one jot, but only created new cravings. In all pursuits that begin and end in this life, it is as if we were drawing water in sieves; and for the brimming cup that we mean to fill, how often do we pour into it only a few scanty drops! And he who has not found access to the water of life keeps on drawing with his sieve at the broken cistern. But have we learned the way to the well-spring, and taken our first draught of its living waters? Then all this experience of earthly disappointment leads our souls to a more constant resort to the source of unfailing joy. We find that we were not made to realize full satisfaction in this world, — that

> "The choicest pleasure earth can give
> Will starve the hungry mind."

And then there reaches us from every earthly scene the invitation, —

> "Come, and the Lord will feed your souls
> With more substantial meat,
> With such as saints in glory love,
> With such as angels eat."

Think not that I speak of this discipline of constant disappointment in the tone of complaint. To my mind there could be no arrangement so merciful for immortal beings, strangers on earth, invited citizens of a better country. Did every thing prosper to our minds, did attainment always answer to expectation, and fruition equal hope, rarely would our thoughts and efforts rise above the passing scene. In the certainty with which we could calculate on earthly joy, we should lose all desire of heavenly blessedness. But now, while God gives us outward blessings enough to make our pilgrimage a happy one, in the perpetual disproportion between what we seek and what we attain, between what we hope and what we enjoy, he is constantly saying to us, "Arise and depart, for this is not your rest." If we have once turned our faces heavenward, heaven gains upon our affections by every hold which our spirits lose upon the passing world. It is through the discipline of daily disappointment that our souls grow in the love of God and the life of duty. The more we feel the uncertainty of all outward dependence and hope, the more does that hidden life which we lead with God, that peace which the world could not give and cannot take away, develop itself in our hearts. Thanks, then, to the heavenly vine-dresser, who daily prunes the lower branches of the vine, that its sap may rise in an ever fuller current to those topmost boughs where the clusters all ripen for heaven.

3. Our text is also verified painfully, yet joyfully, in connection with those severe bereavements, which are the lot of all, and which, grievous

as we find them, are no doubt, in God's eye, the Christian's privilege. Probably there are none who cherish so firm a faith in a Providence always kind, as those disciples of Christ who have sustained the heaviest losses in the circle of their kindred and affection. They have felt these losses only the more severely for their religious faith; for it is the office of religion to make love more tender, and to strengthen the bonds of kindred. But every sorrow has opened to them new sources of spiritual strength, has drawn them into closer communion with God, has made thoughts of heaven dearer and more constant, has removed weights from their spirits and clogs from their feet in the way of duty, has enabled them to run with new vigor and perseverance the race that is set before them, and brought them into more intimate converse with Him whom they follow in trial and suffering, that they may partake of his victory and his glory.

But in order that this discipline of sorrow should perform its due office, there must first be a preparation of spirit. Affliction does not, so often as is supposed, lead to the formation of the religious character, though when it is once formed, it never fails, I believe, to minister to its rapid growth. It often gives expression and firmness to principles that were feeble, to resolutions that were faint, to an embryo piety which the cares and joys of unbroken prosperity might have suppressed and withered. It fixes the religious purpose which had previously flickered and wavered. It fastens on God the trust and love which had been partly his, yet much divided and often turned aside. It rebukes and chastens away sins which had checked the spirit of prayer, and precluded the full enjoyment of religious peace. Often, too, can the afflicted bear testimony that the stroke of a bereaving Providence came just when it was most needed,—at that stage of progress when some decisive experience was essential, to fix the choice, to give a permanent direction to the thoughts and affections, to put the seal to the holiest vows and loftiest purposes, to write the sentence of inviolable consecration on the whole coming life.

Yes, to the eyes of the heavenly witnesses that compass our path, these afflictions from the Divine hand seem to fall, not in desolating showers, but to drop as the gentle rain and to distil like the quiet dew on the plants of our Father's planting, reviving that which was ready to perish, and ripening fruits to be garnered in heaven. While we remain on earth, indeed, our sense of loss and loneliness may never suffer us to carry our resignation to the point of thanksgiving for these sorrows. But I cannot doubt that, when in a better world the innocent and holy who have been taken from us shall be again united with us, we shall look back on these afflictive mercies as among the choicest blessings of a benignant Providence, and shall own, with a fuller evidence than we are now conscious of, that the Father of our spirits pruned the already fruitful plants in his vineyard, only that they might bring forth more fruit.

Such, then, is the course of Providence for our growth in duty and in piety. I close by suggesting one obvious inference from the train of thought in which I have led you, namely, the rich advantage, the priceless privilege, of early piety. It is for the culture and sanctification of our immortal natures, that the whole system under which we live is arranged. God's course of discipline with every individual is precisely that which he needs for the development and perfection of his character. The successive stages of our outward experience are the successive schools, lower and higher, in which we are to be trained for heaven. How essential, then, that we should begin with the first of the series, and gain the teachings of each and all! Under what immense disadvantages must we enter on the later stages of the course, if the instruction and discipline of its earlier portions have been slighted and neglected! What an inconceivable loss is that of any part of a probation season, in which God himself deigns to be our teacher! But that he may fill that office towards us, we must give heed in youth to that fundamental commandment, "My son, give me thy heart."

My young friends, give him your hearts. Then shall his daily Providence nourish and strengthen you. Every event shall prove a blessing, every trial a godsend, every cloud shall rain down righteousness upon you. All things shall be yours. Every experience of life shall be an experience of growing peace and joy as followers of Christ. The discipline of disappointment and sorrow lies before you, — will open upon you sooner than you imagine. Will you encounter its woes, and reject its revenue of spiritual blessedness? — drink the full bitterness of the cup and spurn its healing and strengthening admixture? — bear every burden, bow under every sorrow, and yet refuse that divine ministry which can make the burdens blessings, and the sorrow joy? O that you could see how surely and how soon you must pass through scenes, in which without the spirit of piety all will be dark and desolate, but in which you can feel a heavenly presence and find the darkness light around you! Come young, come now, to the service, and fill your hearts with the love of God, and then shall everything be rich and beautiful in its season, and nothing more so than those sad and sorrowful portions of your lot in life, in which God will reveal himself, and angels minister, and heaven be open to you.

SERMON XXV.

THE MEMORY OF GRIEF AND WRONG.

THESE ARE THEY WHICH CAME OUT OF GREAT TRIBULATION. — Revelation vii. 14.

WHETHER a race of finite and imperfect beings could have been trained for any worthy end, or have reached a state of conscious happiness, without the ministry of suffering, we are not competent to say. It may, however, be plausibly maintained, that, as self-consciousness must precede our knowledge of the outward world, and our cognizance of the finite our conception of the infinite, so must we have had some experience of suffering, in order to obtain the idea of happiness as something over and above existence. Whether this be the case or not, it is certain that very many of our happiest experiences, and of our best frames of mind and traits of character, are to be traced, if not to the direct agency, at least to the memory, of grief and wrong. There is no exaggeration in Dickens's story of the Haunted

Man, in which the supernatural agent, who relieved the hero of his remembrance of evil and sorrow, is represented as having robbed him, not only of the joy of life, but of all the genial, tender, sympathetic elements of his character. The beneficent influences flowing from such remembrances will be my subject this morning.

I might remind you, in the first place, that the lowest degradation into which a human being can sink is a state in which there is no retentiveness, nay, hardly a transient consciousness, of painful emotion. Let a child, born in sin, be cast in very infancy upon the bleak world, without shelter, education, or guidance, exposed to the pelting of the elements, spurned and buffeted at every hand's turn, a vagrant in the lanes and along the wharves of a great city, — that child becomes in his very infancy almost invulnerable to every outward influence, and incapable of feeling neglect or injury; but in this process he grows up an absolute brute. Even in the satisfaction of his bodily appetites there is neither discrimination nor enjoyment; and in cold and hunger the limbs and stomach scarcely tell their story to the intellect. He is incapable of attachment and of gratitude. Gentleness cannot tame him, nor can severity awe him. As the frozen limb must be made sensitive to pain, before it is capable of healthy circulation or free motion, the first step towards making him happy will be to unseal the fountain of sorrow. He must weep before he can enjoy. His awakening into moral life will be attended at least with pensiveness, probably with intense suffering; and without this he will live and die like a brute.

Take next the case of one who has fallen into loathsome degradation from a favored and happy early lot. That fall was not without frequent and severe suffering, probably not without full as much wrong received as committed. But the degraded being has lost his sensibility. The fountain of tears is dried up. He now bears physical privation or distress with a dogged resoluteness, — with a depraved stoicism. You cannot arouse such a being to the consciousness of present misery. Rags, hunger, blows, the almshouse, the prison-cell, have become congenial; and the traces of every new hardship or infliction are like those of the arrow in the air. Nor yet can you excite penitence or remorse by any moral representation, however pungent or attractive, of the evil and misery of guilt or the loveliness of virtue. You must go back to the days of innocence, — to the earliest steps in the evil path. You must awaken the remembrance of obsolete wrong and sorrow. You must recall the prodigal's first wretched pilgrimage from the father's house. You must arouse in the present self sympathy with the past, the long past self. In this way alone can you call forth the resolution, "I will arise and go to my father." Thus true to nature is our Saviour's parable, when he makes the lost son come to himself, remember his father's house, and derive from this remembrance the germ of penitence, the purpose of return. Thus true to all experience was the prolonged weeping of the outcast sinner at the feet of Jesus; and, had she not sorrowed much, she could not have loved much, or have been much forgiven.

Let us pass now to experiences that lie more within our own sphere of consciousness, and, first, to domestic happiness. We can hardly be aware how much of the joy, how much of the purity and tenderness, of our home relations springs from the very events which we most dread, or from the shadow or apprehension of them. Two young hearts are plighted to each other in the most fervent love, and enter on their united life under the most prosperous auspices and with the highest hopes. Let everything answer to their anticipations, — let their life flow on without grief or fear, — avert from them the cares from which they shrink, the responsibilities which they deprecate, — and their love is either suddenly exhaled, or gradually frittered away. They grow mutually intolerant of their necessary differences of taste, opinion, and feeling. The glaring sunlight in which they live shows them in exaggerated forms each other's defects and foibles. The hot glow of unintermitted prosperity withers those filaments of tender, delicate respect, confidence, forbearance, and attachment which are essential to their permanent union. If they remain without mutual discord or dislike, it is through the negative power of passive good-nature, while the heart-ties are all the while growing weaker, so that their dissolution would be more and more slightly and transiently felt.

But, with their first weighty cares or solicitudes, they are drawn into an intimacy of feeling closer than they had ever imagined before. The anxiety, the suffering, the remembrance of which thrills through their hearts over the cradle of their first-born, while it consecrates the child to their love, renews with double emphasis every obligation of the marriage covenant. The peril, the transient shadow of death, through which the new-born has passed into life, is the most blessed experience to the parents, who thenceforth can cherish a mutual forbearance, sympathy, and helpfulness, to create which the ardor of youthful passion would have been wholly inadequate. Similar is the ministry of every painful domestic epoch. Every watching by the sick-bed, every weary night and anxious day, every anxiety and grief borne together, evokes from the depths of sympathy a still lower deep, and binds the kindred hearts in still closer bonds.

After every such passage in life, each member of the household circle seems more essential to the rest than ever before; and, in this strengthening of mutual dependence and attachment, their joy in each other, though more sober in its manifestations, is constantly becoming more deep, full, and satisfying.

Then, when bereavement comes, it comes with its mission of love. One voice hushed, every other voice grows more tender. One kind ministry suspended, each of the surviving circle becomes more assiduous, considerate, and faithful. The love withdrawn from earth seems not so much lost, as diffused through the hearts of those who yet remain; and though outward sources of joy can never flow so bright and high as before, their joy in one another, their mutual trust and sympathy, are rendered more pure, entire, and fervent. The cup of bereavement is indeed bitter, and the whole heart recoils when it is offered, and even more from its repetition than when it is first mingled for us; nor would we ever lose the fresh and regretful remembrance of those no longer with us. Yet we have felt that these griefs have unsealed hidden fountains of affection in our own hearts, and in those of our near kindred, and enabled us at once to impart and to receive more richly all the kindly commerce of domestic intimacy. Then, too, with the very seasons of our severest apprehension or sorrow there are associated so many thoughts of peace, so many expressions of kindness, so many offices of friendship and affection, that they make green spots for memory to look back upon, and are among the last of our life-experiences of which we would willingly have the remembrance blotted out.

A similar view presents itself with regard to our religious characters. Could those of us, who are endeavoring to live in the fear of God and the love of Christ, trace back the growth of the religious life in our hearts, we should find that, while the germ was there before care or sorrow had taken strong hold upon us, yet in many instances its first decided development and rapid increase were in connection with pain, perplexity, or grief. It was the clouding over of earthly prospects, that opened to us a clear and realizing view of heaven. It was the failure of fond hopes, that sealed our determination to lay up treasures where hope cannot fail. It was the falling away of objects of our most confident dependence, that cast us upon the Most High as our only enduring refuge and support. It was keen disappointment in things outward, that turned our earnest and anxious thought to those inward resources, to that spiritual life, which wells up from an inexhaustible fountain in the heart at one with God and Christ. Were we to lose the more pensive or sorrowful chapters of the past, we must tear up by the roots and cast away with them the very portions of our natures and characters that fill the present with peace and the future with hope.

I have spoken of the sheltered scenes of home, and of the interior life of the soul. In the outward relations of society, we are equally indebted to the ministry of affliction. How many are the pure and virtuous friendships, now sources of unalloyed gladness and improvement, which had their commencement in a common grief, or in a burden of solicitude or sorrow, which one, whom previously we had not known how to prize, hastened to bear with us, or we with him! Of the many bonds of cordial esteem and affection, which cross and recross each other around the same communion-altar or in the same worshipping assembly, between a pastor and his flock, or between fellow-worshippers, how many there are, (and those the most sacred and tender,) that had their origin in trial or in grief! How many of the most devoted offices of Christian kindness, which give a glow and charm to prosperity, first began to be extended in adversity! Take away, my friends, from our religious union all that has borne a sad aspect, — our mutual counsel and consolation in doubt or sorrow, our united prayers by the bedside, our last joint offices of piety over the dead, our intercessions for one another in the sanctuary, — there would be little left to unite us, little reason why we should worship and commune together, and we should fall asunder as isolated human units, each to feel out his own solitary way to the grave and to heaven.

In old age we can also trace the genial influence of sorrow. As the cloud, that has flashed its angry lightnings and poured its desolating showers, retreats fringed with gold and crimson, and spanned with the glorious bow of God's unchanging promise, so do the griefs that have been the heaviest and the most cheerless, when they lie in the remote horizon of the past, glow with celestial radiance and divine beauty. As the aged Christian looks back on the conflicts and sorrows of earlier years, every cloud has its rainbow, every retreating storm dies away in whispers of peace. Not in its bitterness and agony does the past come up, but with its thoughts of consolation and promise, its breathings of immortality, its hopes triumphant over death and the grave. There lie in the background conflicts stern and arduous, — they can never be renewed; but the Christian's victory in them was once and for ever. There recur to the memory vanished joys that cannot be restored; but the peace of God that came in and filled the heart when they fled remains there still. Friends, from whom it seemed more than death to part, yet live in dear remembrance; but from their vacant places the soul turns to the goodly company of the beloved and the holy, who are making ready the heavenly welcome. Take away the remembrance of what life has had of sadness, and you would startle the aged disciple from the brink of heaven, drown the hope of immortality, and bring back the thronging interests and joys of former years to run riot in the worn-out heart. It is the softened, painless memory of trial and of grief, that feeds the spirit of patient, cheerful resignation, reconciles the soul to dissolution as it draws near, and sustains the willingness to depart, the desire to be with Christ.

I have spoken chiefly of the sorrows that come to us by the direct appointment of Providence. Are there any of us who can look back on wrong and injury done to us by our fellow-men? Even this, if we were wise, we would not wish to forget. Far more noble is it to remember in full, and yet forgive, — to retain our sensitiveness unimpaired, and yet to take the offending brother to our hearts as if he had done us no wrong. Thus only can we make the wounds of carelessness, unkindness, envy, or malice, permitted, though not wrought by Providence, coincide in their blessed ministry with the griefs that flow from the hand of God. Thus do we turn our enemy into a benefactor, by making him the unconscious instrument of calling out in our hearts traits more elevated, Christlike, Godlike, than without his agency we could have put into exercise. The diadem of universal sovereignty on our Saviour's head would have been a silly bawble. Those who platted the crown of thorns for his brow prepared for him a diadem, which, labelled with the FATHER, FORGIVE THEM, can never fade from the faith and love of humanity.

Finally, the connection in which our text stands leads us to extend the benign ministry of sorrow to the world where sorrow is unknown. You must have been struck, I think, with the constant reference to earthly trial and grief in St. John's representations of heaven. Their redemption from it is the burden of the ascriptions of the ransomed host to their glorified Saviour. Freedom from all the ills, hardships, and sufferings of earth furnishes the most glowing portions of the picture of the New Jerusalem. The frequent trials of the present state, its disappointed hopes, defeated plans, withered joys, may, far along in the heavenly life, supply the term of comparison, reveal the measure of our happiness, quicken the flow of adoring gratitude, and sustain a full consciousness of the felicity in which we are embosomed. The ever-new ardor of enjoyment, the unceasing flow of thankfulness, the idea of deliverance, of redemption, inseparable from the song of praise to God and the Lamb, will no doubt distinguish ransomed men from those of the heavenly host who have never suffered, so that it shall be said of them, not in pity, but in sympathy with their intense gladness, "These are they which came out of great tribulation."

SERMON XXVI.

COMMUNION OF THE DEAD WITH THE LIVING.

I AM THY FELLOW-SERVANT, AND OF THY BRETHREN THE PROPHETS. — Revelation xxii. 9.

So said the angel that showed St. John the tree of life, and talked with him of the joys of heaven. He was an earth-born angel, trained by arduous duty and stern conflict for a holy and exalted ministry in God's nearer presence. It was in a *vision* that the Apostle beheld him; and a *vision* denotes, with emphasis, *seeing;* that is, a clearer, deeper, truer insight than is enjoyed in the usual condition of the faculties. It was not fables or allegories, but realities and truths appertaining to the spiritual world, that were unfolded to the seers of the Old and New Testament in vision. The inward eye was opened. They beheld things of which the external sense cannot take cognizance, and which they could describe only by images and symbols that feebly represented the impressions made upon their own minds. I have chosen this text in order to speak to you of the nearness of heaven to earth, and of our connection and communion with the great spiritual family. I cannot think of heaven as a separate, far-off mansion or city of the redeemed, but as in close connection with the world in which we live. I believe that the members of the heavenly society, even now, sympathize with us, rejoice in our virtue, and minister to our spiritual growth. Let us look at some of the grounds and uses of this belief.

There are many sayings of Jesus, and incidents in his life, which imply the intimate communion of the dead with the living. One of the most striking features of his life is the frequency and nearness of his converse with the spiritual world. He never speaks of angels and just men made perfect, as if there were a weary distance to be crossed from them to us, or from us to them. They are often with him, — at his birth, in his temptation, and in his agony, they come uncalled, — they watch by his sepulchre, and wait on his ascension. The spirits of the long-dead talk with him on the mountain. His voice to the widow's son, his powerful word at the tomb of Lazarus, seem addressed to souls not afar off, but within call, — near the scenes from which they had gone, and among the friends who thought them lost for ever. He promises, also, his own spirit-

29*

ual presence with his followers, when he shall be no longer visible to the outward eye.

Among other touching allusions to the connection between the dead and the living, we cannot but assign a prominent place to that saying of our Saviour, — "Joy shall be in heaven over one sinner that repenteth." In this joy we cannot imagine the higher orders of the spiritual family as partaking, without its being shared by the penitent's kindred and friends in heaven. How intimate is the relation between the two worlds implied in the thought which these words suggest! The faint, lowly sigh of the contrite heart sweeps in glad harmony over the golden lyres, and wakes among the blessed a new song of thanksgiving. The first pulsations of spiritual life in the outcast sinner beat in the souls of the sinless, and every throb of godly sorrow on earth pours new joy through the ranks of the redeemed.

It is said that this near connection of heaven with earth must interfere with the perfect happiness of those in heaven, from their view of the painful discipline appointed to many of their nearest and best friends? I reply, that, whether they behold the trials of their friends or not, they must know, from their own remembered experience, that sorrow awaits all who enter into life. But they no longer dread for others the angel-ministries of adversity, which they now fully recognize for themselves. They behold universal Providence everywhere from seeming evil educing the highest good, and thus can acquiesce with solemn joy in whatever afflictions are appointed for those whom they hope one day to welcome as their companions in glory, even as the Father himself, who loves us all better than we can love each other, dwells in serene and eternal happiness, while he mingles the cup of sorrow and agony for his children.

Is it asked, how heaven can be thus near, and yet unseen? I reply, that the invisible presence of the children of God is no more mysterious than his own. They may be all around us, without our discerning them, because our spiritual vision is not strong and clear enough to behold them,—even as the minute creation, that fills air, earth, and sea, remained for ages unknown, for lack of a proper medium through which to view it. Our Saviour saw the dead and talked with them; for in him the spiritual vision was clear and full. And when his religion shall become supreme and all-pervading, and generations shall come forward, as they will in the latter days, bathed from infancy in the light and love of his Gospel, the free communion with heaven may be opened, the tabernacle of God be with men, and the union of the two worlds form as much a part of the distinct consciousness of every disciple as it did of the Saviour himself.

I prize the belief of the communion of the

dead with the living, on account of the encouragement to religious effort which their sympathy gives us. We all seek sympathy, and to secure it we often become followers of each other more than of Jesus. We walk slower than we need, that we may not part company with our halting fellow-pilgrims. We hang about our persons the same weights, and cherish the same easily besetting sins, as those who run the race at our side. And when, in any way, our consciences prompt us to walk otherwise or move on faster than our fellow-Christians, we cannot help looking back with a painful sense of solitude and desertion. But our friends in heaven are the more intimately associated with us, the farther we are in advance of the inert and sluggish. When we seem to be alone, we can say as did the prophet, when he saw himself environed and guarded by the host of heaven, — "They that be with us are more than they that be with them." Those of our friends who have entered the heavenly rest have endured what we must encounter, and know how severe are the conflicts through which we must struggle into the higher life. They themselves felt the loneliness and desolation which sometimes press so heavily upon our spirits. Their sensibilities are now touched to the finest issues. They are familiar with every mode of inward experience, and can enter into our hearts, where the closest sympathy of the living fails us.

Again, we can hardly entertain the idea of the communion of our departed friends with us, without its prompting the desire for their continued approbation. Can we bear their inspection, and willingly remain unworthy of their esteem? Can we cherish the thought that they are with us, and yet harbor principles and habits from which they would turn with disapproval and loathing? Shall they behold us clinging to the weights which we should lay aside, and hugging the sins which we should crucify? Our friends who have gone from us, perhaps, in the weakness of partial affection, could see no fault in us. Our parents were, it may be, blind to our failings. Our children looked up to us with unmingled reverence, as if we had been the incarnation of every virtue. Our gentle and loving fellow-Christians, while they were with us, threw over our weaknesses the beautiful mantle of their charity, and read our characters through the hazy medium of their own kindness. But the scales have now dropped from their eyes. If they see and know us, it is with a just appreciation of what we are. And have we fallen in their esteem? Do they find us less worthy of their love than they used to think us? Do they look upon us as less their companions and fellow-disciples than when they were here? As we, parents and children, neighbors and friends, hope to find the long lost, but unforgotten, still true and loving, still and for ever ours,

O, let us cut off these sources of alienation and disappointment on their part, — let us not break fellowship with them, by so living in negligence and sin, that they must often avert their eyes from our unprofitable lives to the eternal throne in pitying intercession for us.

The idea of this discourse appeals with peculiar power to those who have never entered upon the spiritual life. Is there here a son who has a mother in heaven? Had God spared your mother, my young friend, would you not have held her happiness sacred, anticipated her desires, and shielded her from disappointment and sorrow? You can even now make her happier. Full as her joy is, it is not perfect while you remain out of the circle of her communion. Your mother's soul still yearns for your salvation. Her intercessions, which first rose over your cradle, now ascend for you near the throne Enter on the life of heaven, and you hang new jewels on her eternal crown of rejoicing. Is there a parent, still living without prayer and without the Christian's hope, who has committed a child to the grave in spotless infancy? How gladly, my friend, would you have guarded your child from peril and from grief, and borne him in the arms of an all-enduring love along the rugged path of life! A work of love yet remains for you in that child's behalf. He prays that he may not be left an orphan spirit, though it be in heaven; and for your first steps in the footmarks of the Lord Jesus, the voice, lost to earth before it could say *My Father* or *My Mother*, will be lifted in glad thanksgiving for you. Brothers and sisters, from whose circle Heaven has chosen the pure and lovely, were you here united by cordial sympathy and deep affection? Their prayer is, that the divided household may again be made one. Are you the bond-slaves of gain, or pleasure, or self-indulgence? The spirits of the departed mark your downward steps, and turn away from the scenes of your levity or your guilt in earnest deprecation of the fatal issue to which they see you hastening. By a renewed heart and life, you can make yet happier those whom God has made happy, and satisfy the only longing of their souls which eternal love has left unfilled.

Finally, what a momentous interest is given to our whole earthly life by the thought that it is passed in the presence and communion of the great spiritual family? To my mind there is hardly a text of Scripture, or form of speech, that rolls on with such a depth and fulness of meaning as those words, — "Seeing that we are compassed about with so great a cloud of witnesses." Vast and bewildering is the philosophical speculation which tells us that we cannot lift a finger without moving the distant spheres. But far more grand and unspeakably solemn is the thought that our daily lives, our conduct in lowly and sheltered scenes, our speech and walk in the retirement of our homes, are felt through the universe of ever-living souls, — that the laws of attraction and repulsion that reach through all orders of being extend to our least words and deeds, — that in every worthy, generous, holy impulse all heaven bears part, — that from the trail of our meanness and selfishness, our waywardness and levity, all heaven recoils. Let the august witnesses, the adoring multitude, in whose presence we dwell and worship, arouse us to growing diligence in duty, and awaken in us increasing fervor of spirit, that we may run with patience the race that is set before us, and, found faithful unto death, may receive the crown of life.

SERMON XXVII.

THE LORD'S SUPPER.

AS OFTEN AS YE EAT THIS BREAD, AND DRINK THIS CUP, YE DO SHOW THE LORD'S DEATH TILL HE COME. — 1 Corinthians xi. 26.

It is an hour of love. The toils of death are spread for the great Teacher. The traitor has commenced his plotting. The great council of the nation have decreed that Jesus shall die. He knows that his hour has come, — that the shepherd is to be smitten, and the sheep scattered. Regardless of his own sufferings, but full of tender solicitude for his disciples, he gathers the faithful few around the paschal table, and there pours forth over them his love, his counsels, and his prayers, in words of the most thrilling pathos, which must have made even the traitor's heart die within him, and which alone will suffice to account for the agony of remorse that seized him, when he found his crime committed past recall. Not for them alone does Jesus pray; but for those who shall believe on him through their word. He looks far down the vista of time, and far-off generations rise before him. He sees the growing ranks of the redeemed from every kindred and people. For all these is he to bear the cross and endure the shame. For these is the crown of thorns to lacerate his brow, and the knotted scourge to tear his flesh. Their sins he bears, their griefs he carries on his interceding breast. Through him is the voice of pardon to reach them, and the peace of God to be shed abroad in their souls. How stupendous an interest hangs around this hour! He has uttered the testament of love, and is going to seal it with his blood. It is "a night much to be remembered unto all generations." "And it will be remembered," we may suppose our Saviour inwardly to have said. "My disciples in every age will look back to this hour, to learn the depth of my humiliation and the fervor of my love. They will revert to these words of mine, when they are smitten of God and afflicted. My voice will vibrate to the end of time, saying to the tried and stricken everywhere, Let not your hearts be troubled,—believe in me,—in my father's house are many mansions. And now am I to be offered up a sacrifice to my own quenchless love. Let those for whom I die love me as I have loved them. Let them know how sore an anguish weighs me down in view of their guilt and woe, and how deep their names are engraven on the palms of my hands and on my heart; and they will, they must, love me."

Full of these emotions, with the simplicity of true and deep feeling, he seeks no far-fetched memorial of the interview, — he institutes no pompous ceremony; but takes the bread and the wine before him, breaks and pours them, gives them to his disciples, and says, — "Thus do ye in remembrance of me. Thus perpetuate this hour of love, renew its memory, ponder on its hallowed communings. When I have ascended on high, and you are treading after me the deep vale of humiliation, or the flinty path of the world's scorn and hatred, thus recall my love and kindle yours. And when you shall preach the word of the kingdom from city to city, and gather here and there a little flock in the name of the despised Nazarene, tell them of this festival of love, let them in memory of me act over the scene, and, as they recall my prayers and counsels, and muse sadly on my broken body and flowing blood, break for them the bread and pour the cup, as I do now. Thus, when the world has grown old, and the time arrives that it should pass away, — when I shall stand at the latter day upon the earth, not, as now, in the weeds of poverty and sorrow, but in the glory of the Father and his holy angels, — shall I find those here who still keep the feast, and show forth their Lord's death till he come."

Such is the request, — such the memorial, — the dying wish of our best friend, — of him who suffered for us then, and intercedes for us and loves us still. Let us now consider the dispositions of mind and heart with which it becomes us to approach the holy table.

1. We should come with deep humility. For who are we who thus meet to commemorate the Saviour? Most or all of us, I trust, persons who have felt something of the power of his death and resurrection. But from what experiences of life have we come hither? From homes and from paths of duty, in which Jesus has been constantly with us? Or rather, in this holy presence, must not confession precede thanksgiving with the most faithful of us? One comes to the altar from an active and busy life, in which the love of gain has often been the overmastering principle, and selfishness has usurped the place of brotherly love. Here is another, in the main a careful and faithful wife and mother, who yet, when troubled about many things, has sometimes forgotten the good part, and let worldly cares shut out God and heaven from her thoughts. Here is one in the flush of youth, who at times has loitered over long, or transgressed the bounds of Christian soberness, in the pursuit of mere gratification, has spurned the yoke of duty when its weight was felt, and cast away the cross when it began to be a burden. Another has left a home, where he

finds it hard to preserve the meek and serene aspect in which the eyes of the world sustain him, where he often lets forbearance give place to wrath, fretfulness cloud his brow, and discontent rankle in his heart. Some come from neglected family altars; some from want and misery which they have known without relieving; some from calls of religious charity to which they have lent no ear; some without an effort, since we last met, to hasten the fulfilment of the prayer which we always offer, — "Thy kingdom come." How cold and languid has the flow of our devotion often been! How much imperfection, how large an admixture of inferior and unworthy motives, mingles with our holiest seasons and our best services! How often does the shadow of self come in between our own spirits, and both our brother whom we have seen, and our Father whom we have not seen! How various, how heavy, how humiliating, the burden, which we, communicants, bear to the footstool of Divine mercy, when we lift our united supplication, and say, — "Father, forgive us, take away our sins, and make us all that thou wouldst have us!"

With all these frailties, we come hither to commune with one who bore part in our temptations and trials, yet knew no sin, — with one for whom no shadow of self ever lay across the path of duty, or between him and the throne of the Most High. We come to measure our spirits with his, — to make his piety and love the standard for ours, — to try the question, whether we are like or unlike him, and, if like him, how nearly resembling him, and in what traits still lacking kindred with him. This self-comparison we ought to make, whenever we come to the table of the Lord. We should admit him as Judge into the recesses of our hearts, and listen with reverence for the sentence that he may pass upon us. Did we bow at the altar in conscious lowliness, — did we, while owning the Saviour's love, behold in truthful hues our own negligence and sin, — did godly sorrow for what we have not attained blend with our thanksgivings over the emblematic bread and cup, — did we, making a mirror of our Lord's countenance, get the just reflection of our own characters, — as many days as these communion seasons lie apart, so many Sabbath-day's journeys on the path to heaven would they mark, and each would be a starting-point for a yet higher aim and a yet more vigorous pursuit of treasures incorruptible and eternal.

2. While we come to the altar with deep self-abasement, let us come also with sentiments of gratitude to Jesus personally, for what he has done and suffered in our behalf. This is not a season for general praise, prayer, and meditation, or for the contemplation of duty, virtue, and piety in the abstract. But one image should be before our minds, — that of a loving, suffering,

interceding Redeemer, considered as standing in the closest personal relation to us, as the medium of God's best gifts, as the friend and benefactor of each of us individually. It was with emphasis that Jesus said, — "*This* do in remembrance of me." In other religious services, while we recognize him as our Mediator, his and our common Father is the direct object of regard. Here, though all is to the glory of God the Father, our vows and thanksgivings should pause and linger on their way to the eternal throne, to retrace the steps and rehearse the love of Jesus, and to dwell with a prolonged and intense regard on the benefits of which he has been made the sole agent and almoner.

I love to go back in fancy to those early communion seasons when the Apostles themselves broke bread from house to house, and when often there might not have been one present who had not talked with Jesus, sat at meat with him, and received special favors directly from his hand. At such a scene there may have frequently met Lazarus of Bethany and the widow's son of Nain, both "recalled upon earth to testify the powers of Heaven," made mortal again to bear witness of immortality. There may the maniac of Gadara and the grateful Samaritan leper have told, each in his turn, what great things the Lord had done for him. There, too, met the self-made maniacs, and the victims of spiritual leprosy, whom the good Shepherd had called back from their mad wanderings and healed of their infirmities. And then, as years passed, what inward gladness and gratitude must have beamed from the countenances of the little children on whom the Lord's hands had been laid in blessing, as they came forward to join the company of his professed disciples! How must the Master's form and face have been all outrayed before the inward eye of each and all! How closely felt must have been his spiritual presence with them! And, as each told his own story of the Saviour's compassion and love for him personally, as they retraced one and another of the scenes when they had been with him on the lake-side or in the desert, and especially when one of the chosen twelve unfolded the dread mystery of sorrow and agony on the night on which he was betrayed, I can almost see the furtive eye turned to the closed door, in expectation of his visible appearance among them, saying, — "Peace be unto you."

But are these communion seasons never to be repeated, and these dear remembrances never to be recalled? Far from it. They were what ours ought to be, — seasons of personal remembrance and gratitude for the great things that the Lord has done for us individually. If we are in our true place at the altar, he has done great things for us, — greater things than those outward miracles for which we imagine such heart-swelling praises to have gone forth. He has done more than to awaken us to a dying life; he has breathed into our souls a life to which there is no death. He has done more than to raise us from the couch of chronic illness; some of us, we trust, he has cleansed from old iniquities, and restored our palsied powers and diseased affections to health and soundness. He has done more for us than to pronounce a blessing on our infant heads; for many of us his blessing rested always on our very cradles, his baptism was on our spirits when they first unfolded, his gentle influences were shed all around our infancy and childhood, and have never for a moment left us, except when by our own perverseness we have shut them out or grieved them away. His image blends, or ought to blend, with every comfort, hope, and joy. There is not a gift of Providence which he does not sanctify for our use, not a sorrow in which his words of peace are not breathed for us, not a cup of consolation or gladness mingled for us by the Father, which he does not help fill.

Now, why did not God rain down righteousness upon us? Why, instead of sending his spiritual favors as he does the dew and the summer shower, did he give them to us through the hands of a Mediator? Was it not that he might make that Mediator a central object of reverence, love, and gratitude, and fix our hearts upon him with the warmest devotion, so that, when we lifted our thanks to the Father of all, we might praise him, not only for his gifts, but even more for that chosen Son and elder Brother through whom he had bestowed them? Let us, then, prepare at the holy table inwardly to recount our Saviour's benefits to us. Ought not each of us to be able to make such grateful acknowledgments as these?—"This virtue I learned of him on the Mount. That sin he rebuked in me, as he taught by the Sea of Galilee. This spiritual grace I have copied from the living law which he held forth. His meekness has made me gentle. His prayer for his murderers has taught me to forgive. I mourn with hope for my pious kindred; for his words at the tomb of Lazarus give me peace. I bow with submission under trial, I take the bitter cup without repining, I murmur not when the cross is laid upon my shoulders; for I have watched with him in Gethsemane, and have trodden with him the path to Calvary. Death has no terror for me; for I have seen his countenance in dying. Eternity is full of hope for me; for it is lighted by rays from his broken sepulchre."

3. Let us, also, approach the holy table, as a place of enlarged communion with the members, no less than with the Head,—with all who bear the name and breathe the spirit of our Master. Not only let there be peace, cordial good-will, and intimate sympathy with those of our own

little flock, but here especially let our hearts go forth beyond our own enclosure, and extend a sincere fellowship to all that love the Lord Jesus, under whatever form or creed they worship. Nor let our communion be with those on earth alone. Heaven and earth lie, with regard to each other, as did the holy place and the holy of holies in the old Jewish temple, close together, and yet a thick veil between them, which veil Jesus came to rend away, and will rend it utterly away in the latter days for all who shall dwell upon the regenerated earth. If the veil is ever parted now, may it not be, ought it not to be, at the festival of him who is Lord both of the living and the dead, — in whom the whole family in heaven and on earth is one? If there is a point of close union between the two worlds, must it not be on heaven's part, should it not be on ours, at this our special meeting-time with him whom the Church above and below unite to reverence? Nay, with regard to some, the veil almost visibly divides. We can almost see with the bodily eye the revered forms, the benignant faces, of those fathers and mothers in Israel, who loved this sanctuary as the very gate of heaven; and with them come back, in lifelike remembrance, many who went behind the veil in the full prime of usefulness and piety, — many, too, who to mortal eye faded as the summer flower, but whom faith beheld passing from the outer courts to the inner sanctuary of their God. Let these communings with heaven be cherished as among the choicest means of lifting us above grovelling cares and petty sorrows, of sustaining us in arduous duty and elevated devotion, and making our daily conversation, where our best treasures and unfading hopes are, in heaven.

4. Finally, we should meet at the holy table, not only as friends of the Redeemer, but as fellow-workers with him, — as those on whom his parting command has rested, and who are pledged to sustain his cause and extend his reign upon earth. The prayer, "Thy kingdom come," should here be offered with peculiar fervor, and with the earnest resolve that it shall come in part through our own instrumentality. We here commemorate the great work of redemption; shall not we bear part in it? We render our thank-offering to him whose name was *Jesus*, — *he shall save;* shall we not labor with him in the saving of souls?

I have sometimes thought, from the apathy of so many professed Christians to the great work of the Saviour and his Church, that the flow of their reflections at the altar must be directly the opposite of all this, — that many a self-complacent communicant, with a sunny smile upon his countenance, and with a really grateful and benevolent cast of feeling, yet with a most unchrist-like narrowness of spirit, may say to himself, as the consecrated elements are distributed,—"How mercifully are we surrounded by bulwarks of salvation and walls of praise! How kindly are we cared for, with the word of truth regularly dispensed, and the feast of love spread in its due season, with no weary length to go that we may worship God, with no sacrifice to make for the truth's sake, with no form or mode of self-denial, in order that we may win Christ and be found in him! All that we have to do is to sit quietly on the favoring tide, and float to heaven." These thoughts may pass, and the communicant may deem them pious thoughts, and may go away imagining that he has had a season of refreshing from the Divine presence; while yet there has not been a single outgoing of spirit for a world lying in ignorance and sin, not a single purpose of effort or of charity in any cause of human progress or redemption, not a shadowy idea that Christ has established a bond of sacred obligation between the well nourished and the hungering and thirsting spirit. Brethren, we have not thus learned Christ. Let us not, then, in heart and in practice receive him thus. By his appointment, every disciple is a missionary of his cross, bound in some way or form, by prayer, by influence, by effort, by the mite or the talent, as God shall endow him, to urge on the cause in which the Saviour died, and for which he ever lives to intercede. Let vows and purposes of faithfulness to the work which he has given his Church to do mingle with the solemnities of our approaching communion season. And may we so eat and drink at his table, discerning the Lord's body, that the bread may nourish us, and the cup strengthen us, for a walk of growing duty, piety, and love.

SERMON XXVIII.

THE SOUL'S SOLITUDE.

I HAVE TRODDEN THE WINE-PRESS ALONE; AND OF THE PEOPLE THERE WAS NONE WITH ME. — Isaiah lxiii. 3.

We are solitary more than we are social beings. More of our life is hidden from one another than is revealed to one another. Much as we can communicate, there is more which we can never disclose. Intimate as the union of spirits often is, they are like trees that interlace their lower branches, while each has its own separate root, and each its own separate coronal of verdure. These bodies keep our souls apart, dwelling in their several tabernacles, and looking at one another and holding restricted converse from behind the curtains of their tents. Especially is this the case with those who are leading spiritual lives and aspiring after spiritual excellence. In speaking thus, I do not undervalue such communion as we have; though, as I shall show you, the most precious part of it is not direct, but through common media of intercourse. Yet, much as we enjoy the fellowship of those like-minded with us, there are chambers of the soul which the keenest mortal vision can never penetrate, — secrets of the heart which can never be revealed or discovered on earth. Are you not all conscious of this? Is there one of you, who feels sure that he thoroughly knows any fellow-mortal, or believes himself to be thoroughly known by any fellow-mortal?

Language, — how utterly inadequate to convey our deepest experiences, our keenest trials, our profoundest consolations, our richest joys! Child of earth and of sense, her ministry is perfect only when outward and earthly objects are the theme, and grows less and less sufficing as she approaches the deep things of God and of eternity. The spirit has groanings that cannot be uttered, — thoughts which it can revolve in silent musing, and pour into the ear of Heaven in silent prayer, but which in great part elude the drapery of words, and refuse to take shape in the conventional forms of speech. Language is strictly accurate and fully intelligible, only when it relates to those material things which we can identify and compare by the organs of sense. When I speak of a house or a tree, of the sun or the stars, of music or of thunder, I describe what must needs be substantially the same to other eyes and ears as it is to my own.

But when I speak of motive, desire, temptation, aspiration, love, peace, I can convey only the same sort of conception, not precisely the same conception, that is in my own mind. I may convey more; I may convey less. The person to whom I speak measures my consciousness by his own, and how widely apart these may be neither he nor I can tell. And then how frequently is thought forced into the very mode of utterance most unlike itself! Thus the most frigid words proceed as often from the profoundest emotion, as from a superficial and passionless nature. We are so painfully conscious of feeling more than we can express, as to utter very much less than we might say. Thus some of the warmest hearts are among the most reserved, and those who the most earnestly long for sympathy frequently obtain the least of it

In temptation and in spiritual conflict, we must tread the wine-press alone. No human eye can behold the embattled hosts of passions and affections, of the thoughts that grovel and the thoughts that climb, of the earth-spirit with its evil angels and the spirit of the Father with the powers of the world to come. The warfare is within. Voices of encouragement may help us. The intercessions of those who love us may make our prayer flow with a freer current. But, after all, the brunt of the battle we must sustain alone, and in the momentous decisions on which depends our fall or our rising as spiritual beings no man can give an answer for his neighbor.

In our trials and griefs we must tread the wine-press alone. There are indeed portions of every sorrow that are common with others, and in these we court sympathy, and it gives us comfort. Widow can condole with widow; the bereaved parent is solaced by communion with those who have passed through similar affliction; the infirm and suffering rejoice in the converse of those who have borne burdens like their own. But in every deep grief there is some profounder depth, which only he who bears it has sounded or can sound. There is a limit beyond which fellow-feeling cannot pass. In every bereavement there are wounded some of those peculiar chords of tender feeling, which we can trace in no other heart, and no one else can discern in ours. There is a portion of our burden which we cannot impart. There are lacerated sensibilities which we cannot describe. There are painful reflections, regretful remembrances, burningly distinct to our own souls, to which we know not how to give utterance.

In the responsibilities of life we must tread the wine-press alone. The precise measure of each one's stewardship, the adjustment of his conflicting obligations, the right balance of mutually limited duties, the due proportions of activity in this and in that direction, — these depend on circumstances which the individual alone can fully know. Fundamental principles may indeed be expounded and urged by others. The great heads of obligation may be enforced with persuasive power by the pulpit or the press. Religious counsel or exhortation may awaken the slumbering conscience, and stimulate to vigorous action the dormant powers of the moral nature. But when all this is done, there are many questions of detail — those too of the most solemn import — which no man can answer for another, and in which he who yields passively to the best advice, to the most importunate appeal, to the purest example short of the all-perfect, may be false to his trust and to his own soul. Duty is in the last resort to be determined by the individual conscience, and to his own Master must each one stand or fall.

In the hour of death, of judgment, and of retribution, we must tread the wine-press alone. In its own strength or weakness, unclothed or clothed in its own Christ-bought robe of penitence and piety, must the soul wage the fearful conflict with the last enemy. The prayer of faith may indeed go up by the deathbed; but only the prayer of the dying soul can bring down the ministry of angels and the peace of God. And who shall stand as his brother's advocate before the Judge of the living and the dead? How solemn the thought of that first interview of the disembodied spirit with its Father, — no human charity at hand to cover the sins it cannot heal; no faulty examples or imperfect standards to justify its shortcomings; no surrounding circle of the equally frail and erring to drown the consciousness of its frailties and to palliate its errors! Alone with God, — unveiled, self-knowing, the depths of memory and of consciousness broken up, the secrets of the heart laid open, — thus must we meet the omniscient eye, and receive the sentence which consigns us to the company of kindred spirits, to the kingdom prepared for us, to joy unspeakable or to unknown woe.

Thus must we, in our most momentous experiences, living and dying, tread the wine-press alone, and of the people, nay, of the dearest and best beloved, there can be none with us. What are the appointed resources for this spiritual loneliness?

In the first place, there is, or ought to be, a reality in Christian fellowship, as bringing human hearts into more intimate union than can subsist through any other agency. Our direct knowledge of one another and communication with one another are, as I have said, greatly restricted by the essential poverty and inadequacy of language. We need a mediator, not only between man and God, but between man and man; and in the latter office no less than in the former, Christ stands to his disciples.

We are one in him. Our fellowship is with him, and through him with one another. He is the common standard and measure of spirit and character for his followers. So far as we are united with him, we are conscious of possessing the same spirit; the same life-tide throbs in our hearts; the same aspirations go forth; the same inward peace, gladness, and strength settle down upon our souls. He is absolute goodness, — not only the same yesterday, to-day, and for ever, but the same in his moral lineaments to you and to me, to men of diverse nations, unlike forms, and conflicting creeds; and by conversance with the beauty of holiness in him, we may learn to trace, with clear recognition and cordial sympathy, the Christian elements — the "Christ-side," if I may so speak — of every character.

Thus your temptations may be widely unlike mine, and neither could convey to the other the map of his battle-ground or the history of his conflicts; but of the principles through which we have overcome, of the helping spirit from the Father which has made its strength perfect in our weakness, of the Divine Form which has preceded us as the Captain of our salvation, we can freely commune, and hardly need words to make our communion perfect, so fully conscious are we of the identity of the Saviour's part in the experience of both. Our trials and our griefs too have much that we cannot impart; but the consolations of the Gospel, the words of peace, the promises of Christ, the spirit of implicit trust and serene resignation, the "one like unto the Son of Man" that is with us in the furnace seven times heated, — these are the same to every Christian heart, the tokens of that presence which is without variableness or shadow of turning. Thus, also, we may not fully enter into one another's position and circumstances, so as to answer one for another those delicate questions of duty in which the Christian must take chief or sole counsel of his conscience and his God; but we can fully sympathize in the loyalty to our common Master, which sustains us on our separate paths, and gives a harmony of purpose and action to all the various forms and aspects of Christian obedience.

The term "Christian" has for all whose experience has helped them to define it a fixed and absolute meaning, and so far as we realize its meaning in our own souls, we know what it means in every other soul and life. Thus is it that, with no other bond and with everything else dissimilar, the sincere followers of Christ can easily enter into the most intimate relations, and can know more of each other in an hour than if they stood side by side for a lifetime on any worldly arena. Thus, in those great emergencies of trial, grief, and arduous duty, when ordinary sympathy becomes distant and the closest associates seem to move as in an outer circle, Christian may approach Christian, though they never saw each other's face before, may converse in a known language, and from heart to heart may flow the consolations that are in Christ Jesus, the breathings of the hope full of immortality, the emanations of a peace which the world cannot give. And in the last conflict, when kindred that are not kindred in Christ must leave the soul alone, and must feel that intercourse has ceased though consciousness still remains, the Christian can go down with his fellow-Christian to the margin of the stream that divides the unseen world from this, and can know the joy that fills his heart, the communion with heaven that looses for him the pains of death, the glad visions of eternity that play before his departing spirit, the voice of "God that justifieth" calling him from the outer courts of the Father's house into the holy of holies.

We have also direct communion with Christ. We rely on his word, "Lo, I am with you always." Tempted as we have been, touched with the feeling of our infirmities, our brother in trial and in grief, our forerunner through the shadow of death and the darkness of the grave, he can enter into our every experience, into the depths of our inmost consciousness, and we can feel assured of his entire sympathy in thoughts too profound for utterance, in conflicts which have no human witness, in our peculiar and incommunicable griefs, in doubts and fears which the nearest earthly friend knows not and can never know. O, it is a thought rich in comfort and encouragement that he is thus with us, — that the fellow-feeling which we can fully realize in no human friend is with him entire and intimate, so that there is for us no unshared burden, no undivided sorrow, no worthy desire which he proffers not for and with us, no fervent prayer which is not upborne and seconded by him who "ever liveth to make intercession for us."

Among the many uses of our Saviour's incarnation, — among the many reasons why God has ordained that his richest spiritual favors shall flow to us not directly from himself, but through a Mediator in human form, — we cannot attach an unduly high importance to this provision for the spiritual solitude in which we are often left, so far as man is concerned. It is not a mere fancy, but a blessed experience, as I trust many of you can bear witness with me. In arduous and thankless duty, has it not seemed to us as if Jesus were treading the wine-press with us, and were saying in our inward ear, "Be thou faithful unto death, — be thou of good cheer; for I have overcome the world"? When the lives of those dear both to us and to him have trembled on the verge of death, has there not been that in our hearts which corresponded to the message sent by the sisters of Bethany, — "Lord, behold, he whom thou lovest is sick"? Has it not been an unspeakable consolation to us, that he, whom diseases obeyed, is no less near to mortal homes and hearts than in the days of his flesh, and, though he may not as then speak the healing word, that he can impart to the dying and the living peace not as the world gives? In the death of those whom the Lord loves, can we divest ourselves, or would we if we could, of the simple, beautiful faith of the hymn, —

> "'T is but the voice that Jesus sends,
> To call them to his arms"?

When we look forward to our own death, is it on the abstract truths of religion that we rely; or is it not rather on the personal presence and sympathy of our Redeemer, and are not our dearest hopes expressed when we can say to the Good Shepherd, "Though I pass through the valley of the shadow of death, I will fear no evil, for thou art with me"?

Again, we are not alone; for the Father is with us. He has restricted our fellowship with man, that we may seek the closer communion with him. He has ordained that we should be alone, that we may be alone with him. Prayer, though cherished by utterance, needs not words, nor even the capacity of utterance, but may often be most fervent when we know not what to pray for as we ought. The spirit of adoption — the cry,

"Abba, Father," as it trembles in the heart — is in itself a perpetual prayer. It is prayer, when we are profoundly conscious that God is more closely conversant with our spirits than we ourselves are, though we can only say, — "Lord, thou knowest all things; thou knowest that I love thee." What an unspeakable relief is it, — when we are misapprehended by others, when our attainments fall short of our aspirations, when diffidence represses the utterances of which the heart is full, when we can let no mortal friend into our deepest emotions and our warmest desires, when we are alone in conflict or in sorrow, — in those crises of the inward nature which no human sympathy can reach or human help avail, — to feel that God sees us as we are, that the darkness which veils our spirits from mortal sight hides them not from him to whom the night shineth as the day! Let this then be our constant resort in the loneliness of the soul. Let us rejoice that to him are our hearts known, our desires open, and no secret thing hidden; and let the consciousness that he is thus with us make the words of our lips and the meditations of our hearts always acceptable in his sight.

Finally, this solitude of the spirit directs our thoughts and hopes to the sphere of being where we shall fully know and be fully known, where the separating wall of the body shall fall away, soul spring to soul, and heart unite with heart. We cannot but believe that closer society, more intimate union than we can enjoy here, is reserved for us in heaven, — that there will be a blending of spirit with spirit of which the present laws of intercourse are but an imperfect type and a vague shadow. This is one of the visions of the future life which is adapted to give richer zest to our hope of reunion in heaven with those whom we love best on earth. How have we often longed for a deeper insight into the souls of those who have been our exemplars and guides in duty, who have here breathed the most of the spirit of heaven! When we have drawn close the bonds of our communion, how have we desired that they might be closer still, — that there might be a fuller interchange of sentiment and feeling than could be borne from heart to heart by lip or look! Of the mode of spiritual intercourse we can indeed form no clear conception. This only we know, — that from the Divine Spirit there are thoughts communicated to our minds, impressions borne in upon our souls, without voice, or sound, or any of the outward machinery of intercourse. Why may not spirit, in the future, commune with spirit, as the Father of our spirits now communes with us all? Why may not each spiritual presence be, as it were, translucent to every other, and sentiment, affection, adoration, be transfused, as it is even now in our best and happiest moments from the pressure of the hand, the quivering of the lip, the glow of the countenance? However this may be, there can be no division-walls in the heavenly household,—there must be there unrestricted converse, perfect mutual knowledge, society so close that spirit shall answer to spirit as face to face does now.

Shall not this hope bring us into nearer and happier fellowship even here? Shall not our communings be such as we shall delight to renew and prolong in heaven? O, while we must tread the wine-press alone, let us aspire after the closer communion that pervades the ranks of the redeemed. In our households, let our converse be not only of the things that change and perish, but of those things which the angels desire to look into. As fellow-disciples let hand join hand, and heart draw nigh to heart, as we move on in our Christ-marked way. Let the chosen, dearest themes of our converse be those which we shall rejoice to recall in the New Jerusalem, in the assembly of the redeemed, among the adoring hosts near the eternal throne.

SERMON XXIX.

HOPE THE SOUL'S ANCHOR.

WHICH HOPE WE HAVE AS AN ANCHOR OF THE SOUL, BOTH SURE AND STEADFAST, AND WHICH ENTERETH INTO THAT WITHIN THE VEIL. — Hebrews vi. 19.

THIS comparison of hope with an anchor is opposed to common modes of thought and expression. The more natural figure to most minds would be that of a buoy. I apprehend that, where that of the anchor is employed, in nine cases out of ten it is quoted from the Bible without any definite meaning. Yet I do not believe that it was used at haphazard in our text; but it seems to me one of the numerous cases in which a profound wealth of spiritual significance is condensed into a single word of Scripture. All hope is not anchor-like; or, if it be, there are many hopes which are anchors with cables too short to reach the bottom, and which therefore only expose the vessel to quicker, more irregular, and more violent pitches and plunges in the storm-lifted deep.

32*

Following out our figure with regard to worldly affairs, we can easily see that the length of the cable makes a surprising difference. The strong hope of some gratification of to-morrow unsettles to-day's life, unfits us for to-day's duty, and sustains a feverish excitement, under which time is wasted, obligation violated, and even principle endangered. The approaching holiday crazes the schoolboy, and the teacher must expect only slighted tasks and incessant mischief till the holiday is over. The near prospect of intense but evanescent joy is hardly less a disturbing force to the else contented and industrious adult, whose continuous toil thus becomes spasmodic, while his usually sober habits of thought lapse into reverie. But a distant hope has a very different effect. The boy who hopes at some future time to support his impoverished parents; the youth who hopes for a good name and a fair place in his chosen profession; the man who hopes for competence and honor, which he can win only by patient effort, — all these find hope an availing anchor. It moors them; it steadies them against breeze and current, gale and storm; it keeps them from temptation, and delivers them from evil.

The anchor needs a length of cable sufficient, but not too great; adequate weight; and the adjustment of stock, shank, and flukes, which will most effectually hold the ship to her moorings. These characteristics applied to spiritual things would give us adequate remoteness, vastness, and certainty as the requisite properties of a hope that shall be an anchor to the soul.

I. Adequate remoteness. Remote in point of time we cannot, indeed, pronounce the objects of the Christian hope; for there may be at any moment but a step between us and death. Yet the due effect of distance is produced, in part by the indefiniteness of our term of life here, and in part by our imperfect knowledge of the details of our future condition. Did we know that our lives would be greatly prolonged on the earth, our anchor would then have indeed a superfluous length of cable, and we should be tempted to give unrestrained scope to the enjoyments of the passing day, and to postpone till the last few years or months the work which belongs to all our time, and is the easier and more entire the earlier it is begun. On the other hand, did we know the day of our death to be very near, the cable of our anchor would be injuriously shortened, — the prospect would impair our active powers, derange our plans both of self-improvement and of social duty, and transfer us from the list of workers to that of anxious expectants. So, too, had we the same clear conception of the life of heaven which we have of approaching seasons of earthly festivity and gladness, the view would be so overpoweringly grand and attractive as to throw all temporal interests and enjoyments into undue insignificance, to make us impatient for the time of our departure, and discontented under the yoke of daily duty. But now the uncertainty that rests on the closing hour is adapted to make us diligent without impatience, to help us use the world without abusing it, to keep the field of duty and discipline fully open for us, without inspiring disgust, weariness, or inordinate longing for a change. At the same time, just enough of the unseen future is revealed to feed desire, without casting too deep a shadow on earthly good, to make us willing to depart, and yet willing to await God's time and way for our removal. The hopeful Christian sees heaven near enough to furnish every possible motive for virtue, fidelity, and spiritual affections, yet not near enough to detach him from the relations in which God would have him conscientiously faithful, — from the field of duty of which the Master says, "Occupy till I come."

II. Our Christian anchor is of sufficient weight. The prospect of heaven, though indefinite, is vast. Though a veil hangs before the glory and joy to be revealed, it is a semi-transparent veil, through which we get grand and gorgeous glimpses of the celestial city. What an unspeakable amount of happiness is proffered us here, in the crowded godsends of a benignant Providence, compassing our path and our lying down, poured out with unstinted hand on all our ways, — in the kindly course and beautiful harmony of nature,—in our homes, and in those genial relations with our fellow-beings by which blessings are multiplied because divided, magnified because shared! Yet, with the full perception of all that can here minister to our joy, it is a far more exceeding and eternal weight of glory that lies before us. The earthly fades when brought into comparison with the heavenly. Time presents no attractions that can vie with the promises of eternity. Our conceptions of heaven are enough to more than fill the soul with their fulness, and to outshine all things else by their divine radiance. The imagery of the New Testament carries fancy on to its utmost limits, and up till its pinions can soar no higher. In these boundless and infinite prospects, we have more than a counterpoise for whatever might beguile our souls from their high calling and destiny.

III. Our Christian anchor has its firm hold of certain and immovable evidence. Little as we know where or what heaven is, no law of our being is made more sure to us than our immortality. Its evidence is not intuition, surmise, speculation, or longing, but fact which cannot be gainsaid, unless we pronounce the whole past a dream and all history a fable. We have the same proof that the dead have risen, which we have that countless multitudes have sunk into the death-slumber. The resurrection of Christ is not even an isolated fact of authentic history, but a fact which has left surer traces of its reality, deeper channels of its influence, than any other event that has occurred since the creation of man. It was the initial cause, and the only possible cause, of a series of events and experiences that have been developing themselves for eighteen hundred years. There is no ground on which we believe anything beyond the range of our senses, on which the whole Gospel history, with Christ's resurrection for its culminating incident, does not commend itself to belief. Thus, do we receive human testimony? Here we have its blended and manifold voices. Do effects indicate a cause? Here we have numberless and vast effects, which were all uncaused unless the Gospel narrative be true. Is the consenting voice of large and varied experience a valid ground of argument? What a cloud of witnesses have we here to the reality of every spiritual phenomenon that should result from the fact of a resurrection and the demonstrated certainty of the life to come! Is the Author of our being competent to attest its laws and its destiny? If so, what conceivable testimony other than miracle could he bear, and how could that attestation be clearer and stronger than he has made it in the Gospel?

In thus laying intense stress on the historical argument, I forget not the intimations of immortality, the hopeful analogies, the onward pointings, of which nature and life are full. When Nature wakes from her wintry slumber, and the life-current throbs anew in the withered trees, and field and forest resume their robes of praise, we revisit the mounds in the graveyard with a renewed glow of hope. In the outblooming of the world around us, we feel a more elastic assurance that the blighted blossoms of our homes and hearts bloom in celestial gardens. But when in autumn all looks worn and faded, a troop of mournful associations and sad analogies come thronging into the mind again; the soul that relies on the teachings of Nature yields to the surrounding gloom; and the snow that falls upon the late green graves falls with deadening weight upon the hope of man. But the spring flowers that bloom around the sepulchre of Jesus never wither.

Again, there are times when our souls seem almost conscious of immortality, spring forth into a higher sphere, behold their celestial birthright, and read the words of eternal life in capacities which they have no room to develop here, in longings which earth cannot satisfy, in aspirations that transcend all created good. But weariness, care, or sorrow comes; and then the wings of the spirit droop, its heaven is clouded over, and to him who depends on his own clear intuition all looks dark and desolate. But the

Christian thus bowed down stoops to look into the place where the Lord lay, hears the voice of the resurrection angel, and sees, through a cleft in the clouds, the shining path of the ascending Redeemer.

No one can recognize more cordially than I would the correspondences between the outward and the spiritual world, — the Scriptures old as the creation, on which God has inscribed images and symbols of the very same truths that he has revealed in the written word. To my eye, the law of man's immortality is typified in the wheat-sheaf springing from the dry and shrunken kernel, in the butterfly soaring aloft from the tomb which the earth-worm had spun, in the tendency, through all departments of nature, of lower forms of life to merge themselves in higher. I would own, too, with the warmest gratitude, those elements of our spiritual nature, which, confined and crippled here, like the germ in the unplanted seed, claim a more genial soil, a more propitious sky, for their full development. But I always find that these views come the most readily to my mind when it is free, unburdened, and happy. Under the pressure of bereavement or despondency, like summer friends, they vanish, or linger at the threshold, cold and ungenial comforters. It is then that we need to see immortality revealed, the eternal life made manifest; and more would I prize in the season of need a single realizing glimpse of the scene at the gate of Nain or the tomb of Lazarus, or a single glance of implicit faith at the forsaken sepulchre of Jesus, than all sources of belief from beyond the Gospel record, were they brought to one fountain-head, and poured over my spirit in their fullest flow.

We have, then, a hope fitted to be an anchor of the soul, and we need it to give us stability equally among the temptations, the duties, and the trials of life.

1. Among its temptations. How close their pressure! How intense their disturbing force! Like the swell of a storm-lifted ocean, they break upon our youth, dash against the strength of our maturer years, and burst over the hoary head. Appetite and passion, pride and gain, ease and indolence, how do they essay by turns their single and their combined power upon every soul of man! How do they toss and dash from breaker to breaker, and from shallow to shallow, every unanchored spirit! And their hold upon us is as unanchored spirits, — through our intense desire of immediate gratification and our detachment from the unseen future. Their talisman is the infidel's creed; their watchword, "Immortality is a dream." They get influence over us solely by shaking our conviction, or drowning our consciousness, of a life beyond the present. They assail us, not as children of God and heirs of immortality, but as offspring of the dust and vic-

tims of the grave. And did I believe myself so, I would seize the nearest and the cheapest pleasures. I would crown myself with rosebuds before they were withered, and let no flower of the spring pass by me. I would never face opposition, or gird myself for self-denying duty. The utmost calculation that I would make would be as to the greatest amount of pleasurable sensation that could be crowded into the probable period of my life on earth. But let me only behold in faith my risen Saviour, and hear from him those divine words, "Because I live, ye shall live also," then I can cast away the withering wreath from the earthly vine for the amaranthine crown. I can dash from me the cup of sensual gratification, for the water which I may drink, and thirst no more for ever. I can tread the rough and steep path, while at every step the celestial city rises clearer and brighter to my view. I can throw the whole energy of an immortal being into the defiant mandate,—"Tempter, depart; get thee behind me, Satan."

2. But we no less need this anchor when we have escaped the temptations which assail the lower nature, and find ourselves on the shoreless sea of duty. Here again the waves lift up their voice. How vast the extent, how complex the demands, how imperative the claims, how earnest the calls, of spiritual obligation! How liable we are, even with a quick and tender con-

science, to let some of these voices drown others, — to select our easy or our favorite departments of duty, instead of aiming at entire fidelity, — to let waywardness modify principle, and convenience limit obligation! How does the random, erratic course of many who mean to do right and well, resemble that of a ship driven by the wind and tossed on the billows! And here our anchor comes into use, to keep us in the moorings where God has placed us. It is earthly breezes — human opinion, fear, and favor — that sway us hither and thither. The consciousness of our immortality alone can make us firm and resolute, with every real demand of duty before us in its relative claims and just proportions, with the work given us to do present to the inward vision, and with the whole power of the world to come making its strength perfect in our weakness.

There is, in this view, a wonderful impressiveness in the close of the fifteenth chapter of St. Paul's First Epistle to the Corinthians. The whole theme of the chapter is the resurrection and the life to come. The corner-stone of the Apostle's reasoning is the great stone which the angel rolled away from the Saviour's sepulchre, — "If Christ be not risen, our preaching is vain, and your faith is also vain." From this, he ascends step by step to the contemplation of the still distant day when he, who conquered, shall destroy death, and "all things shall be put under his feet." He rebuts by unanswerable analogies the scepticism of those who ask, "How are the dead raised up, and with what body do they come?" He shows us the corruptible putting on incorruption, the mortal clothing itself in immortality. Then, as if for himself the change were already passed, and heaven won, he breaks forth into the shout of eternal triumph, — "O death, where is thy sting? O grave, where is thy victory?" And now comes the climax in the calm, deliberate exhortation, — "Wherefore, my beloved brethren, be ye *steadfast, unmovable*, always abounding in the work of the Lord, forasmuch as ye know that your labor is not in vain in the Lord." Thus does the great Apostle forge, as it were among the lightnings that play before the sapphire throne, the anchor to be dropped down into the sea of conflicting interests, opinions, and passions, to hold the individual soul to its divinely appointed roadstead of duty.

3. We need our anchor among the trials and sorrows which are the lot of all. However calmly the sea of life may roll for a while, there are times when the waves and the billows go over us, and the floods lift up their voices around us, — times when, if in this life only we have hope, we are ready to pronounce ourselves of all men the most miserable. When the gains of a lifetime are swept away in an hour, and a prime spent in

affluence sinks into a needy old age; when, agonized by violent disease, we pass at once from vigorous health into the very jaws of death, or, crippled by chronic infirmity, we drag our limbs after us as a prisoner his chain; when the light of our eyes is quenched, and the voices that made sweet melody in our hearts are silent in the grave; when, as with not a few among us, our dead outnumber our living, and the monuments in the cemetery are more than the olive-plants around our table, — we then have encountered griefs beyond the reach of human comforters. They set adrift the soul that has no hold on heaven. They abandon it to empty regrets, fruitless complainings, — often to a despondency which can find relief only in the self-forgetfulness of sensual indulgence. They are, in an earthly point of view, intense and unmitigated evils. Yet, with the anchor of an immortal hope, how serenely may the Christian outride these storms, and at the very acme of their violence hear the voice which ever says to the winds and to the waves, "Peace! be still!" How does the great thought, the swelling, bounding hope of immortality belittle earthly trials, so that, when it fills our souls, we can borrow the Apostle's words, and pronounce our sorrows "light" and "but for a moment," and "not worthy to be compared with the glory that shall be revealed"! For what is loss, what is penury, if the soul have its wealth, boundless, infinite, eternal? What is bodily pain or infirmity, if there be within the health and soundness which the Divine Physician guarantees as the pledge of everlasting life? And what are these partings on the brief voyage? — severe indeed, I know from repeated experience, yet not for a single moment hopeless or despairing, when we can yield up the dying to the covenant love of our risen Redeemer, and feel assured that we shall meet them again in the ranks of the ransomed, and renew the worship of the home altar in the redemption song of the Father's house on high. O how blessed the anchor, "which entereth into that within the veil, whither," adds our context, "the Forerunner is for us entered, even Jesus," — whither so many of the beloved have passed on before us, and await our coming!

"There, in the soft and beautiful belief
Flows the true Lethe for the lips of Grief;
There Penury, Hunger, Misery, cast their eyes,
How soon the bright republic of the skies!
There Love, heart-broken, sees prepared the bower,
And hears the bridal step, and waits the nuptial hour!
There smiles the mother we have wept! There bloom
Again the buds asleep within the tomb.
There, o'er bright gates inscribed, NO MORE TO PART,
Soul springs to soul, and heart unites to heart!"

SERMON XXX.

THE CLOUD OF WITNESSES.

WHEREFORE, SEEING WE ALSO ARE COMPASSED ABOUT WITH SO GREAT A CLOUD OF WITNESSES, LET US LAY ASIDE EVERY WEIGHT, AND THE SIN WHICH DOTH SO EASILY BESET US, AND LET US RUN WITH PATIENCE THE RACE THAT IS SET BEFORE US. — Hebrews xii. 1.

THE author of this Epistle had in his mind the games, or contests of speed and strength, which were the most august occasions, and convened the most illustrious and brilliant assemblies, in all classic antiquity. The athlete who ran on the Olympic course had been for months training himself for the trial, — had abstained not only from guilty, but from innocent indulgence, — had sought by the most rigid regimen and the most vigorous exercise to lay aside every weight, that is, all superfluous heaviness of the flesh, and to reduce himself to that precise degree of thinness which combines strength with activity, lightness and elasticity of limb with full muscular development and tension. And the day of his race was the most eventful day of his life. He ran in an area, around which stood all the great men of Greece and her colonies, and not unfrequently crowned and laurelled heads from foreign and distant lands. There were poets ready to embalm the victor's name in immortal verse. There were artists who would transmit his form and features to far-off generations. It was indeed the highest honor that the world had to bestow ; and those who had won the first place in empire or in arms deemed the summit of glory unattained while the Olympic wreath was wanting.

It is unfortunate that our text, in the arbitrary arrangement which you know is a device of modern times, stands at the beginning of a chapter. It belongs to the preceding chapter In that the writer gives a long list, from Abel downward, of those whose faith had made them dear to God, and won for them an inheritance among the just made perfect At first he goes into detail, and describes the peculiar forms of trial and modes of fidelity of those whom he commemorates. Then, as one after another crowds upon his memory, he gives simply the names of Gideon, Barak, Samson, Jephthah, David, and Samuel. Then, as the very names oppress him with their multitude, he suspends the catalogue, and enumerates the various sufferings and conflicts in which a number beyond thought of devout men and holy women had obtained a good report through faith, and received the promises. And now he sees the world transformed into a race-ground. Christians are running for the prize. These illustrious dead, each decked with the crown of victory, are the dense cloud of witnesses, watching the conflict with intense interest, urging the laggards, cheering on those who are rapidly nearing the goal, shouting their plaudit whenever the goal is reached and the laurel wreath is twined around the victor's brow. "Seeing, then," says our writer, "that we are on the race of life, with the amaranthine crown for our prize, and encircled by all who in every age have won the victory, have reached the summit of spiritual glory, have their name written on records more durable than brass or adamant, let us lay aside every weight, every desire, love, propensity, or habit that can make us loiter on the race-course, especially our constitutional or besetting faults, — those sins to which we are the most inclined, and for which we find the readiest apology; and thus unencumbered, in full strength, with every power and affection concentrated on the goal and the prize, let us run with perseverance the race that is set before us."

This idea of the presence of the departed, and their surviving interest in the scenes among which their trophies were won, is a familiar one with the sacred writers, though nowhere else exhibited with the scenic effect with which it is here placed before the imagination. What a glorious and inspiring thought, that we are acting our parts, fulfilling our mission, beneath the loving and solicitous regards — when faithful, under the approving eye — of patriarchs, prophets, and apostles, — of Abel, the first mortal who put on immortality, — of Abraham, the father of the faithful, — of Moses, the mediator of that early covenant which embosomed the promise of the Messiah and the spiritual destiny of all his followers, — of the intrepid Peter, the fervent Paul, the loving John, — of the noble army of martyrs, — of the great and good, as their ranks have been multiplied all down through the Christian ages! Nor can we confine our thoughts to these. With them we associate those whom we have known and loved, — our home-born saints, those who have taken sweet counsel and lived in holy fellowship with us, the tutelar spirits of our households, — the parents whose prayers consecrated our infancy, and whose ripened virtue strengthened us on our opening way, — the children translated in their innocence from our embrace to the Good Shepherd's arms, — the companions of our youth cut off in the bloom of their beautiful promise. These are the cloud of witnesses that encompass us; and, could they be but for one moment made visible to the outward eye, how would they

> "reprove each dull delay,
> Allure to brighter worlds, and lead the way"!

Nor is this view attended by any intrinsic improbability, which makes it hard for our faith. We are the unrecognized witnesses of the habits and movements of the lower orders of animated existence. Why may not the translated spirits that have preceded us to heaven be in like manner the unseen witnesses of our conflicts, failures, and successes? Science brings to view numberless tribes of sentient beings too minute for our unaided sight. Why may not religion equally reveal to us forms and modes of life too ethereal for our bodily vision to discern? Almost every spot of earth has its double occupancy; every green leaf, every drop of water, has its myriads of living tenants; the realm of inanimate and that of sentient existence interpenetrate each other, mingle without confusion, occupy the same space, yet appertain to separate systems. Why may not the realms of matter and of spirit similarly interpenetrate each other, and blend throughout without collision or disturbance? The stirring of the summer air, so gentle as to elude our senses, wakes melody in the Æolian harp. Why may not converse and communion, too subtile for detection by the dull organs of the perishing body, transpire near and around us among glorified spirits? And if, through faith in things unseen, through a yearning after the fellowship of the holy dead, we clarify the inward sense, and attune aright the chords of the spiritual nature, why may not we become wind-harps, to vibrate strains of celestial harmony, and to echo loftier praise than can float on the broken song of our vocal worship?

Nor need any questionings about a local heaven disturb our faith in the presence of these witnesses. The laws of spiritual existence, knowledge, presence, and intercourse, whether in the body or out of it, transcend our philosophy. There may be a local heaven, and yet it may be heaven *here* and everywhere; as in our material firmament it is heaven where the sun walks in glory and the stars keep their watches, and, at the same time, heaven at our fingers' ends. Must not the very process of disembodiment bring the pure spirit into the intimate presence of God, — reveal to it its due place in the ranks of the redeemed, — suffuse its whole being with the welcome of the Saviour and the benediction of the Father? And if this be so, it must be heaven wherever the spirit can remain in communion with God and Christ, and in full consciousness of its immortal heritage. Especially must it be heaven where the affections love to linger, among the scenes of past conflict and triumph, among the friends yet militant, but pressing on for the prize of their high calling. By the form from which life has fled, when survivors have clustered around the bed of death with calm resignation and unwavering trust; when on the waters that threatened to go over their souls they have found fast moorings by the Rock of Ages; when the voice of praise has gone up for the translation of the departed saint; when the Saviour's words of peace have been breathed into every heart, and his loving presence is as consciously felt as it was beheld by the sisters at the tomb of Bethany, — it has seemed to me as if the dying soul need not leave the chamber for heaven, but might receive the light of life eternal in that very room, might remain in the bosom of the stricken household, and yet be bathed in the gladness and glory of the house not made with hands; and that to the vision purged and clarified by death every tear of bereaved affection might seem a morning dew-drop of renewed spiritual life, every sigh an aspiration heavenward, every sad thought a harbinger of God's own thoughts of peace. And when those survivors, instead of sinking under sorrow into supineness and selfishness, have heard in the death-summons for one of their number the call to a more earnest and devoted life; when they have gone forth with a chastened, yet hopeful spirit to meet the demands of daily duty; when their prayers have flowed with a freedom and fervor unknown before; when their social sympathies have been touched to finer issues; when a richer beauty of holiness has attested that the earthly vine had not been pruned in vain, — I cannot conceive that heaven should have a purer joy for the departed, than he might find in watching the spiritual growth, the successive attainments and victories, of those who were dearest to his heart. When I witness such fruits of sorrow, I always think of the spirit recently removed as removed only from outward sight, — as the happy witness of the path on which, one by one, those for whom the earthly household has been dissolved are to attain the end of their faith, the salvation of their souls.

Nowhere, it seems to me, may we more appropriately welcome these thoughts, than at the altar, when the memorials of him who is the Lord of the dead and the living, of him in whom the whole family in heaven and on earth is one, are spread before us. If there is a spot on earth peculiarly dear to those who have gone from us, it is this where they pledged their early vows, consecrated their riper years, felt the presence and power of the Redeemer, and rejoiced in the fellowship of those who were as tendrils of the same branch of the Heavenly Vine. How many are the revered and tenderly beloved forms that come up in our remembrance, when we sing around the holy table our favorite hymn, —

"The saints on earth and those above
But one communion make"!

There is the pastor, whose eloquent eye, whose fervent exhortations and prayers, whose saintly and loving walk, are as fresh in the memory of many of us, as on that sad day when his body reposed before this altar on its way to the grave. With his image there comes up before us the numerous array of those who wrought with him in every cause of Christ and man; — those who brought to the service the best fruits of genius and of liberal culture; those whose wisdom, matured among the busy scenes of life, was consecrated in the patience of faith to the labor of love; those formed for the more tender, gentle ministries of Christian benevolence; the bowed in age whose dying prayers were for our peace and prosperity; the fathers and mothers in our Israel; the young translated from their brief altar-service to the worship of the upper sanctuary. How fast thickens for us the cloud of witnesses! Since our last communion, we have performed the parting rites of religion for no less than three of our circle; — the veteran disciple, whose ripened sheaves were bound, and who was calmly awaiting the summons to bear them home; the earnest, whole-souled laborer in the vineyard, called to go up higher when every heart that could breathe a prayer would have interceded for his longer stay; the venerable matron, with mental vigor unimpaired, and faith clear as sight, removed from the home which she could not have made happier than it was under the serene sunset of her day, to the larger circle of the beloved that have bid her welcome to the Father's house in heaven.

What should be for us the voice of these bereavements? We think of them with sadness, nor can it be otherwise. God means that by such removals our spirits should be more and more unearthed, — that our affections should not be withdrawn from those that go, but should follow them, and through our love for them should take a stronger hold on the home where we may rejoin them. But are they our witnesses, more closely present than when they walked with us here, more familiarly conversant with our characters, more solicitous for our spiritual well-being? Have they at once an enlarged comprehension of all that we ought to be, and a clearer view of what we are? And do we love them still? Then may they — then should they — form a golden chain to bind our affections, desires, and hopes to the throne of God and the fellowship of his ransomed. We would not pain them while they were with us here; shall we not much more court their approval, now that they are even more intimately with us? We cherished their communion; shall it not be even dearer to us, now that it may assume the form of heavenly benediction from guardian angels? We loved to walk with them in mutual counsel and helpfulness; shall we part from their company, now that we cannot take a step with them which urges us not Christward and Godward? They indeed have replaced the intermittent strength of their earthly state by immortal vigor, — they mount up on wings as eagles, they run and are not weary, they walk and faint not; and lame may be our progress compared with theirs. But as none sympathize so cordially with the beginnings of the religious life, — with the feeblest sincere efforts and aspirations for spiritual excellence, — as those of the most advanced experience and mature piety, I cannot but feel that the bond of our fellowship with our friends in heaven is in no wise weakened by their and our different rates of progress, if we are only true to our means of inward growth, faithful to the utmost measure of our ability, — if we do God's will on earth in the same loving spirit in which they do it in heaven. Only let me thus live, and I cannot feel that there is any separating gulf between the two worlds, or that, when we are all in one world, those who went before me will be too far advanced to welcome and enjoy my society as cordially as I would theirs. The earlier dead will indeed be to us as elder brethren, yet brethren still; and none the less so because they can be, not only our companions, but our guides, — not only our fellow-worshippers, but our teachers in the redemption-song, — not only our co-workers, but our forerunners in every shining path of the Divine service.

SERMON XXXI.

AUTUMN.

WE ALL DO FADE AS A LEAF. — Isaiah lxiv. 6.

THE outward world is full of the types of spiritual things. Like the roll in Ezekiel's vision, it is written within and without, though often in a cipher to which Christ alone can furnish the right key. Especially do the alternations and transfers of life in the creation around us correspond to those in the human family, so that every year seems an epitome of man's life, death, and resurrection. What more obvious symbol of man's transitory condition can there be, than the fading leaves of autumn? And it is a symbol which bears a closer and more varied application than might appear at first thought, — one which we may begin to contemplate in sadness, and pass on to joy and gratitude; for the fading leaves have not only their lessons of frailty and mortality, but their suggestions of a hidden life to be preserved through death, and to be restored in vigor and beauty.

"We all do fade as a leaf." Hardly has the prime of summer passed, when here and there a dry and wilted leaf begins to wake autumnal musings, and to remind us that in the midst of life we are in death; while on the very verge of winter there hangs in sheltered nooks leafage still unblighted,—the type of those rare exceptions to the common lot of humanity, the few who remain unchanged while all is changed around them, whose leaf withers not, and whatsoever they do prospers. The varied hues of our autumnal foliage bring to our thought different classes of the death-doomed;—the deep scarlet, those who smile when all around them weep, and dream sweetly of life while they are sinking into the death-slumber; the pale orange, those who seem born but to die, and wither in their earliest bloom; the russet-brown, those who go down to the grave in ripened age like a shock of corn in its season. And when the work of desolation is completed,—when

> "these trees,
> Each, like a fleshless skeleton, shall stretch
> Its bare brown boughs; when not a flower shall spread
> Its colors to the day, and not a bird
> Carol its joyance, but all nature wears
> One sullen aspect, bleak and desolate,
> To eye, ear, feeling, comfortless alike,"—

have we not in this sable close of autumn an apt

type of the wintry grave, where the rich and the poor lie down together, and the storms of earth beat unheeded over their silent dust? O, let not nature wither and sink into the tomb, without reminding us that for man too the grave-clothes are ready and the sepulchre is open, — that all

> "the sons of men,
> The youth in life's green spring, and he who goes
> In the full strength of years, matron, and maid,
> And the sweet babe, and the gray-headed man,
> Shall one by one be gathered side by side"

But let us not forget that this season of desolation is the very reign of beauty. All gorgeous hues blend and alternate. There was sameness in the summer's green. It was charming; yet the eye could promptly receive and easily retain the impress of the scene. But now, every turn of the street, every angle of the forest pathway, each individual tree, presents its separate panorama of colors variously grouped and shaded, interpenetrating one another at every opening, and, as they glance in the sunlight or wave in the cool breeze, giving us a kaleidoscope with ever new combinations from moment to moment. Thus does splendor immeasurably beyond that of its spring and its prime cover the retreat of vegetable life, and spread its multifaced smile over the dying year.

Thus it it, too, with seasons of decline and

death among men. If aught that is human awakens admiration among the heavenly witnesses, it is not in the buoyancy and gladness of opening life, nor yet in the heat and turmoil of its busy and care-cumbered prime. The very virtues of the true and upright are liable to present a soiled and doubtful aspect, on account of the dust and strife of the crowded arena, the conflicting opinions, passions, and prejudices of its actors, the hiddenness of motives, and the prevailing tendency to misrepresent or depreciate whatever departs from the average standard, even though the departure be Christward and heavenward. Then, even in the best men, prior to severe vicissitudes, there is a tinge of earthiness. They look to heaven with eyes dazzled by the glare and glitter of this transitory life. They find it hard to retain the singleness of vision and purpose for which they aim. There are, also, depths of spiritual experience, which are not opened while hope is undimmed and prosperity unimpaired. There is an intimacy of converse with God, a fellow-feeling with the suffering, glorified Redeemer, a home-longing for the house not made with hands, which cannot be fully reached in the bloom and flush of happy youth or busy manhood. There are, too, human sympathies, tender and beautiful, which do not begin to flow, till disappointment, blighting, or decay has passed over some portion of the earthly heritage. In our bright and active days, the heavenly witnesses may indeed be — we trust they are — our ministering angels, yet with a remoter sense of kindred. It is under the approaches of the autumnal chill and frost, that they begin to discern a life more entirely resembling their own. It is then that Faith puts on her beautiful apparel; Hope, her queenly robes; Love, her wedding garment, as the heavenly Bridegroom's steps draw near. The richest manifestations of character; the communings that can never be forgotten; the heroic forms of devotion and submission; the outgoings of affection too intense for utterance, overflowing from the faltering tongue on eye and lip and brow, — these belong to the chamber of illness and the bed of death.

Often is there during the active season of life sincere faith and profound religious feeling, while an insurmountable diffidence or unreadiness seals the lips and ties the tongue, so that the loving and devout thoughts, which are all ready to leap forth in burning words, are locked up in the disciple's heart. But in such cases, approaching death opens the floodgates; the lips grow suddenly eloquent; the treasures of a rich life-experience are poured out for the instruction and comfort of surrounding friends; and we are ready to deem the death-chamber a Bethel, — the house of God and the gate of heaven.

Still oftener may we witness the gradual transforming and spiritualizing of character under the process of decay and the slow approaches of dissolution. Here is a man, with serious dispositions and purposes, but without a distinctly marked religious character. The world goes prosperously with him, and he loves it more than is consistent with supreme love to the Father. His life is more outward than inward. He has held infrequent and slight communion with his own soul. Not wholly undevout, he yet has known little of the joy of fervent and prolonged converse with the Author of his being. But now comes the early frost. His leaf begins to wither, and he knows that it can never be green again. Under this consciousness, his thoughts are gradually drawn in upon himself; they go forth to the prospect of a higher life, which is all that remains for his hope; they seek after God, if haply they may find him; they cluster around the Redeemer, as the Author of pardon and the Herald of immortality; they are detached from passing and perishing objects, and fixed on those that are unseen and eternal. And now submission makes his sufferings beautiful. Patience has her perfect work. Serenity and cheerfulness present an unruffled front to the approaches of disease. In his uncomplaining endurance, his gratitude for sympathy and kindness, his calm reliance on the Heavenly Shepherd as he passes through the valley of the death-shadow, friends find their post of service near him a place of privilege, and feel that the darkest scenes through which they pass with him are irradiated by the clear outshining of omnipotent love. Every trait of his character that had previously won their regard is touched to its finest issues. Sincerity was never before so transparent, nor kindness so genial, nor affection so tender. Winning graces, which till now had hardly revealed themselves, grow with every stage of decline, and brighten with every day's march to the grave. The spirit seems unclothed of all that is not heavenly, and tints of celestial beauty replace the earth-hues that had clung to it in the walks of busy life.

Nor is it only such as I have described that feel these blessed influences. The softening, elevating ministry of decline and decay imparts new richness even to the loftiest types of virtue and devotion. Rigidness and austerity then become gentle. Exclusive sympathies grow catholic. Sectarianism expands into a genial sentiment of brotherhood. Stern legality yields place to that perfect love which is the fulfilling of the law. The entire energy of faith and principle, which had sufficed for strong temptations and large responsibilities, is now all converged on the intercourse, trials, privations, and infirmities of a wasting frame and an ebbing life. And as duties of a new class arise, — as it is the disciple's mission no longer actively to do, but meekly to bear,

God's will, — the passive virtues, which may have been but feebly developed for lack of exercise, are called into prominent relief, and bring the character into a closer kindred than ever before with the Saviour who was made perfect through sufferings. There is choice fruit, which is hard and acrid all summer long, but which, when the oblique rays of the autumnal sun make their way to it through the thinned leafage, grows mellow and luscious. In like manner, there are characters of rare excellence, which present a rough exterior, till they are laid open to the mellowing influences of infirmity and decline. So, too, there are traits of spiritual loveliness and beauty, which are hidden from the only influences under which they could grow by the interests, cares, and pleasures of the more active years, — shrouded by the summer foliage of the life-tree, — and can ripen only when the last of earth and the dawn of heaven are near.

I would call your attention to yet another analogy. Under what gorgeous celestial scenery does the leaf wither and fall! How rich in picturesque beauty is the autumnal sky! How soft, yet how radiant, its every-day robe of dewy azure! Its sunset drapery how resplendent! The sun sinks upon a couch of the richest purple, fringed with burnished gold, with curtains of the purest violet and the brightest orange. The western clouds seem lakes of liquid amber; while, above and around, the heavens are suffused, and the tree-tops and hill-sides bathed in the tranquil smile of departing day. Then, too, how glorious those nights, when the harvest moon chases every cloud from the sky, and rides conqueror and queen ; and when, in its wane, mystic fires shoot up from the horizon, dart in lambent rays from pole to pole, span the firmament with their radiant bow, encircle the zenith with their rejoicing crown, and the whole heavens glow as with an altar-flame of praise to the Most High !

Equally do the heavens brighten over the scenes of man's decay and dissolution. Nowhere does the Divine love seem so visibly and consciously present. Nowhere does prayer flow with so genial an utterance, and meet so prompt an answer. Nowhere reigns so serene a spirit of trust and gratitude. Beneath the pensiveness of the death-shadow, beneath the very paroxysms of agony that rend the hearts of those so soon to be bereaved, flows a current of tranquil gladness, of joy that the Lord God Omnipotent reigneth, that the issues of life and death are in his hands, that the dying are wrapped in the mantle of his love, that his thoughts of peace may be poured into their souls when the dearest earthly voices can no longer reach them. These are the seasons — however severe the conflict of feeling while they last — on which we love to look back, and recall the tokens of a guiding spirit, an all-sufficient love, a Father who "forsaketh not his children when their strength faileth them."

Yet another analogy presents itself. The fading of the leaf is not death, but a rallying of life to its source and centre. Never is the vitality of the tree more vigorous than when its juices and its energies are concentrated in the roots, to withstand the winter's cold and storms, and to elaborate, deep beneath the frost and snow, the elements of renewed bloom, more ample growth, and richer beauty when returning spring shall issue the resurrection fiat. Thus, when the pure and good fade and sink into the grave, our faith tells us they are not dead. Only the leaf has withered. Only the outer form has perished. The life which glowed in the countenance, nerved the arm, and clothed the frame with strength, has been gathered up in its fulness into the soul, whence it emanated, and, with the winter of but a moment, has already grown green and vigorous again, — for ever green, for ever young, where

> "everlasting spring abides,
> And never-withering flowers."

The fading of the leaf, too, reminds us of the things that change not and die not. The same earth from which God first brought forth the herb yielding seed and the tree yielding fruit, receives the dying trust of every herb and tree. The same mountains that emerged from the waters of the flood hide their summits in the clouds. The same heavens wherein the psalmist beheld the glory of God array themselves in their autumnal robe of splendor. The same moon by which Boaz wrought his harvest task makes our nights glorious as day. The same stars that kept watch over the infant world perform their unchanging circuits. Thus is it among the vicissitudes of life and the ravages of death. Mortal affairs are ever fluctuating. The current of time sweeps on, undermining and ingulfing man, with all his possessions, plans, and hopes. Generation after generation is borne away to join the great congregation of the dead. Meanwhile God sits serene and unchangeable, and while the waves of time wash over his footstool, they shake not the foundations of his throne. And, as Nature trustingly commits her germs of vernal life to the bosom of an unchanging earth and the kindly influences of an unchanging sky, so let us, in humble faith, — while our bodies fade as the leaves fade and die as the flowers die, — yield up the germs of immortality within us to Him in whom the dead live, and to whom all flesh shall come.

The day will arrive when Nature's trust must fail. This earth, these heavens, though now in their age-long spring, will have their autumn, when the stars will fade and fall like leaves, when the sun will cut short his circuits, when the visible monuments of creative power will cease to be.

> "The seas shall waste, the skies to smoke decay,
> Rocks fall to dust, and mountains melt away."

But our souls, in faith and love committed to the keeping of Him who is the same yesterday, to-day, and for ever, shall live on in fairer scenes and among purer joys, though the earth be removed and the heavens be no more.

SERMON XXXII.

GREATER THAN MIRACLES.

VERILY, VERILY, I SAY UNTO YOU, HE THAT BELIEVETH ON ME, THE WORKS THAT I DO SHALL HE DO ALSO; AND GREATER WORKS THAN THESE SHALL HE DO; BECAUSE I GO UNTO MY FATHER, AND WHATSOEVER YE SHALL ASK IN MY NAME THAT WILL I DO, THAT THE FATHER MAY BE GLORIFIED IN THE SON. — John xiv. 12, 13.

In the phrase "greater works than these," *works* is printed in Italics, to show the absence of any corresponding word in the original Greek. Had the Evangelist written "greater *works*," as this word is usually employed by him to denote *miracles*, I should suppose that he meant "greater miracles"; and yet it would be hard to say what were or could be greater than those wrought by Jesus in his own person. But in the absence of that word, I would expound our text as follows: — "You, my disciples, after I have left the world will indeed be endowed, for the propagation of my religion, with the power of working miracles like my own. But you will do greater things than miracles. Your victories over your own souls, your sacrifice and self-denial, your lofty moral attainments, will possess a far higher spiritual beauty and glory than can belong even to the healing of the sick or the raising of the dead. And such gifts will be bestowed upon you through my continued sympathy and aid; for I am going from you to your Father and my Father, and, in heaven as here, I shall still be a medium of holy influence for you, shedding upon you the choicest of heaven's blessings, granting you all that you pray for, that thus, through my mediation, God's name and grace may be honored in your obedience and holiness."

There is a narrative in the tenth chapter of Luke, in which our Saviour gives utterance to the same sentiment under very impressive circumstances. He had sent forth the seventy disciples endowed with power to heal the sick, and commissioned to preach the Gospel. They return to him with joy, and, it would seem, with some leaven of vanity; for the foremost item of their report is, "Lord, even the demons are subject to us through thy name," — that is, they had cured not only common diseases, but epilepsy and insanity, which the Jews of that age ascribed to demoniacal possession. Jesus rejoins: "*I* beheld Satan [the impersonation of moral evil] fall like lightning from heaven"; that is, "*My* thoughts were occupied, not with the outward miracles to be wrought through your instrumentality, but with the inroad which you might make on the reign of irreligion and guilt. You have started Satan from his exalted throne. The powers of darkness are no longer in the ascendant. You have inaugurated a new era, not for suffering bodies, but for sin-bound souls." And then he goes on to say: "Behold, I give unto you power to tread uninjured on serpents and scorpions, and over all the power of the enemy, — over whatever can do you harm, — and nothing shall by any means hurt you. Yet no gift of this kind is for your own sakes, or is a fit object of self-congratulation. Rejoice not that the demons are subject unto you; for these are works wrought rather through you than by you, — they imply the power of God, but furnish no test of your own characters. Rather, then, rejoice that your names are written in heaven, — that you have the faith, devout feeling, and holy purpose which can fit you for heavenly happiness."

Our text, thus illustrated, simply teaches the transcendent greatness and glory of goodness. In this sense, it derives its richest illustration from our Saviour's own character. His miracles, indeed, we cannot over-estimate; but they teach us less of himself than of God. They open the depths of the Divine attributes and counsels, not of the Saviour's soul. They call forth the glad shout, "God hath visited and redeemed his people," but would not of themselves elicit the outpouring of the heart, "Lord, thou knowest that I love thee." In truth, they derive their greatest attractiveness from the manifestations of his own character connected with them, — from the tenderness of his compassion, the profoundness of his sympathy, the warmth of his love. It was before he had called Lazarus from the tomb, that the by no means friendly by-standers exclaimed, "Behold how he loved him!" We look upon his miracles without surprise, because we feel that there was that in his whole life and spirit which was greater than they, — that which made his lordly walk among the powers of nature no less the type and expression of his godlike personality, than is our subjection to them the token of souls often clouded by error and sin. But our associations of his spiritual glory linger chiefly around the scenes of his humiliation, distress, and suffering; — when he overcame the gainsaying of his enemies by the meekness of wisdom; when he lifted his midnight prayer on the lone mountain; when he raised the weeping penitent with words of good cheer which no other lips in Judæa would have dared to utter; when, having power to save his life, he chose to lay it down; when he poured forth his sympathy and intercessions at the paschal table; when, in Gethsemane, mortal agony soothed itself into calm resignation, and rose in godlike strength to meet the impending doom; when the crown of thorns lacerated that benignant brow; when he trod the way of grief under the burden of the cross; when from that instrument of torture, as from a regal throne, he dispensed pardons, loving mandates, heavenly benedictions. We spontaneously feel that there was more glory in these manifestations of character than in the creation of a world,— a universe.

As regards the Apostles, though they were endowed with miraculous gifts, to excite the attention and help the faith of those to whom they carried the word of the Lord, do those gifts enter at all into our estimate of their characters? Does not Paul's shaking the viper from his hand without harm seem a very small matter, compared with his renunciation of emolument, office, and honor, of the high places in society which he might have adorned, of the halls of learning in which he might have shone pre-eminent, and his adhering to the despised cause of the crucified Nazarene? Are not the chains which clanked upon his wrists, as he wrote those words of unearthly trust, gladness, hope, and triumph, immeasurably more glorious than the garlands and sacrifices which the idolaters of Lystra, astounded by his miracles, brought to him as a god in the likeness of man?

But our concern is chiefly with our own characters; and our constant danger is that we neglect or undervalue, for outward doings, successes, and attainments, the greater than miracles which we may achieve and be in our spiritual conflicts and victories, — in the virtues that may clothe and the graces that may adorn our souls, — in the Divine image which we may transcribe and bear with ever-growing vividness of resemblance, — in the realization, which may be ours, of those good words of the Saviour, "The glory that thou gavest me, I have given them." Let us look, for our instruction, at some of the modes in which the sentiment of our text may be verified in our experience.

1. There is that which is greater than miracle in resistance to evil. The self-emancipated from the thraldom of appetite and vicious habit are among the strongest and noblest of the race. Those of us whose early nurture was under favoring circumstances, so that our faults never developed themselves into vices, can hardly know how intense is the power of the degrading and destructive appetites and passions which hold so many in bondage. We speak with literal truth, when we say that it is more than a miracle for one thus fallen to rise again. And yet he may. The energy of his will slumbers, yet is not dead. The power of that name, in which the impotent man walked and leaped and praised God, is proffered for his rescue. He may, by agonizing prayer, get a purchase on the throne of the Om-

nipotent, by which he can lift the mountain-load of sensual habit and longing, and cast it into the sea. But he must gird himself as to a great work. He must be resolute, imperative, in his self-denial; heedless of the thousand pretences on which the expelléd demon will strive to open, as by a mere hand's breadth, the door closed against him; deaf to friendly voices that would lure him a little way back on the steps which he cannot begin to retrace without measuring them all back again. And, above all, he must fortify himself by earnest prayer, by a profound consciousness of the present God, by a deep sense of the powers of the world to come, by the constant feeling that he is doing battle for his soul, — for all that can be worth living for, — for all that can minister to his acceptance and gladness when he stands before the Divine tribunal. He who shall thus wrestle with the foul fiend, and pluck from his brow the palm of victory, has won for himself lofty praise and enduring glory, has written his name high among those great in the sight of God, has wrought that of which the miracles of the first Christian age were but the symbol and shadow.

2. Love is greater than miracle; for "prophecy shall fail, tongues shall cease, knowledge shall vanish away, but love never faileth." The miracles which our Saviour wrought for suffering humanity were types and models of the still

greater achievements wrought by his followers through his helping spirit. His word, which bade the paralytic take up his bed and walk, has sent its echo all down through the Christian ages. It breathes in the hospitals of the Old World and the New, where even corporations and communities take the place of the good Samaritan, and tenderly woo back health to the diseased organs and soundness to the shattered frame. It inspires those who move as angels of mercy through the streets swept by swift and deadly pestilence, smooth the brow knotted in mortal agony, and pour thoughts of peace into the departing soul. It prompts and gladdens the steps of those who, without parade or ostentation, carry comfort and hope to the home of destitute illness and infirmity, and watch as with a daughter's assiduity the flickering life-lamp of desolate and helpless age. The touch which healed the loathsome leper has been transmitted through all the lineage of the Saviour, and is still put forth to relieve those forms of guilt and degradation, from which fastidiousness recoils and sensibility stands aloof, and which the worldly-wise would leave to perish uncared for. It is this that reaches the prisoner in his cell, the slave in his house of bondage, the squalid heathen of our great cities, the despised and rejected of all but Christian hearts. The power which gave sight to the man born blind is put forth, through the followers of Christ, in world-embracing efforts for the enlightenment of those that sit in darkness, in the instruction of the children of ignorance and vice, in the outstretching of Gospel ministries till the vast globe is girdled by responses to the Divine call, — " Say to the north, Give up, and to the south, Keep not back; bring my sons from afar, my daughters from the ends of the earth." These various forms of philanthropy are greater than miracles, inasmuch as the effect is greater than the cause, the oak than the acorn, the field white for the harvest than the handful of seed-corn cast into its bosom.

3. There is a power of endurance that is greater than miracle. No spectacle is more sublime than that of a truly Christian soul in severe affliction. No soul can feel so deeply; for religion intensifies the affections which a bereaving Providence may wound, adds tenderness to the sensibilities which may be lacerated by the thorns on the life-road, enhances the power of suffering no less than of gladness. It is not, then, indifference, it is not an impassible nature that checks the rising murmur, and calls forth the voice of serene submission, "Thy will, not mine, be done." That sufferer has gone down into the profoundest depths of agony, — has trodden with bleeding feet the bloody wine-press; but He who trod it for us all is at his side, breathes into the disciple his own spirit, dictates the words of his own prayer, and holds forth the trophies of his own victory.

And when, in the wreck of human joy, faith can kneel and adore; when "Father, I thank thee!" goes up from the home and heart made desolate; when heavenly Peace folds her wings over the stricken spirit; when the hope of immortality irradiates the gloom of bereavement or of penury, — we then witness more than miracle, — a more subtile, a more penetrating power of Jesus, than when lifeless matter moved at his word, though that matter were the lifeless tenement of a living soul.

4. Finally, there are phenomena greater than miracle in the death of the Christian. Only those who are familiar with the scene can appreciate the awful, momentous solemnity of the closing hour of life. The sundering of every tie of home and of society, the separation from all that has been pursued and enjoyed, the inconceivable change that awaits the soul, the plunge into the dread unknown, the dense, palpable blackness which to the earthly vision lies beyond the parting moment, — no wonder that, with all these things in view, the soul, shuddering

> "to o'erleap the bounds,
> Yet clings to being's severing link."

How sublime, then, the faith which looks within the veil, which feels and anticipates no evil, which can express its willingness, its joy to depart and be with Christ, which has not a lingering doubt or fear, but can say, — "I know in whom I have believed; I know that my Redeemer liveth!" The soul puts forth in life no power to be compared with that thus manifested in dying, — not indeed its own strength, but the overcoming might of Him who conquered death. Nowhere are we so sure, beyond the shadow of a doubt, of the fulfilment of his words, — "Lo, I am with you alway, even unto the end of the world." The voice that waked the widow's son from the bier and Lazarus from the tomb, vibrates along the ages, and is heard anew by the disciple as the death-shadow closes over him. The resurrection-touch thrills through his spirit, before life has left its mortal habitation. The Lord's call, COME FORTH, echoes through the walls of that crumbling tenement, as once through those of the sepulchre in Bethany. The miracle of that hour reproduces itself in more than miracle for the strong man and him who bows under the weight of many years, matron and maid, the unlettered follower of Jesus and the great, wise, and noble among the ranks of his disciples, as with one voice they take up the glorious strain of apostolic triumph, — "O death, where is thy sting? O grave, where is thy victory? Thanks be to God, which giveth us the victory through our Lord Jesus Christ."

SERMON XXXIII.

ALL POWER GOD'S.

"GOD HATH SPOKEN ONCE; TWICE HAVE I HEARD THIS, THAT POWER BELONGETH UNTO GOD. ALSO UNTO THEE, O LORD, BELONGETH MERCY: FOR THOU RENDEREST TO EVERY MAN ACCORDING TO HIS WORK." — Psalm lxii. 11, 12.

THE very being of God includes omnipotence. If he exists, he is the ultimate source of all power. Yet with regard to the Divine power there are two tenable theories, differing widely, as it seems to me, alike in their intrinsic claims on our credence, in their hold on Scriptural authority, and in their adaptation to our spiritual nature and needs. According to the one view, the Almighty has lodged in the various agencies of the material world capacities and tendencies, by virtue of which they prolong the order and harmony of nature, perpetuate the races of organized and animated being, and work out a course of events, incidentally disastrous, yet in the main beneficial, and adapted to produce a vast and ever-increasing preponderance of happiness over misery, and of good over evil. But as to incidental evil, God in no way interposes, directly or indirectly, to avert it, or to transform it into good, so that we have no guaranty, as regards any disastrous event, of its actually beneficent use or capacity, nor yet is such an event to be regarded as good, except as inseparable from a generally beneficent plan. According to this theory, human agency is uncontrolled in its own sphere, and the mischief which man may do to his fellow-man is limited only by the strength of his will and the range of his activity; while there is no happy or hopeful view that we can take even of the external evil which guilt and crime produce in the world.

According to the other view, God is actively present in the entire universe, upholding all things by the word of his power, guiding the course of events by his own perpetual fiat,—preserving, indeed, a certain uniformity in sequences which we call cause and effect, so far as is needed to assist human calculation and to give definite aim to human endeavor, but behind the order of visible causes adjusting whatever takes place with immediate and constant reference to the needs, the deserts, and the ultimate well-being of his creatures; ordaining the seeming evil no less than the seeming good, making even wicked men his sword; so overruling malignity and evil passion as to work out their own ultimate extinction and the ascendency of truth and right; so modifying the results of vicious agency, that they shall either, on the one hand, harmonize with the salutary affliction which flows confessedly from his appointment, or, on the other, subserve the essential ends of moral demonstration, rebuke, and retribution.

I hardly need say, that this last is the view directly sanctioned by the express language and the entire tenor of Scripture. Indeed, as much as this is admitted by the Christian advocates of the former theory, who regard the sacred writers as by a bold, yet legitimate figure ascribing to the direct action of the Almighty whatever takes place under a system initiated by his power and sanctioned by his wisdom. But there was, it seems to me, immeasurably more than figure in their minds. To them the curtain of general laws, which hangs in so dense drapery before the eyes of modern philosophy, was transparent, and they saw no intervening agency, no intermediate force, between the Creator and the development of his purposes in nature and in providence. "He maketh the winds his angels, and flames of fire his ministers." "The voice of the Lord is upon the waters; the God of glory thundereth." "These wait all upon thee, that thou mayest give them their meat in due season." "Shall there be evil in a city, and the Lord hath not done it?"

"The Lord killeth, and maketh alive; he bringeth low, and lifteth up." "Surely the wrath of man shall praise thee; the remainder of wrath thou wilt restrain." "The hairs of your head are all numbered." "The sparrow falleth not to the ground without your Father." If these are mere figures, I know not how we are to assign limits to figurative interpretation, or what Scriptural language there is, of which we may be sure that it means what it seems to mean.

But without pressing phraseology of this class, which occurs on almost every page of the Bible, we might derive the same inference from the duty of unlimited, unqualified trust constantly inculcated in Scripture by explicit precept, by the examples of saints under both the Old and the New Covenant, and by that of the Divine Founder of our religion. This trust is impossible under anything less than a perfect Providence; for under a system only generally beneficent, how know we but that we are the destined victims? In a lottery with but one blank to a thousand prizes, how know we that the one blank is not ours? Nay, we shall be sure to think and to feel that it is ours in the stress of impending, or the fresh sorrow of realized, calamity; and the philosophic trust which we may cherish in a general Providence will fail us at the very times when all that we can do is to submit, believe, trust, and hope.

Our view of the direct administration and perfect providence of God is confirmed by the results, or rather by the non-results, of science. Six thousand years of research have failed to reveal the latent forces, to lay bare the hidden springs, of nature. Gravitation, cohesion, crystallization, organization, decomposition, — these are but names for our ignorance, — fence-words set up at the extremest limits of our knowledge. That Nature pursues her course and events take place under such and such conditions, is the utmost that we can say. We find it impossible to conceive of any innate or permanently inherent force in brute matter, but by the very laws of thought we are constrained to attribute all power to mind, intelligence, volition.

I admit, however, that without the revelation of immortality there would be great difficulty in the admission of a Providence always benignant; and while we might even then well hesitate to ascribe power to lifeless matter, we might be driven to the Oriental hypothesis of conflicting spiritual agencies, — a semi-omnipotent evil intelligence in perpetual antagonism with the Supremely Good. The difficulty does not attach itself to the afflictions, however severe, which fall to the lot of those who are growing in moral excellence; for we always see in a progressive character an alembic in which sorrow is transformed into spiritual nutriment, — a divine alchemy through which all things work together for good; and the heaviest trials which are thus converted to beneficent uses are no more a mystery than are the lowering days and dreary rains of the spring as regards the fields and meadows. Nor yet need the calamities that befall the highly privileged, but non-improving, create an insuperable difficulty; for they may be regarded, on the one hand, as a merited retribution, or, on the other, (and I believe with greater fitness,) as proffering the best adapted and most hopeful means — for the inefficacy of which they themselves are accountable — of awakening them to a sense of their relation to God, their obligation to him, and their amenableness at his tribunal.

But there are numerous cases, in which heavy calamity falls, and rests prolongedly, on those whose unprivileged condition renders trial utterly useless. Here we are fully relieved by the assurance of immortality; for the period of their endurance bears no assignable proportion to the eternal life at the threshold of which they wait and suffer. Their time of privilege is beyond our earth-bound vision, but it is hastening on for each and all; and it is entirely conceivable that the remembered sufferings of their sojourn here may be among the choicest means of their spiritual nurture in heaven, and that, for the fervor of their zeal, and the strength of their allegiance to the Saviour whom they will first know when they emerge on the farther side of the shadow of death, it may be said of them, as of such multitudes that belonged to his earthly fold,—"These are they which came out of great tribulation." We do wrong to our Christian faith, if sincere, when we exclude it from our philosophy,—when we fail to concentrate its full radiance on the else dark passages of the Divine Providence. We do equal wrong to our intuitive sense of justice and to the benign spirit of our religion, when, because tribulation and anguish in the world to come are the destined lot of those who, having the full light of the Gospel, refuse to avail themselves of it, we tacitly include in the same doom, or, from complaisance to the advocates of a sterner theology, we refuse in thought to exempt from that doom, those to whose case we might apply the spirit of our Saviour's words, —"If I had not come and spoken unto them, they had not had sin."

We may thus set aside such objections as flow from unavoidable human suffering, so far as it is the direct act of God. And, these objections set aside, do not insuperable difficulties lie in the way of any supposition other than the direct action of the Almighty in the entire external universe? Omnipresence, omniscience, is implied in the very conception of God. But can his, at any moment or in any part of his creation, be a powerless knowledge, an inert presence,—a mere watching of machinery wound up and put in motion in unknown ages past, and to run for unknown ages yet to come? Can we conceive of him as present, and not vitally, actively present? I cannot, and I rejoice that I cannot. To my thought, the bloom and verdure that clothe the earth this day are no less his immediate handiwork, than were those on which Adam's eyes opened in Eden. The trees and shrubs that now wave and rustle in the breeze are no less suffused with his just-spoken blessing, than the burning bush on Horeb was vocal with his audible voice. The waves are no less upheaved this morning by the direct action of his power, than the waters were of old piled up by his might to wall in a safe path for his ransomed to pass through. The scanty seed-corn of late committed to the earth will be no less multiplied thirty, sixty, and a hundred-fold by his wonder-working providence, than the widow's handful of meal grew by his benediction during the weary months of famine. Do you say that there is something belittling in the thought of this minute agency of the Infinite God? What is not minute, — what concerns of nations, planets, or systems are vast and grand to him, whose worlds crowd the telescopic vision by myriads, and stud the heavens as countless as the sand on the sea-shore? These distinctions of magnitude and importance vanish in his sight.

> "To him no high, no low, no great, no small;
> He fills, he bounds, connects, and equals all."

But what shall we say of man's power over outward nature and events? We are conscious of free volition. Is it ours to execute our own volitions; or is it literally in God that we live, and move, and have our being? I cannot conceive of divided power, of concurrent sovereignty, in the same domain, — of our ability to do what he would not have us do. That we can will what he wills not, we know only too well; but must we not reach the conclusion that he executes our volitions for us whether they be good or evil, — nay, that the execution of these volitions, whatever they are, is always good, — that he literally makes "the wrath of man" to praise him, and "the remainder of wrath" — that whose mission would be unavailing for the purposes of his righteous administration — he will so "restrain" as to frustrate of its end? Do we thus make God the author of evil? Far otherwise. So long as his spiritual children are endowed with freedom of volition, sin is possible; and so long as sin exists, the occurrence and continuance of its consequences in all their vileness and deformity is an essential part of the system, which is ultimately to abolish sin, to establish the reign of universal righteousness, and to weld free agency and right volition in a union to be made sacred and permanent by the finished and transmitted experience of the long ages of violence, wrong, and guilt.

Let me illustrate this thought by a supposed case. You have a child whom you would train in habits of soberness, self-control, and rigid virtue. Your time is at your own command; your resources are unlimited. You determine that he shall see in some outward form the reflection of every disposition that he cherishes, of every wayward choice and every right purpose. For each forthputting of genial feeling, of conscientiousness, of kindness, you create before his eye some form of beauty or utility. You follow up his peevishness and petulance by placing and keeping in his sight some repulsive object or scene, — the fit embodiment of the temper you would rebuke. You produce, and compel him to witness prolongedly, havoc and desolation among objects under his cognizance, for every fit of groundless or excessive anger. You thus write out his whole moral history in the aspect of his nursery or playground, and sustain under his constant inspection mementos that he must needs see and feel of whatever good and whatever evil there is in his mind and character. Had you the ability thus to educate your child, think you not that it would be the readiest and most effectual way of eradicating the evil and establishing the supremacy of the good?

It is thus, it seems to me, that God is educating the races and the generations of men. To suppress the consequences of sin would be to manifest indifference to moral distinctions, to perpetuate the supremacy of guilt, to make evil grow with the march of the ages, and fasten its eternal hold on the heart of humanity without remedy or hope. So long as man will sin, it is immeasurably for the best that his sin should do its appropriate work in the eyes of the sinful and the tempted. So far as that work is external in the form of calamity, there is nothing that need distinguish it from the so-called direct visitation of an afflictive Providence. For those who are in successful training for a higher sphere of being, it has its double ministry, in the winnowing, hallowing power of all sorrow over the principles and affections; and in sustaining the hatred and dread of moral evil by the innocent experience of its bitter fruits. For those who are yet to be won to duty, the unsightly and odious consequences of sin are the most effective preachers of repentance and righteousness, often heard and heeded by those who have turned a deaf ear to every other mode of appeal. For the unprivileged and irresponsible sufferers by the guilt of their brethren, we know not what essential and blessed ministries such remembered experiences may subserve in that spiritual education which, we cannot but believe, is destined for them, under better auspices, in other realms of being.

Nor can we suppose that God will give effect to a guilty disposition or purpose in any other way or instance than may serve the ends of discipline, warning, rebuke, or merited punishment. In thousands of ways his providence may and does make void the thought of evil, the counsel of violence, — avert the blow which guilty man would aim at the peace of his fellow-men. Where his wisdom sees fit to save, he can say as effectually to human malice as to wind and wave, "Touch not mine anointed, and do my servants no harm." Over the agitated sea of depraved passions, over the field of reckless carnage, over the haunts of those who lurk privily for the blood of their brethren, the fan of his discriminating providence waves with no less unerring choice, with no less merited or merciful doom, or needed and signal deliverance, than over the daily paths of disease and death among the walks of quiet and peaceful life. Evil and death come to none, for whom it is not the fit time and way in the counsels of retributive justice, or the best time and way in the counsels of paternal love.

I am aware that this view may to some minds seem at first thought harsh and revolting. But not so when we consider the only alternative. For can God have left us unsheltered, to be preyed upon and sacrificed by the evil passions of our brethren? Are we cast solely at the mercy of our fellow-men? In our exposure to the unnumbered forms of violence and recklessness that not unfrequently beset us, is our only security the chance that they may not select us as their victims? Can we suffer or perish in a time or way in which God sees and knows that it is not best, not good, and only evil, for us? — and yet the sparrow falleth not to the ground without him. In our ignorance of what a day may bring forth, are we liable, not alone to what our Father may appoint, but to what may be done in defiance of his will and contravention of his purpose concerning us? If so, what or where is our ground of trust for the life that now is? Where shall we roll off the burden of agonizing solicitude? How shall we dismiss our care because God careth for us? Our faith in Providence must extend to human agency no less than to the so-called direct action of the Almighty; else it can have but little practical influence as regards the present life, can be of little avail in evil times and among evil men.

There are indeed mysteries in Providence, — heights which we cannot scale, depths which we cannot fathom. We seek only to look between the leaves of the immeasurable volume, where Jesus has unloosed the seals. I have barely endeavored to develop what we must believe, if we would receive our Saviour's lessons, and imbibe his spirit, of implicit trust and self-surrender. Where Reason fails, let Faith usurp her place, and let us rest in the calm assurance that what we know not now we shall know hereafter. This we do know now, — that our times are in our Father's hands, our path through life marked and guarded by his watchful providence, and that to the soul that stays itself on him all things must work together for good. And in the destined home of our spirits, while the heavens shall declare his righteousness, the dark forms of evil will disclose their ministries of love; from the caverns of the grave will come voices of praise; and even sin — mercifully punished in time that it might not weigh down our souls to perdition, repented, forsaken, forgiven — will only swell with deeper ıoy the anthem of unceasing adoration.

THE END.

www.ingramcontent.com/pod-product-compliance
Lightning Source LLC
LaVergne TN
LVHW021133110826
845150LV00005B/1015

* 9 7 8 1 4 2 5 5 4 9 9 8 5 *